4747

D1084465

THE CHICAGO BOARD OF TRADE HANDBOOK OF FUTURES AND OPTIONS

Chicago Board of Trade

McGraw-Hill

New York Chicago San Francisco
Lisbon London Madrid Mexico City
Milan New Delhi San Juan Seoul
Singapore Sydney Toronto

This book was previously published by Glenlake Publishing Company, Ltd., under the title *Commodity Trading Manual.*

3 4 5 6 7 8 9 10 IBT/IBT 1 9 8 7 6 5 4 3 2 1 0

ISBN 0-07-145751-8

The information in this publication is taken from sources believed to be reliable, but it is not guaranteed by either the publisher or the Chicago Board of Trade as to accuracy or completeness, and is intended for purposes of information and education only. The rules and regulations of the individual exchanges should be consulted as the authoritative sources on all current contract specifications and regulations. Nothing herein should be considered a trading recommendation of the Chicago Board of Trade. An attorney should be consulted concerning legal restrictions applicable to your business that might preclude or limit your use of any of the futures and options on futures markets described in this publication.

LIFFE-CONNECT is a trademark of LIFFE Administration and Management and is registered in Australia, Hong Kong, Singapore, the United States, and the United Kingdom, is a registered community trademark, and is the subject of a pending application for registration in Japan.

"Dow Jones," "The Dow," "Dow Jones Industrial Average," "DJIA," are service marks of Dow Jones & Company, Inc., and have been licensed for use for certain purposes by the Board of Trade of the City of Chicago, Inc. ("CBOT"). The CBOT futures and futures options contracts based on the Dow Jones' indexes are not sponsored, endorsed, sold, or promoted by Dow Jones, and Dow Jones makes no representation regarding the advisability of trading in such products.

Throughout this book, trademarked names are used. Rather than put a trademark symbol after every occurrence of a trademarked name, we use names in an editorial fashion only, and to the benefit of the trademark owner, with no intention of infringement of the trademark.

Library of Congress Cataloging-in-Publication Data
The Chicago Board of Trade handbook of futures and options / by Chicago Board of Trade.
    p. cm.
   ISBN 0-07-145751-8 (hardcover : alk. paper)
1. Futures—Handbooks, manuals, etc. 2. Options (Finance)—Handbooks, manuals, etc.
I. Chicago Board of Trade
   HG6024.U6C45 2006
   332.64'52—dc22

2005027316

This book is dedicated to the memory of
Coleen O'Donnell Craig
CBOT employee
1984–2005

CONTENTS

Chapter 15

Metals Markets: Gold, Silver, Copper, Platinum   323

Chapter 16

Forest, Fiber, and Food Markets: Lumber, Cotton, Orange Juice, Sugar, Cocoa, Coffee   341

Chapter 17

Energy Markets: Crude Oil, Gasoline, Heating Oil, Natural Gas, Electricity   361

ACKNOWLEDGMENTS

Chicago Board of Trade (CBOT) Handbook of Futures and Options prepared by Mark Melin and Julie Collins

Julie Collins is a talented business communicator who has helped professional service firms reach their audience for over 20 years. In 2001, she founded her own marketing agency, BlueStem Marketing. Her clients have included futures exchanges and brokerages, financial institutions, consulting and research companies, real estate organizations, lawyers, and accounting firms.

Mark Melin is a registered commodity trading advisor at www.dowoptionstrader.com whose fund trades futures and options on futures. Mr. Melin, author of two books, has served as a consultant to major futures commission merchants, broker/dealers as well as many of the major derivative exchanges in Chicago including the Chicago Board of Trade and OneChicago, the single stock futures exchange.

Chicago Board of Trade Editors
Barbara Kodlubanski
Lisa MacDonald

Chicago Board of Trade Contributors
Joseph Benning
James Boudreault
Ted Doukas
Daniel Grombacher
Lewis Hagedorn
David Mitchell
Carol O'Shea
Remmie Vail

Project Coordinators
Kristen Carlson, Trungale, Egan & Associates
Elizabeth Hoeppel, Trungale, Egan & Associates

For further information, please contact:

Chicago Board of Trade
141 West Jackson Boulevard
Chicago, IL 60604-2994
Telephone: (312) 341-7955
Fax: (312) 341-3027
Web address: www.cbot.com

PART ONE

Market Overview: Structure and Safeguards

CHAPTER 1

Why Futures? An Overview of Futures Trading

Price risk is present in practically every business transaction. Whether you're buying or selling stocks, bonds, or soybeans, managing the risk of price change can mean the difference between financial success and financial ruin. Managing price risk is one of the key purposes of futures. In this chapter and the next, we provide an overview of key topics in the futures industry, and perhaps no topic can be more important in the futures market than that of managing risk.

FUTURES MARKETS WERE CREATED TO MANAGE RISK

Futures and options markets evolved to help people manage price risk—and even to take advantage of it. Risk doesn't simply go away, though. Therein lies the elegance of futures and options as risk management tools. Futures and options markets make it possible for those who want to manage price risk, called *hedgers,* to transfer that risk to those who are willing to accept it, called *speculators.* It's a classic win-win situation, and it is the basic underpinning of how the futures markets work.

Of course, managing price risk requires information. The grain markets of 1800s Chicago, for instance, suffered not just from supply and demand chaos, but also from a lack of timely, accurate, and public information about price. Processors had no established way to learn what other processors might be paying or what the market deemed a fair price. And farmers had no idea what buyers had offered other sellers. Grain pricing remained opaque for both sides, and price risk grew. However, today's centralized marketplaces like futures exchanges solve that problem. Beyond trading, futures markets provide price information that the world looks to as a benchmark in determining the value of a particular commodity or financial instrument at a given time. By requiring open market bids and offers and disseminating price information to all interested parties, futures and options exchanges give everyone a better understanding of business—and eliminate the risk that comes from not knowing.

These important benefits—risk transfer and price discovery—reach every sector of the world where changing market conditions create economic risk, from agricultural products to foreign exchange to investment and finance.

PRICE THEORY

Price risk stems from fairly straightforward economic fundamentals. Quite simply, the price of a product is discovered by changes in its supply and demand.

Supply is the relationship between a product's price and the amount of that product sellers are willing to provide. Supply can be graphed as a curve with quantity shown on the horizontal axis and price shown on the vertical axis. (See Fig. 1.1.) The curve slants upward from left to right, as shown, to indicate the quantity supplied at a given price. When prices are high, sellers are willing to provide larger quantities of their products to the market. At lower prices, sellers are willing to furnish smaller quantities to the market. This relationship between product supply and price is known as *the law of supply*.

FIGURE 1.1

Supply Curve

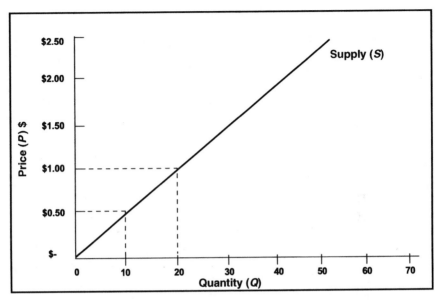

A variety of economic factors can cause supply to increase or decrease, thus shifting the supply curve. These factors include changes in production costs, prices of related goods, and the number of sellers in the market.

Demand is the relationship between a product's price and the amount of that product that buyers are willing to purchase. Demand can be graphed as a curve with quantity shown on the horizontal axis and price shown on the vertical axis. (See Fig. 1.2.) The curve slants downward from left to right, as shown, to indicate the quantity demanded at a given price. When prices are low, buyers are willing to purchase greater quantities of a product. At higher prices, buyers will purchase less. This relationship between product demand and price is known as _the law of demand._

A variety of economic factors can cause demand to increase or decrease, thus shifting the demand curve. These factors in-

FIGURE 1.2

Demand Curve

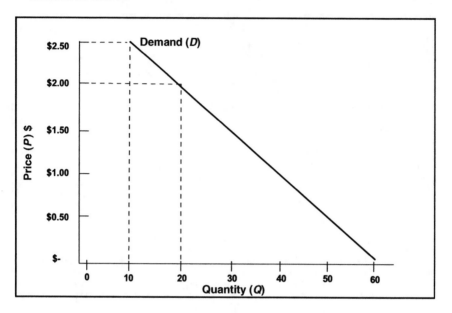

clude changes in personal income, prices of related goods, and the number of buyers in the market.

In competitive markets, the price of a product, commodity, or financial instrument—even money—depends on the relationship between supply and demand. If the supply and demand curves of a product are placed on the same graph, the point at which they intersect is the product's market price, also known as the *equilibrium price*. (See Fig. 1.3.) At this market or equilibrium price, the quantity supplied equals the quantity demanded.

A change in the supply of or demand for a product will cause a shift in the respective supply or demand curve. As these curves shift, the market price changes to the new point where supply and demand intersect. For example, as good weather increases agricultural production, the supply curve will shift right, and, with all else equal, the market price will fall accordingly (i.e., equilibrium moves from A to B).

FIGURE 1.3

Equilibrium Price

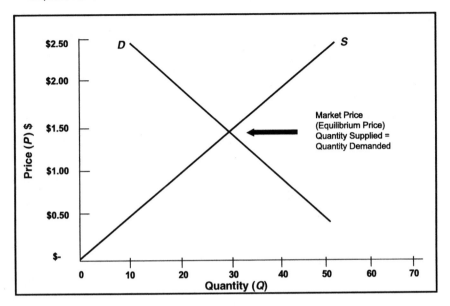

Of course, supply and demand curves are shifting all the time. New information about factors affecting supply and demand comes into the market almost constantly. Centralized markets digest this information, balance it against other information and market opinions about what new information will soon arise, and come up with an equilibrium price—the sum total of all market data and opinions. This equilibrium price, as a result of constant supply and demand shifts, changes minute by minute—sometimes even more frequently when the market attempts to digest significantly different information from that already reflected in the market price. (See Fig. 1.4.)

When price moves—whether for beans or bonds, corn or money—risk results. The corn you grow today could be worth more or less at harvest, more or less by the time you sell it. The money you agree to accept as payment today could be worth more or less by the time you receive it, more or less by the time

FIGURE 1.4

Equilibrium Price with Supply Shift

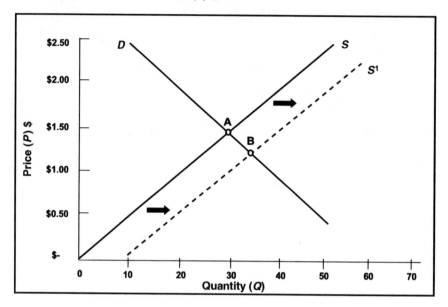

you put it in the bank. Supply and demand shifts create risk. Fortunately, they also create opportunity.

CASH TRANSACTIONS

In their early years, exchanges were essentially cash markets where physical commodities were bought and sold. As the volume of trading increased, buyers and sellers began trading futures contracts—standardized, legal agreements to make or take delivery of a given commodity or instrument at a designated place at a specified future time. While cash and futures contracts have common elements, they serve different market functions. Cash contracts in the agricultural markets, for instance, are sales agreements for either immediate or future delivery of a commodity. The quality and quantity of the commodity and the delivery terms are agreed upon by both the buyer and the seller. Each of these factors affects the sales price. For instance, if a lower or higher quality of grain than the buyer agreed to purchase is delivered, a price discount or premium is calculated in the final price. Quantity also affects the price. If a greater quantity is delivered than was initially agreed upon, a price discount is sometimes negotiated.

As an example, a cash transaction involves a farmer who wants to sell his grain and a grain elevator operator who wants to purchase it. Typically, the grain elevator operator acts as an intermediary between farmers and grain buyers, such as flour millers, who eventually purchase the grain to process. Farmers, grain elevator operators, and other marketers can use a variety of cash sales agreements in this situation.

Another type of cash transaction involves immediate delivery of the commodity. Many farmers use this marketing alternative in the fall. After harvest, they haul grain to the local elevator, where it is priced on the spot based on the quantity and quality of the crop.

CASH FORWARD CONTRACT

Another alternative is a cash forward contract—in which a seller agrees to deliver a specific cash commodity to a buyer some time in the future. For example, a farmer could enter into a cash forward contract with a grain elevator operator in the winter to deliver 10,000 bushels of wheat the following July. At contract initiation, the farmer and grain elevator operator agree on the quality and quantity of grain, the delivery time and location, and the price. When delivery occurs, the farmer's wheat is carefully inspected, and price adjustments are made according to quality and quantity.

In many instances, a cash forward contract might be more appropriate than an immediate cash sale, because it allows both buyers and sellers to plan ahead. Not only do they know, in advance, the price they will have to pay or the price they will receive for a specific commodity, but they can also hold off delivery until they have possession of the grain or are ready to process it. This saves the expense of tying up storage facilities.

Similar cash forward transactions are prevalent in all sectors of the economy. "Tailor-made" forward rate agreements (FRAs), for example, are offered by numerous commercial and investment banks through over-the-counter dealer markets. *Forward rate agreements* are legally binding agreements to lend or borrow money from a specified future date to a specified maturity date at a rate agreed upon today. Like agricultural forward agreements, the terms of an FRA are specific to each individual agreement. The dollar amount and the payment and maturity dates are negotiated between borrower and lender, as is the interest rate charged. That rate includes the lender's credit risk premium and so depends in part on his or her institution's relationship with the lender.

Whether made in the agricultural or financial markets, forward contracts are not actively traded on exchanges nor are they standardized, as are futures. They are customized, privately negotiated agreements. They thus expose both parties in the agreement to the risk that one side is negotiating in bad faith or without sufficient funds or that future events could prevent one or both sides from fulfilling the contract.

FUTURES CONTRACTS

Unlike forward agreements, futures contracts are standardized instruments traded only on organized futures exchanges. A *futures contract* is a legally binding agreement to buy or sell a commodity or financial instrument some time in the future at a price agreed upon at the time of the trade. Unlike cash transactions and forward transactions, physical delivery of the underlying commodity seldom takes place with a futures contract. Nonetheless, futures contracts are standardized according to delivery specifications, including the quality, quantity, and time and location. The only variable is price, which is discovered through the trading process, which takes place on the exchange's physical trading floor or "virtual" trading conducted electronically through the computer. As Todd Petzel notes in *Financial Futures and Options,* "Successful futures contracts have enough standard elements to insure that the buyer and the seller have a clear understanding about what performance is expected."

Offset

Ironically, this standardization actually affords tremendous flexibility. Because futures contracts are standardized, sellers and buyers can exchange one contract for another and actually *offset* their obligation to deliver or take delivery of the commodity or instrument underlying the futures contract. While delivery can take place, most traders simply offset their positions before the expiration of the contract. *Offset* in the futures market means taking another futures position opposite and equal to one's initial futures transaction. For example, suppose an investor bought two December mini-sized silver contracts before the contracts called for delivery. To offset this position, the investor must sell two December mini-sized silver contracts before the contracts call for delivery. On the other hand, if the investor first sold two December silver contracts, to offset the position, the investor must buy two December silver contracts before delivery.

Standardization of contract terms and the ability to offset contracts quickly led to the increasing use of the futures markets by hedgers such as commercial firms and by speculators. Commercial firms began to realize that they could use futures to hedge against price volatility without the need to make or take delivery of the cash commodity underlying the futures contract. Speculators found that standardization added trading appeal because they could buy and later sell, or sell and later buy, futures contracts at a profit if they could correctly forecast price movement.

Indeed, eliminating all other variables through standardization and focusing exclusively on price affords additional benefits as well. Trading occurs in a competitive public auction with bid and offer prices available to all market participants. That facilitates price discovery and removes user concern about credit and price tiering, typical features of less public markets. For this reason, the standardization of futures contracts make futures prices extraordinarily efficient—and the delivery of the underlying commodity easy to manage, that is, if delivery ever takes place.

Delivery

While the potential for delivery is vital to linking cash and futures prices, in reality, very few futures trades result in delivery. Remember that buyers and sellers of futures contracts are required to take or make delivery of the commodity or financial instrument represented by the contract unless they liquidate their position before contract expiration. While most futures traders liquidate their contracts before expiration, if a futures contract is not offset, the trader must be ready to accept or make delivery of the underlying commodity. Futures contracts for most physical commodities, such as grains, require market participants holding contracts at expiration to either take or make delivery of the underlying contract. It is this responsibility to make or take delivery that forces futures prices to reflect the actual cash value of the commodity.

PRICE DISCOVERY

Futures markets provide a centralized marketplace for buyers and sellers to continuously evaluate supply and demand factors and other market indicators. Based on analysis of current market information and expectations of future price movements, trades are made, and prices are discovered.

That's not to say, however, that futures exchanges "set" prices. The market price of any given futures contract at any given time represents the sum total of all market data and opinions. In other words, the equilibrium price at any given market moment balances the myriad supply and demand factors driving the market. Futures markets are barometers, not referees. They measure the market's equilibrium price; they do not dictate it.

Of course, that equilibrium price is in constant flux. Traders constantly adjust their bids and offers in relation to a continuous flow of worldwide market information. News of Brazilian soybean crop conditions, for instance, is sought, analyzed, and then reflected almost instantaneously in the prices of soybean, soybean meal, and soybean oil futures. The impact of nationalization of foreign-owned copper mines is registered in the price of copper, silver, and related futures in New York, London, and Chicago. And announcements or indications that the Federal Reserve is putting more money into the economy are immediately absorbed by the market and noted in the price of U.S. Treasury futures.

Futures prices are the most widely used pricing reference in domestic and international financial, metals, and agricultural markets. Once prices are discovered, futures exchanges disseminate those prices to the public. In fact because of the popularization of the Internet, price discovery is instantly communicated around the globe in real time as the transactions occur.

HEDGING

Hedging, the other major economic purpose of futures markets, is buying or selling futures contracts to offset the risks of changing prices in the cash markets. This risk-transfer mechanism makes futures contracts extremely useful tools for controlling costs and protecting profit margins.

In the agricultural markets, for example, commercial firms, producers, merchandisers, and processors of commodities use futures to protect themselves from changing cash prices. They can do so because cash and futures prices usually respond to the same economic factors and tend to move together in the same direction. News of bad weather likely to result in crop losses and tighter supplies is reflected immediately in higher cash prices, as buyers seek to buy and store the commodity in anticipation of later shortages. Correspondingly, futures prices rise in response as well, as buyers anticipate a commodity shortage not only at harvest but throughout the marketing year.

On the other hand, economic news signaling higher than expected supplies immediately registers in weakening cash prices, as buyers anticipating easily available supplies relax their buying efforts. At the same time, buyers in the futures markets scale down their bids, given the prospect of increased supplies.

Merchandisers at commercial firms realize that although a single set of economic factors might result in a loss on a cash transaction, that loss could be hedged, and sometimes turned into a profit in the futures market, if they initiate a futures position equal and opposite to their cash market position. For example, suppose a Midwest wheat miller agrees to ship 500,000 pounds of flour in six months to a cookie baker in Minnesota. Both agree on a price today, even though the flour will not be delivered for another six months. The miller does not own the wheat that will eventually be processed and is concerned that prices will rise during the six-month period.

To hedge against the risk of rising cash prices, the miller buys wheat futures contracts for delivery in six months. When the time comes to acquire the wheat, cash prices have risen. But futures prices have also increased, driven up by the same economic fundamentals. The miller can then sell two futures contracts with the same expiration as those originally purchased to offset the initial long futures position and earn a profit on the futures transactions. Even though the miller will have to pay more for the cash wheat than was originally planned, the futures market gain largely negates that loss.

The economic principles that apply to traditional commodity futures contracts, such as wheat futures, also apply to financial contracts such as currencies, stock indexes, and government debt. A portfolio manager waiting for cash inflows to make a planned bond purchase can buy Treasury bond futures to hedge against an increase in the price of bonds, just as the miller hedged against a rise in wheat prices by buying wheat futures. A corporate treasurer planning to issue a bond can hedge against higher interest rates and lower bond prices by selling T-bond futures. Similarly, an institution can hedge to protect the market value of stocks from a possible decline in value with stock index futures.

For example, suppose a financial institution plans to sell a portion of its bond portfolio in four months. The company, however, expects interest rates to rise over that time, which would result in lower bond prices. To take advantage of the current market price, the company can sell U.S. Treasury bond futures contracts. If the bond market falls, as expected, the company can then sell its Treasury bonds in the cash market and offset its futures position by buying Treasury bond futures contracts with the same expiration as those originally sold. Even though the institution will receive less in the cash market than it would have four months ago for the same portfolio of bonds, it has gained in the futures market, thus reducing the potential loss.

Other users of financial futures contracts include commercial and investment bankers, corporate treasurers, state and local government officers, portfolio and money managers, mortgage bankers, pension and trust fund managers, and insurance companies. (See Chapter 8 for a more complete discussion of hedging.)

In all hedging strategies, the common denominator is the desire to establish, in advance, an acceptable price. Every business, regardless of whether it performs a service or manufactures a product, faces some type of financial risk. Remember, though, risk doesn't simply go away. For each individual or institution attempting to minimize risk, there must be another willing to assume it. Futures exchanges act as a magnet, attracting risk avoiders (hedgers) and risk takers (speculators) alike.

SPECULATING

Speculators assume the risk that hedgers try to avoid. Driven by potential profits, speculators provide the marketplace with an essential element—liquidity. *Liquidity* is a characteristic of a market to absorb transactions of any size without a substantial change in the price. Liquid markets easily match a buyer with a seller, enabling traders to quickly transact their business at a fair price. Without liquidity, hedgers' attempts to buy and sell contracts would immediately drive prices up or down in response. Having this liquidity is crucial to institutional investors, processors of commodities, and other commercial and financial firms that buy or sell hundreds or thousands of futures contracts to hedge cash market positions.

Although speculators usually have no commercial interest in the commodities or financial instruments underlying the futures contracts they trade, the potential for profit motivates them to gather market information regarding supply and demand and to anticipate its effect on prices. Thus, by buying and selling futures contracts, speculators provide additional information to the market about the impact of current events on expected future demands.

In short, speculators are essential to effective markets. Speculators make the market more liquid, bridging the gap between the prices bid and the prices offered by other futures traders. They close the risk-transfer circle by taking the other side of hedgers' trades and improve price discovery by contributing additional information to the market.

PROFIT OPPORTUNITIES WITH FUTURES

With futures the speculator can profit under a number of different circumstances. When traders purchase a futures contract, they are said to be "long" and profit when the market moves higher. When traders sell a futures contract, they are said to be "short" and profit when the market moves lower. Shorting in a futures market is much easier than shorting other cash markets, which require the person shorting the market to actually borrow the security or commodity they are shorting to make delivery.

With futures a trader can easily trade different products and create a diverse investment portfolio. For instance, a trader can easily sell the CBOT soybean future and buy the corn future, creating a unique investment opportunity that takes advantage of changing price relationships between these various markets. This is referred to as a *spread trade,* and it is just one of the many opportunities a trader can leverage with futures and options.

CLEARING

An exchange's clearing mechanism is absolutely essential to the marketplace. Clearinghouses settle the accounts of their members, clear trades, collect and maintain margin monies, regulate delivery, and report trading data. More important, though, clearinghouses are an integral part of the guarantee system that protects futures users from contract default.

The guarantee system used at futures exchanges also severs the direct relationship between buyer and seller, so that each is free to buy and sell independently of the other. The system does this by placing a third party—the clearinghouse—between the buyer and seller in futures and options trades. Each of the trading firms that holds membership in the clearinghouse becomes liable to the clearinghouse for all the trades made for itself and its customers. The clearinghouse itself acts as a buyer to every clearing member seller and a seller to every clearing member buyer. Buyers and sellers of futures and options contracts thus do not create financial obligations to one another, but, rather, to their clearing member firms, which in turn have obligations to the clearinghouse. This multipart system creates several levels of safeguards for futures and options users.

Traditionally futures exchanges used their own clearing mechanisms to clear trades. Recently, however, the Chicago Board of Trade (CBOT) and the Chicago Mercantile Exchange (CME) reached agreement to create a common clearing link. This system, which now clears 85 percent of all U.S. futures trades, reduced transaction costs for traders and improved cross-margining capabilities with corresponding products on both exchanges.

MARGIN

To minimize the risk of a contract default ever happening, exchange clearinghouses require their members to deposit performance bond money called *margins,* just as clearing members require margins from their customers. Remember that buyers and sellers of futures contracts are required to take or make delivery of the commodity or financial instrument unless they liquidate the position before the contract's expiration. Margins are good-faith deposits required of both buyers and sellers to ensure fulfillment of these contract obligations.

Margins are determined on the basis of market risk. As such, they help preserve the financial soundness of futures exchanges and provide valuable price protection for hedgers with a minimum tie-up of capital. Margins are normally set at 2 to 5 percent of the value of the commodity or financial instrument represented by a futures contract.

WHY TRADE A FUTURES CONTRACT?

There are several reasons to trade a futures contract, including liquidity, transparency, and leverage.

Liquidity

A key benefit of futures trading is liquidity. Liquid markets easily match a buyer with a seller, enabling traders to quickly transact their business at a fair price. To view liquidity in action, you can visit the CBOT Web (www.cbot.com) site and view the live gold "book." This shows all the bids (to buy) and offers (to sell) on both sides of the CBOT gold contract. You will notice that within the first five price increments, known as *tics,* there is an average of 300 contracts to either buy or sell. This is considered a very liquid market, meaning that for all practical purposes the trader can buy or sell at a fair price.

Some beginning traders often equate liquidity with trading volume, concluding that only markets with the highest actual volume of contracts traded are the most liquid. While this holds true in many markets, with the advent of electronic trading, exchanges can provide substantially more liquidity, or opportunity to trade, than the actual number of contracts traded. We explore liquidity and electronic trading in Chapter 3.

Transparency

Many futures markets such as those at the CBOT are considered to be "transparent" because the order flow is open and easily observable. When an order enters the marketplace, the order fills at the best price for the customer. With the advent of electronic trading, transparency has reached new heights because all transactions can be viewed online in real time.

Leverage

For speculators, hedgers, and other traders, a key benefit of trading in the futures markets is that it offers financial leverage. *Leverage* is the ability of a trader to control large dollar amounts of a commodity with a comparatively small amount of capital. Leverage is possible because of margin. Rather than pay for the full value of the contract (as one would in a cash transaction) or pay margin rates as high as 50 percent (as one would in a stock transaction), futures margin amounts require a trader to post a fraction of those amounts. As such, leverage magnifies both gains and losses in the futures markets.

For example, if a trader buys one soybean futures contract at $6.50 per bushel, he or she then controls 5,000 bushels of actual soybeans at a contract value of $32,500 per futures contract. So for $1,400 in "margin," or $0.28 per bushel, the trader can purchase a contract that has a delivery value of $32,500.

Margins are good-faith deposits required of both buyers and sellers to ensure fulfillment of these contract obligations. Margins are determined on the basis of market risk. As such, they help preserve the financial soundness of futures exchanges and provide valuable price protection for hedgers with a minimum tie-up of capital. Margins are normally set at 2 to 5 percent of the value of the commodity or financial instrument represented by a futures contract.

FURTHER READING

Hull, John, *Options, Futures, and Other Derivative Securities,* 2d ed. Englewood Cliffs, NJ: Prentice Hall, 1993.

Kolb, Robert W., *Futures, Options and Swaps.* New York: Blackwell Publishers, 2002.

Kolb, Robert W., *Understanding Futures Markets,* 3d ed. New York: New York Institute of Finance, 1991.

Lofton, Todd, *Getting Started in Futures,* 4th ed. New York: John Wiley and Sons, 2001.

Siegel, Daniel R., and Diane F. Siegel, *The Futures Markets: The Professional Trader's Guide to Portfolio Strategies, Risk Management, and Arbitrage.* Chicago: Probus Publishing, 1990.

Stoll, Hans R., and Robert E. Whaley, *Futures and Options: Theory and Applications.* Cincinnati: Southwestern Publishing, 1993.

Veale, Stuart R., *Stocks, Bonds, Options, Futures.* New York: New York Institute of Finance, 2001.

CHAPTER 2

Futures Fundamentals: Auction in Action

Futures exchanges provide a venue for buyers and sellers to transact business through an open-auction system, be it a physical trading pit on the exchange floor or virtual trading pits on a computer. Through this trading, a price for specific futures and options contracts is discovered.

This chapter outlines the structure and processes of trading. Whether the action takes place in a trading pit or on the computer, this fast-paced action is what many regard as the hallmark of futures exchanges. As in most things, there's much more than meets the eye.

EXCHANGE STRUCTURE

Although all U.S. futures exchanges share some general characteristics, no two are exactly alike. While futures exchanges were initially established as not-for-profit membership associations, the Chicago Mercantile Exchange and the Chicago Board of Trade are now publicly traded for-profit enterprises, as are a handful of other start-up all-electronic futures and options exchanges. Membership in each exchange traditionally is limited to a specific number of individuals, although some exchanges permit the holding of multiple memberships. Companies, corporations, partnerships, and cooperatives may register for certain membership privileges, but every membership in many exchanges is held in the name of an individual person. In fact, exchanges conduct a thorough investigation of each member applicant, focusing on the applicant's credit standing, financial responsibility, character, and integrity. Electronic exchanges have more flexible exchange rules that encourage a large, geographically diverse group of members.

Electronic Exchanges

Many of the major futures exchanges rely on electronic platforms to conduct some or all of their trading. Like a physical trading pit located on the exchange floor, electronic exchanges use electronic trading technology to create a gathering place where buyers and sellers transact business. The electronic exchange is open to many types of traders using a variety of strategies. The primary difference between the electronic exchange and the physical trading pit is that the electronic exchange transacts business over the computer networks and the Internet and does not require the trader to be located in a particular place. We discuss electronic exchanges and electronic trading and its impact on futures and options trading in Chapter 3.

Memberships

In recent years, some exchanges have offered special memberships or trading privileges. While membership is not required to trade exchange products, membership for the most part enables people to trade at a discounted rate and to directly trade from the exchange's physical trading floor. Other special membership interests permit more restricted trading. In an effort to become more inclusive, exchanges have started to broaden their membership to include groups of traders typically considered "customers." For instance, the CME and CBOT now offer membership privileges to accredited hedge funds, a trading group that previously received only "public trader" status.

Governance

The governance of each membership-based exchange is vested in a board (variously called the *board of directors, board of governors,* or *board of managers*) and its officers. Exchange members elect the board, and the board appoints appropriate officers. Other responsibilities rest with various committees. These committees are composed of exchange or board members either appointed by the board or elected by the exchange membership. They advise and assist the board and perform specific duties related to exchange operations.

Most exchanges have committees for the following purposes: nomination of board candidates, officers, and those committees elected by the exchange membership; management of the exchange; supervision of finances; supervision and investigation of the business conduct of members; arbitration of disputes; appeal of disciplinary committee decisions; examination of member applicants; supervision of trading floor activity; supervision of market price reporting; management of the physical facilities of the exchange; amendments to rules and regulations; public relations; marketing and education; supervision of trading and changes in traded contracts; and supervision of weighing, warehousing, and inspecting of commodities for delivery against futures contracts.

The administrative staff of an exchange carries out the policies and decisions of the board, its officers, and the committees. Departmental organization of the staff frequently parallels the functions of the various committees, with each department responsible to an executive officer of the exchange. The titles, responsibilities, and numbers of these executive officers and staff members vary among the exchanges.

EXCHANGE OPERATIONS

Activity at each futures exchange has traditionally been centralized on the trading floor; however, the trend is away from floor trading and toward electronic trading.

The Trading Floor

Only exchange members have the privilege of actually trading on the exchange floor, although all market participants have indirect access to the floor through their brokers. The size, arrangement, and facilities of the trading floor vary among the exchanges, but many features are common to all. Futures trading is conducted in octagonal and polygonal pits or rings, with steps leading to the center of each pit. Traders stand in groups on the steps, in the center of the pit, or around the waist-high ring according to the contract month of the commodity or financial instrument they are trading. Buyers and sellers stand throughout the pit, since any trader can buy or sell at any given moment. Generally, one pit or ring is devoted to each futures or options contract traded on the exchange.

Adjacent to the pit or ring (or sometimes in its center) are market reporters, employed by the exchange to record price changes as they occur. The recorded prices are then displayed on computer-operated electronic wallboards, which are designed to be visible from any spot on the floor. Futures prices of commodities traded on other exchanges are also displayed so that traders can stay abreast of the most current price movements. Indeed, electronic displays and video monitors on the exchange floor provide a constant stream of the latest financial, business, and commodity news from major wire services and futures and securities exchanges. Large maps and video displays show weather development in relevant agricultural areas. Cash prices, deliverable supplies, and shipments of various commodities are also available. (See Fig. 2.1.)

To handle the thousands of calls coming from commercial

FIGURE 2.1

The Financial Trading Floor at the Chicago Board of Trade

traders and brokerage firms, batteries of telephone stations and sophisticated electronic equipment are strategically located near the pits. At the Chicago Board of Trade, orders received by phone clerks from various member firms are time-stamped, and then delivered by messengers (called *runners*) or "flashed" (signaled by hand) to brokers in the pit for execution. The floor technology gets some orders to the pit electronically via a computerized order-routing system or, where permitted, headsets. Regardless of how the order makes its way to the pit, the price at which the trade is made and other pertinent information are jotted down by the broker on an order blank and returned by a runner or flashed to the firm's phone desk. The order is time-stamped again, and trade confirmation is relayed to the office where the order originated. The trade information then enters the Chicago Board of Trade's reporting and information system, where it is reported to the general public through various reporting services. (See Chapter 5 for more information on order routing.)

Electronic Trading

While floor trading relies on the physical location of traders in a centralized pit, electronic trading enables traders from disparate geographic locations to trade through computer networks as well as the Internet. Anyone with or without membership in the exchange can trade electronically, and all traders have the same opportunity to transact business.

Traders make trades through a trading application (front-end software) that is located on their computer. The trade is then routed to one of several "points of presence" (POPs). For instance, the Chicago Board of Trade has five POPs, one in each of these cities: Chicago, New York, London, Paris, and Amsterdam. The order is then placed into a trading host "matching engine" that pairs appropriate buy and sell orders. When the matching engine executes trades, the resulting trade price is electronically disclosed to all traders. After a trade has been executed, confirmation of execution is sent to the trader's trading application. Trade details are also sent from the trading host to the clearing engine.

From a liquidity standpoint, the backbone of the electronic trading system is the electronic market maker—particularly in lightly traded markets. In similar fashion to "local" market makers in a pit, electronic market makers provide a constant stream of "bids" to buy and "offers" to sell, enabling all types of traders to enter and exit the marketplace at a competitive price. (We discuss electronic trading more fully in Chapter 3.)

TYPES OF TRADERS

Traders are a key component of the exchange structure and play a vital role in the futures markets by providing liquidity. While futures are designed primarily to assist hedgers in managing their exposure to price risk, the market would not be possible without the participation of traders who provide a fluid supply of buyers and sellers. Traders, or speculators, assume the other side of the hedger's trade, enabling hedgers to lay off their price risk on the market.

Futures traders can be categorized in a number of ways. There are full-time professional traders and part-time traders; traders who trade on the trading floor or behind a computer screen; hedgers and institutions that seek to manage risk; and speculators who seek to profit from price movement. Each of these market participants plays an important role in making the markets effective places to conduct business.

The "Local"

Perhaps the most visible and colorful speculator is the professional floor trader, or "local," trading for his or her own account on the floor of an exchange. Locals come from all walks of life and frequently began their careers as runners, clerks, or assistants to other traders and brokers. Locals utilize a variety of trading strategies. Sometimes they act as a market maker, taking the opposite side of orders that enter the pit. Often they "scalp" the market by buying and selling within seconds of each other. Some locals occasionally position trade, which means that they hold on to a contract that was bought or sold for an extended length of time. With the growing popularity of electronic trading and the high cost of participation on the floor, it is increasingly difficult for the local to achieve a high degree of success.

Public Traders

The vast majority of traders is made up of individuals trading off the floor with private funds. This diverse group is generally referred to as "retail" business. With the growing movement from trading on the floor to trading on the computer screen, the retail customer is becoming an increasingly important force in futures trading.

Proprietary Traders

Another major category of trader is the proprietary trader who works off the floor for a professional trading desk. These "upstairs" traders are employees of large investment firms, commercial banks, and trading houses that are typically located in major financial centers. Traders in this group have a number of different trading objectives. Some engage in speculative trading activity, profiting when the market moves in their direction. Such proprietary traders are compensated according to the profits they generate. Other proprietary traders manage risk, hedging or spreading between different markets—both cash and futures—in order to insulate their business from the risk of price fluctuation or exploiting differences and momentary inefficiencies in market-to-market pricing.

Market Makers

Market makers give liquidity to the market, constantly providing both a bid to buy and an offer to sell. While on the physical trading floor, locals often serve this function; on electronic exchanges, sophisticated corporations are emerging that make markets in a variety of different products. Increasingly important in electronic markets, such as the mini-sized Dow futures or the mini-sized Dow options, market makers ensure that traders of all kinds can buy and sell whenever they want. Market makers often profit from the "spread," or the small difference between the bid and ask prices.

HOW TRADERS TRADE

The types of traders described above use different strategies to achieve their goals.

Scalper

A *scalper* trades in and out of the market many times during the day, hoping to make a small profit on a heavy volume of trades. Scalpers attempt to buy at the bid price and sell at the ask price, offsetting their trades within seconds of making the original trade. Scalpers rarely hold a position overnight and often don't trade or make predictions on the future direction of the market. Locals and market makers often employ a scalping strategy, which provides important liquidity to the market.

Day Trader

A *day trader* is similar to a scalper in that he or she also typically does not hold positions overnight and is an active trader during the trading day. Day traders trade both off and on the floor. A day trader makes fewer trades than a scalper does and trades based on a prediction of the future direction of the market. Proprietary traders, locals, and public traders are often day traders.

Position Trader

A *position trader* might make one trading decision and then hold that position for days, weeks, or months. Position traders are not greatly concerned with minor fluctuations and are more focused on long-term trends and market forces. Public traders and proprietary traders are often position traders.

PRICE DISCOVERY, PRICE REPORTING

Futures exchanges are competitive markets where many factors influence supply and demand. Through the open-auction trading process, these many factors converge into one figure—a price. Exchanges thus act as barometers for price, registering the impact of the many worldwide forces on specific commodities and financial instruments.

Because these economic forces influence cash and futures markets similarly, futures prices usually parallel the actual cash values of commodities and financial instruments to a large extent. This characteristic of futures prices allows hedgers and speculators to gauge the value of the underlying instrument in the near or distant future.

FIGURE 2.2

Live Dow Chart

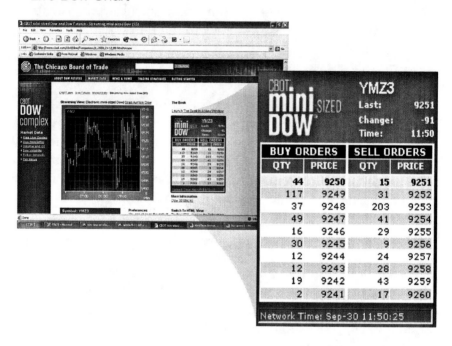

Millions of people all over the world use the price information generated by futures exchanges to make business decisions—whether or not they actually trade futures contracts. The development of new futures exchanges and special futures divisions in older commodity and financial markets in Europe and the Far East underscores the importance of this exchange function.

Of course, in order to use this vital price information, people must have easy access to it. Exchanges must therefore report transactions made to both the exchange membership and the general public. And that mandate means something entirely different today from what it meant even just 20 years ago. Rapid developments in telecommunications have created a global marketplace. Many people have access to price quotations and market data through the Internet. Exchanges like the Chicago Board of Trade and the Chicago Mercantile Exchange now use state-of-the-art technology to transmit price information instantly. In many of its electronic contracts, the Chicago Board of Trade provides immediate and free price reporting over the Internet, including Market Profile technical analysis graphs. The Chicago Mercantile Exchange offers a subscription-based service that provides the feel of the physical trading pit, with simulated pit noise, which increases when the trading volume increases. (See Fig. 2.2.)

READ ALL ABOUT IT

The price discovery function of futures markets is vitally important to the economy. Futures exchanges, recognizing this role, work to disseminate timely and accurate price information and

FIGURE 2.3

Image of a Page from the CBOT Web Site

are constantly improving their price-reporting systems. (See Fig. 2.3.) While the Internet is a primary vehicle for price reporting, newspapers, too, play a role. Major publications, for instance, report select futures and options on futures prices. The newspapers include open, high, low, and closing prices, as well as the net change from the previous day's close and the high-low price range. Prices are quoted in units specific to each futures and options contract. For instance, grains are quoted in cents per bushel, Treasury bonds in points and thirty-seconds of a point, and cattle in cents per pound.

MARKET MECHANICS AND TERMINOLOGY

In order to understand the futures markets, it is essential to become familiar with basic exchange contract terminology and operations. While trading rules and procedures of each futures exchange vary slightly, these terms tend to be used consistently by all U.S. exchanges.

The Contract and Trading Month

All futures are assigned a unique one- or two-letter code that identifies the contract type. This abbreviation, or *ticker symbol*, is used by the clearing platform and others to process all transactions. For instance, the symbol for the Dow future is DJ, while the symbol for the mini-sized Dow future is YM. These symbols are important when you trade electronically because, if you enter the wrong symbol, you could trade the wrong contract. You can obtain a full list of contract symbols on the Web site of the exchange where the contract is traded. (See Table 2.1 for some of the most commonly used ticker symbols.)

When trading futures, you need to know not only the contract code but also the month and year code. For instance, the month code for March is H. So if you were trading the March Dow future in 2004, the code would be DJH4. Table 2.2 contains the month symbols.

TABLE 2.1

Futures Ticker Symbols

Product	Symbol
S&P 500	SP
Mini S&P 500	ES
Dow	DJ
Mini Dow	YM
Corn	C
Mini corn	ZC
Wheat	W
Mini wheat	ZW
Soybeans	S
Soybean meal	SM
Soybean oil	BO
Feeder cattle	FC
Live cattle	LC
10-year U.S. Treasury note	TY
Mini 10-year U.S. Treasury note	ZN
5-year U.S. Treasury note	FV
Mini 5-year U.S. Treasury note	ZF
Eurodollar future	ED

TABLE 2.2

Month Codes

Month	Code
January	F
February	G
March	H
April	J
May	K
June	M
July	N
August	Q
September	U
October	V
November	X
December	Z

Source: Chicago Board of Trade

Contract Pricing in Ticks

It is obviously important to understand a contract's value. This is how you determine profit and loss as well as entry and exit pricing. Each futures contract has a minimum price increment called a *tick size.* The term *tick size,* or simply *tick,* dates back to the old ticker tape machines, which were the original means of conveying price information from the trading floor. Some traders use the words *tick* and *point* interchangeably to express the contract's price movement.

Another term you will have to understand is the *multiplier,* which determines the value of each tick. You can determine the value of a day's price movement by multiplying the movement in ticks by the multiplier. Here are a few examples. The multiplier on the Dow future is $10. If the Dow future moved up 40 ticks in one day, one long contract would have gained $400 in value. The multiplier on the mini-sized Dow future is $5. With the same 40-point price movement, one long contract would have gained $200 in value.

FURTHER READING

Board of Trade of the City of Chicago Rules and Regulations. Chicago Board of Trade Secretary's Office, annually.

Futures and Options Fact Book. Washington, DC: Futures Industry Institute, 1997.

Powers, Mark J., *Starting Out in Futures Trading.* New York: McGraw-Hill, 2001.

Waldron, Richard E., *Futures 101: An Introduction to Commodity Trading.* Quincy, MA: Squantum Publishing Company, 1997.

CHAPTER 3

Electronic Trading

The introduction of the first financial products in the 1970s ushered in a degree of change in the futures industry unprecedented since the founding of the formal futures exchanges in the second half of the nineteenth century. Today financial products—currencies, interest rates, and market indexes—represent more than 80 percent of global trading volume. Since the early nineties, however, the "billboard" story has been the growth of electronic trading and its many supporting technologies.

EVOLUTION OF ELECTRONIC TRADING FUNCTIONALITY

Within a period of a little more than a decade, the vast majority of futures trading has transitioned from open auction to electronic trading environments. Many of the world's leading exchanges are 100 percent electronic, and those few that continue to support both electronic and open-auction markets have seen the bulk of their volume migrate to the electronic markets.

Electronic trading proponents cite greater price transparency, instant trade execution and confirmation, lower costs (particularly marginal cost per trade), and scalability as some of electronic trading's features and benefits that have enhanced the marketplace and enabled the explosive growth of futures and options trading in recent years.

Supporters of the traditional open-auction markets present arguably valid trade-offs that are made when choosing between open-auction and electronic trading platforms: market information gleaned from using floor brokers; ability of skilled brokers to work orders for better fill prices; and an environment more conducive to certain trading strategies. Additionally, we will see that adapting many technology features of electronic trading to open-auction trading is increasingly creating a complimentary overlap between the two—a quasi best of both worlds.

Whichever side one favors, it should be recognized that the fundamental principles of futures trading presented throughout the rest of this book are equally valid for either trading environment.

One could argue that a starting point on the path to electronic trading was the formation of electronic communication networks (ECNs) in the equity markets. The first ECNs were evolving at about the same time as the financial futures product innovations during the seventies and eighties. The first ECN was introduced by Instinet—founded in 1969 and known at the time as Institutional Networks Corporation. The initial objective was to provide a means for large institutional traders to trade directly with one another, thereby reducing trading costs by circumventing the role of third-party intermediaries. Instinet gave traders the ability to display their own or see others' real-time bid and ask prices for nearly every listed stock, and ultimately execute trades.

Also contemporaneous with the introduction of ECNs was the first electronic market, NASDAQ, which began operations in 1971. Today, by allowing market participants to trade through a broad network of ECNs, the NASDAQ market is available on an equal footing from individual retail traders to the large institutional customers. Ultimately, the major ECNs—Instinet, Island, and Archipelago—evolved into fully electronic exchanges in their own right.

The increased global availability of Internet technology during the 1990s was a critical component that enabled the widespread accessibility of electronic markets to small investors desiring to trade their own accounts. While institutional and large professional traders continued to access markets over dedicated networks, proprietary front-end software pioneers such as Ameritrade and E*Trade recognized the potential of the Internet and leveraged it to deliver online brokerage services in 1994 and 1996, respectively. In 1995, Charles Schwab & Co. became the first "traditional" brokerage firm to risk cannibalizing its well-established traditional business model by introducing online trading to its customers.

COMPETITIVE PRESSURES PROMPT ELECTRONIC TRADING

The challenge of satisfying demand for expanded trading hours to meet the needs of a growing global futures community (fueled by the growth of relatively new financial products) was the catalyst for adopting electronic trading platforms in the futures markets. Once established, the efficiencies of the electronic systems vis-à-vis the open-auction trading floors became a new, compelling focal point.

As with the earliest ECNs, the first electronic futures platforms, while serving "cross-border" markets remotely, were closed systems—that is, they required the use of dedicated terminals. This was counterproductive to traders whose limited desktop "real-estate" could ill afford separate terminals for each major market. Traders wanted to use their own terminals and front-end systems to access multiple markets.

Competitive pressures soon prompted all major electronic platforms to provide accessibility through application program interfaces (APIs). An *API* serves as a "translator" that accepts messages—trading instructions—from multiple independent front-end systems, translates those messages into instructions the platform can understand and act upon, and ultimately transmits the results of the instructions back to each respective system user. In other words, APIs enable the use of proprietary terminals and front-end applications.

The segue of futures markets to electronic trading began somewhat concurrently in Chicago, Illinois, and Frankfurt, Germany. In the mid-1980s, the CME leadership recognized that open-auction trading was not practical as a means to support around-the-clock trading and envisioned the use of computers to manage orders and execute trades. This idea led to the development of Globex, the Chicago Mercantile Exchange's electronic platform.

Globex was launched on June 25, 1992, as a joint venture project between the CME and CBOT, with both exchanges trading on the system. The CBOT, however, continued to develop its own proprietary electronic system—Project A. The CBOT launched Project A to support daytime trading of new and low-volume products approximately 4 months after the Globex launch and eventually pulled out of Globex roughly 18 months later, shifting all its electronic trading to Project A.

However, the Chicago Board of Trade's initial solution to overnight trading demand—Asian morning hours—was a special evening open-auction trading session launched in early 1987. Meanwhile, growing global interest and participation in the U.S. Treasury debt futures prompted the London International Financial Futures Exchange (LIFFE) to launch a U.S. T-bond contract. It was estimated that 70 to 80 percent of LIFFE's volume was of European and Asian origin—traded while the CBOT was closed. Additionally, the Tokyo Stock Exchange and the evolving Tokyo International Financial Futures Exchange seemed poised to launch U.S. T-bond futures. The CBOT's evening open-auction session was temporarily successful in staving off the competitive threats by providing superior liquidity. By 1996, however, Project A's overnight volume surpassed the evening open-auction session fourfold, causing the CBOT to eliminate the evening trading session in favor of Project A.

In an effort to better leverage resources and secure greater global distribution of it products, the CBOT abandoned Project A in 2000 when it entered into an alliance with Eurex (known as a/c/e: Alliance Chicago Board of Trade and Eurex) to list CBOT products on the Eurex platform. Today, the CBOT's electronic platform, e-cbot, is supported by the LIFFE-CONNECT trading system.

At about the same time that Chicago's electronic markets were in their formative phase, Deutsche Terminborse (DTB), perceived the solution to the globalization challenge to be an electronic exchange offering remote access from diverse locations. Following development that began in the late 1980s, DTB launched the only all-electronic derivatives exchange at that time in January 1990. By 1994 DTB began expanding throughout Europe and within a few years surprised many skeptics by capturing the German Bund contract from LIFFE through a combination of incentives on fees, technology, and market information. Prior to DTB wresting control of the Bund from LIFFE, the prevailing industry perception was that contracts would stay with well-established and liquid markets. Today Eurex (formed in 1998 by the merger of DTB and Soffex) is the world's largest derivatives exchange with hundreds of direct connections worldwide.

The lesson learned from the loss of the Bund hastened the rate of change at other exchanges, to embrace electronic trading platforms in place of their open-auction trading floors. Stung by the loss of its Bund market to DTB, LIFFE in 1998 discarded plans for renovating its open-auction trading floor and instead initiated an accelerated project moving its markets to a fully electronic platform by the fall of 1999.

MATIF (Marché à Terme International de France) briefly adopted a hybrid side-by-side trading environment that supported trading the same products in tandem in open auction and

TABLE 3.1

Status of Trading at Leading Futures Exchanges

Exchange	Electronic Platform	No. of Trading Hours/Day	Interest Rates	Equity Index	Commodities	Energy	Currencies	Livestock
Chicago Board of Trade	e-cbot (supported by LIFFE-CONNECT technology)	22	Side by side during regular trading hours (RTH); electronic overnight	Side by side during RTH; electronic overnight	Overnight only	NA	NA	NA
Chicago Mercantile Exchange	Globex	23	Side by side during RTH; electronic overnight	Side by side during RTH; electronic overnight	Open auction, RTH	100% electronic	Side by side during RTH; electronic overnight	Side by side during RTH
Euronext LIFFE	LIFFE-CONNECT	14	100% electronic	100% electronic	100% electronic	NA	100% electronic	NA
New York Mercantile Exchange	NYMEX ACCESS	23	NA	NA	NA	Open auction, RTH; electronic overnight	Open auction, RTH; electronic overnight	NA
New York Board of Trade	NA	7.75	NA	Open auction, RTH	Open auction, RTH	Open auction, RTH	Open auction, RTH	NA

Exchange	Platform							
Eurex	Eurex	13	100% electronic	100% electronic	NA	NA	NA	NA
Winnipeg Commodity Exchange	Hosted on e-cbot	3.75	NA	NA	100% electronic	NA	NA	NA
Kansas City Board of Trade	Hosted on e-cbot	14.25	NA	100% electronic	Open auction, RTH; electronic overnight	NA	NA	NA
Minneapolis Grain Exchange	Hosted on e-cbot	14.25	NA	NA	Open auction, RTH; electronic overnight	NA	NA	NA
Sydney Futures Exchange	SYCOM	24	100% electronic	100% electronic	100% electronic	100% electronic	100% electronic	100% electronic
Tokyo International Financial Futures Exchange	Supported by LIFFE-CONNECT	9.25	100% electronic	NA	NA	NA	100% electronic	NA
Singapore Exchange	SGX QUEST	11.5	Side by side	Side by side	NA	NA	NA	NA

on a new electronic platform. Within 30 days, however, the electronic platform enjoyed approximately 99 percent of the volume, thus prompting MATIF to abandon the open-auction market. The Sydney Futures Exchange had already determined in 1997 to go all electronic and launched its SYCOM platform in the fall of 1999.

The threat of the "black box" to open-auction trading was indeed near and present. In over the course of approximately a decade, the futures industry evolved technically from the open-auction scenario that included:

- No public communication networks to support electronic trading
- No electronic order management or trade execution systems
- No straight-through processing from front-end order entry to trade execution, matching, clearing, and back-end accounting systems

Today electronic trading plays a major role in the top exchanges. Many are now 100 percent electronic, while others offer a mix of side-by-side and/or products trading during overnight hours on an electronic platform. Table 3.1 summarizes the status of electronic trading at the world's leading futures exchanges as of August 2005.

SYMBIOTIC RELATIONSHIPS

One early success story of electronic trading was supported by more than cost efficiency and remote distribution features. The development of related nonfutures products in the equities markets and, ironically, symbiotic relationships between electronic and open-auction trading pits contributed to the extraordinary success of stock index futures.

By way of background, the CME introduced the first successful stock index futures on its trading floor in 1982—the Standard & Poor's (S&P) 500 Index. It wasn't until 1997, however, that the CME launched its first fully electronic stock index futures, the E-mini S&P 500. The CME located member trading terminals for the E-mini S&Ps around the full-sized S&P futures trading pit. This arrangement greatly facilitated electronic traders' ability to accurately and quickly provide tight, two-sided markets by providing them a liquid "lay-off" market—a place where the traders providing liquidity for outside users could lay off the risks of their own electronic trades. The E-mini S&P quickly became one of the fastest growing futures contracts in history.

The unprecedented growth of electronically traded stock index futures during the last decade can be attributed in part also to exchange-traded funds (ETFs). Introduced in the early 1990s, ETFs are somewhat analogous to stock index futures to the limited extent that they both have stock indexes as their underlying benchmark. ETFs, however, trade like stocks; that is, people can buy and sell shares of an ETF on major stock exchanges. The most well-known of the early ETFs were the Spiders, which tracked the S&P 500; DIAMONDS, which tracked the Dow Jones Industrial Average; and the "Cubes" (NASDAQ 100 Index Tracking Stock), which tracked the NASDAQ 100 Index. Traders in these products found stock index futures indispensable for hedging or laying off ETF positions—a relationship that was a bonus for both markets.

THE CUSTOMER EXPERIENCE

Futures customers today access electronic trading platforms globally using a wide variety of front-end software applications ranging from browser-based systems to dedicated closed-circuit networks. Access, however, must be made through a firm that is itself a clearing firm of the exchange or has a clearing relationship with a clearing firm. The firm sponsoring a customer's access to the electronic market monitors the customer's risk profile and market position, maintains margin accounts, and provides summary performance reports.

FIGURE 3.1

Electronic Trading Order Flow

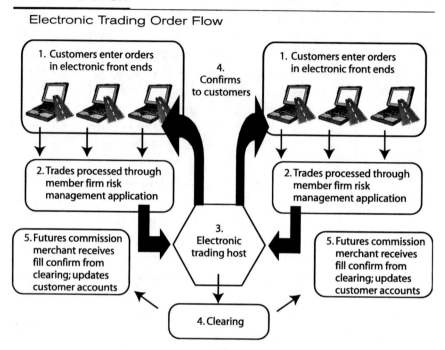

The many front-end systems connect in a standardized manner to electronic platforms through the exchanges' open architecture application program interfaces. As mentioned previously, these APIs translate firms' trading instructions from their proprietary "language" into instructions the trading platform can understand and act upon. This allows the end-user community a wide opportunity of choices in trading systems.

Once customers submit orders through a front-end trading application, the order goes into a central order book within the trading host. The trading host is at the heart of the trading system. It stores all orders in the central order book, determines priority of the order, and matches bids and offers (essentially an electronic representation of the marketplace). Priority of orders and matching is based upon criteria of the relevant matching algorithm. Different algorithms give varying priority weights to price, time received, and pro-rata rules—some with volume caps or minimum volumes.

Prior to a trade being matched, the customer has the ability to cancel or revise orders at any time during a trading session. Once a trade has been matched, however, the results are "locked." Confirmations of matched trades are sent to the trading application and ultimately back to the customer. Trade details are also sent from the trading host to the clearinghouse. Traders are unaware of their actual counterpart both pre- and post-trade.

Figure 3.1 offers a simplified view of the flow of a customer's order on a typical electronic trading platform.

ELECTRONIC TRADING INNOVATION BENEFITS OPEN AUCTION

A long-held goal for proponents of open-auction markets has been a paperless trading environment. The belief is that the requisite communications and processing technology of a paperless environment, combined with the benefits of open-auction trade execution, would generate sufficient efficiencies to sustain the competitiveness of pit trading. The past several years have in fact witnessed the successful adaptation of electronic trading features to the open-auction platform.

The trade order processing system (TOPS), developed jointly by the CBOT and CME, introduced electronic order entry as one of the initial enhancements. TOPS routed orders electronically from the futures commission merchant (see Chapter 4 for more detailed information) to the trading floor and ultimately to brokers' terminals. Electronic order transmission eliminated the need for manually writing paper orders, hand carrying them to the trading pit, and ultimately manually keypunching executed orders. Brokers benefited from electronic order management features. The electronic system also greatly complemented regulatory audit trail requirements by automatically applying electronic time stamps when orders were received.

Electronic order entry systems also automatically transmit filled orders directly to the clearinghouse. This feature not only eliminates the manual steps previously required by the clearing firm, but it also enhances risk management processes by getting trades matched and cleared in near real time. Both the firms and the clearinghouse, as a result, have a much more concurrent status of all trades.

The CBOT's recently implemented Denali system has been at the forefront of recent developments. Denali enhances the efficiency of trade endorsement and confirmation in the open-auction trading environment by fully integrating the electronic clerk (electronic order entry used by floor brokers) and handheld devices used by local traders with a robust two-way communication system. An embedded algorithm matches trades and simultaneously sends them to the clearinghouse and the confirmation to brokerage firms. Trades that fail to match within a specified period of time in the Denali matcher are ultimately delivered to the clearinghouse as single-sided transactions for later matching or reconciliation as out trades.

Once fully embraced, Denali will support paperless straight-through processing for the open-auction environment. Straight-through processing means that there will be no manual intervention in trade handling and processing from the time an order is entered into the system until it is cleared and loaded into the brokerage firms' accounting systems. In this manner, Denali's electronically enhanced open-auction trading system increases operational efficiency; facilitates near real-time risk management; reduces processing costs to customers, the exchange, members, and member firms; eliminates matching errors; and, improves internal reporting capabilities.

The use of electronic devices also has opened the way for pit traders to access electronic platforms, thus providing an added source of liquidity to both environments. The CME's GALAX-C device, imitating its earlier placement of E-mini terminals around the S&P pit, enables traders to access Globex products directly from the trading pits.

LOOKING AHEAD

Competitive and progressive changes in the electronic market-place continue at a rate comparable to the swift emergence of electronic trading. Exchanges and the independent and proprietary developers of front-end and back-end trading support systems are continually improving performance to reduce in-bound and out-bound processing and increase throughput capacity. They are also adding new or enhanced functionality for order management, trade execution, trading strategies, risk management, market and trade data analysis, post-trade processing, and reporting.

As previously mentioned, futures and options on futures trading have grown at an unprecedented rate over the past decade. The virtually unlimited scalability of electronic trading systems has facilitated this growth and will continue to do so in the future. Moreover, the ability to network related markets—for example, cash and futures—electronically is creating even greater trading possibilities and opportunities through the creation of new derivative product classes.

INFORMATION SOURCES

Ameritrade, "Our History," www.ameritrade.com/history.html.

Barber, Brad M., and Terrance Odean, "The Internet and the Investor," *Journal of Economic Perspectives,* Vol. 15, No. 1, Winter 2001, pp. 41–54, http://faculty.haas.berkeley.edu/odean/papers/JEP/InternetAndInvestor.pdf.

Domowitz, Ian, and Benn Steil, "Automation, Trading Costs, and the Structure of the Securities Trading Industry," published in the Brookings-Wharton Papers on Financial Services (1999) and provided with permission to the Financial Markets Group Web site: http://fmg.lse.ac.uk/upload_file/29_domowitz.pdf.

Instinet Group Incorporated, "Certificate Vignette," www.scripophily.net/ingroupin.html.

Mehta, Nina, "Meridien on the Electronic Threat," Derivatives Strategy.com, March 1999, www.derivativesstrategy.com/maga zine/archive/1999/0399shrt.asp.

Schmerken, Ivy, "The Top 10 Financial Technology Innovators of the Decade," *Wall Street & Technology,* December 7, 1999, www. wallstreetandtech.com/story/mag/WST20000601S0047.

Wikipedia, the free electronic encyclopedia, "Electronic Communication Network," http://en.wikipedia.org/wiki/Electronic_ Communication_Network.

Zoller, Joseph H., *Understanding Electronic Trading,* Commodity Research Bureau, 1999: Volume 8, No. 3, www.crbtrader.com/ trader/v08n03/v08n03a02.asp.

CHAPTER 4

Futures Commission Merchants

A *futures commission merchant* (FCM) is a firm that transacts futures and options on futures business on behalf of both financial and commercial institutions and the general public. Also called *wire houses, brokerage houses,* and *commission houses,* FCMs are a highly diversified segment of the financial world. The basic function of an FCM is to represent the interests of those in the market who do not hold seats on futures exchanges. Some of the services provided by FCMs include placing orders; collecting and segregating margin monies; providing basic accounting records; disseminating market information and research; counseling; and training customers in futures and options trading practices and strategies.

Some FCMs conduct business in all types of financial investments; others confine their operations to futures and options markets. There are firms that specialize in hedging accounts, others that concentrate on public speculative trading, and those that do a combination of hedging and speculative business.

FCMs become registered member firms of futures exchanges to trade or handle accounts in the markets conducted by those exchanges. Under the rules of most exchanges, however, only individuals can hold memberships. Usually, partnerships and corporations holding exchange memberships register their

FUTURES MARKET PROFESSIONALS: WHO'S WHO, WHO REGISTERS, WHO IS REQUIRED TO REGISTER

The information that follows should help you determine whether, by law, you are required to seek CFTC (Commodity Futures Trading Commission) registration. If you have any questions as to whether you qualify for a particular exemption from registration, you should seek guidance by referring to the appropriate section of the Commodity Exchange Act or by consulting National Futures Association (NFA) personnel. Requests for exemption or for "no action" opinions with respect to the applicable registration requirements should be submitted to the CFTC, and a copy of the request should be provided to the NFA.

Futures Commission Merchant (FCM)

Generally, an FCM is an individual or organization that does both of the following: (1) solicits or accepts orders to buy or sell futures contracts or commodity options and (2) accepts money or other assets from customers to support such orders.

Registration is required. There are no exemptions.

Introducing Broker (IB)

An IB is an individual or organization that solicits or accepts orders to buy or sell futures contracts or commodity options but does not accept money or other assets from customers to support such orders.

Registration is required unless *one* of the following applies:

1. You are registered as and acting in the capacity of an associated person (see below).

2. You are registered as an FCM.

3. You are registered as a commodity pool operator (see below) and only operate pools.

4. You are registered as a commodity trading advisor (see below) and either solely manage accounts under powers of attorney or don't receive per-trade compensation.

Commodity Pool Operator (CPO)

A CPO is an individual or organization that operates or solicits funds for a commodity pool. A *commodity pool* is an enterprise in which funds contributed by a number of persons are combined for the purpose of trading futures contracts or commodity options or to invest in another pool.

In general, registration is required unless *both* of the following apply:

1. The total gross capital contributions to all pools are less than $200,000.

2. There are no more than 15 participants in any one pool.

Commodity Trading Advisor (CTA)

A CTA is an individual or organization that, for compensation, advises others as to the value or advisability of buying or selling futures contracts or commodity options. Providing advice includes exercising trading authority over a customer's account as well as giving advice through written publications or other media.

Registration is required unless:

1. You have provided advice to 15 or fewer persons during the past 12 months and do not generally present yourself to the public as a CTA.

(Continued)

2. You are a dealer, processor, broker, or seller of a commodity listed in the Futures Trading Practices Act or you are registered in another capacity and your advice is solely incidental to your principal business or profession.

Associated Person (AP)

An AP is an individual who solicits orders, customers, or customer funds or supervises people engaged in these activities on behalf of an FCM, IB, CTA or CPO. An AP is, in effect, anyone who is a salesperson or who supervises salespeople for any of these categories of individuals or firms. The registration requirements apply to any person in the supervisory chain of command and not only to people who directly supervise the solicitation of orders, customers, or funds.

Registration is required unless *one* of the following applies:

1. You are already registered as an FCM, IB, or floor broker (see below).
2. You are already registered as a CPO.
3. You are already registered with the National Association of Securities Dealers and act only in the capacity of an AP associated with a CPO.
4. In certain instances when a firm's commodity interest activity accounts for no more than 10 percent of its annual revenue, the chief operating officer, general partner, or other principal in the supervisory chain of command may be eligible for exception from AP registration. Contact the NFA for details.

Floor Broker (FB) or Floor Trader (FT)

An FB is an individual who executes any orders for the purchase or sale of any commodity futures or options contracts on the floor of any market for another person. An FT is an individual who executes trades for the purchase or sale of any commodity futures or options contract on the floor of any market for his or her individual account. A registered FB need not also register as an FT in order to engage in activity as an FT.

memberships in the name of a key officer. The firm retains full control over the membership and full responsibility for the acts of the firm and its employees under the rules and regulations of the exchange.

REGULATION

Regulation of the futures industry is primarily conducted by the Commodity Futures Trading Commission (CFTC), a government entity, and the National Futures Association (NFA), a nonprofit association.

The CFTC and NFA have strict rules regarding registration of anyone who handles customer accounts. In the mid-1980s, the CFTC ruled that anyone who handles customer accounts must pass the Series 3 National Commodity Futures Examination and register with the NFA. This means that APs, IBs, CTAs, CPOs as well as exchange members who execute customer orders, floor brokers, and even floor traders who trade for their own account must register. For details on the Series 3 examination, visit the NFA Web site at www.nfa.futures.org.

CUSTOMER OPERATIONS

Typically, prospective customers will discuss their financial goals with an AP or IB, who explains the risks associated with trading futures and options. Customer financial requirements may vary from one FCM to another, but they are strictly enforced to protect the customer, the integrity of the firm repre-sented, the exchanges, and the market at large.

Once a prospective customer and the AP establish that trad-ing futures contracts is appropriate for realizing that customer's financial goals and that the prospective customer meets the finan-cial requirements, opening a futures account is quite simple. To open an account, the customer must supply his or her name, address, phone number, social security or tax identification num-ber, and business, personal, and banking references.

CFTC regulations require that the AP provide the prospec-tive customer with a risk disclosure statement. Before the account can be opened, the customer must read the statement and sign a document stating that he or she fully understands it. An addi-tional risk disclosure statement is required for those who want to trade futures and options.

The commodity account agreement form outlines how the account will be handled by the FCM and the obligations of the account holder. The hedge account certificate lists the cash com-modities owned or expected to be owned, or sold or expected to be sold, by the customer. Other documents include a new account fact sheet, a disclosure statement for noncash margin deposits, a bankruptcy disclosure statement for hedge accounts, and sepa-rate risk disclosure statements for futures and for options. These documents can be obtained from any FCM.

All this paperwork may seem daunting at first, but it is designed to ensure that customers understand their financial commitment and the risks associated with a futures and options account. Once the necessary paperwork is completed, the cus-tomer can open the futures and options account on an individual or joint basis. In individual accounts, only one person can make trading decisions; in joint accounts, all parties may have input. The customer can open either type of account for hedging or spec-ulating purposes. Generally, hedging accounts require lower mar-gins because they carry less risk than do speculating accounts.

A third type of account—a discretionary account, also known as a controlled or managed account—is another possibility. Here the customer authorizes another person to make all the trading decisions. The only way to terminate the trading authority established in a discretionary account is by written revocation of the power of attorney either on the part of the customer or on the part of the person controlling the account. Each exchange and FCM has specific rules for handling discretionary accounts, especially if an AP will exercise discretion with that account. On the Chicago Board of Trade, for example, only those APs who have been registered for at least two continuous years may handle such accounts. All discretionary accounts must be supervised by an officer or partner of the FCM. The AP must record, in writing, every transaction for the account, with subsequent confirmation sent to the customer. The customer also receives a detailed monthly statement showing the number, size, and terms of the transactions with net and open positions.

MARGINS

When someone purchases stock or a physical commodity, the cost of that transaction is the value of the commodity. When someone buys or sells a futures contract, the cost is not the value of the contract. Rather, market participants must post performance bond margins that are often a fraction of the value of the contract. These margins are financial guarantees in the form of cash or T-bills required of both buyers and sellers to ensure that they fulfill their futures contract obligations. For example, if a trader buys one soybean contract (5,000 bushels) at $6.50 per bushel, the value of that contract is $32,500 but the margin required to trade that contract is only $1,400 (approximately 4 percent of the contract value). So for $1,400 the trader can purchase a contract that has a delivery value of $32,500.

Margin requirements for futures contracts, which are set by the exchanges where the contracts are traded, usually range from between 2 and 5 percent of the contract's face value. Brokerage firms, however, can and often do require a larger margin than the exchange minimum, but they can never require less.

Exchanges determine futures margins on the basis of risk. They can change the required margin at any time as volatility increases or decreases. In a volatile (or risky) market, exchanges usually require higher margins; in a less volatile (or less risky) market, they may require lower margins. Margin levels also vary for hedging and speculating accounts. For example, exchanges and brokerage firms generally require lower margins for hedging accounts because they carry less risk than do speculating accounts.

Original margin is the amount a market participant must deposit into a margin account at the time an order to buy or sell a futures contract is placed. Then, each day, the margin account is debited or credited relative to the account's profit or loss based on the close of that day's trading session. This debiting and crediting is referred to as *marking-to-market*. In this way, buyers and sellers maintain sufficient equity cushions in their accounts.

A customer must maintain a set minimum margin known as a *maintenance margin* (per outstanding futures contract) in the account. On any day that debits resulting from a market loss reduce the funds in the account below the maintenance margin, the broker will call on the customer for an additional deposit to restore the account to the initial margin level. Requests for additional money are known as *margin calls*.

FCMs must see that their customers deposit the required margin promptly. The CFTC also requires FCMs to hold customer margin monies in accounts segregated from commission house assets, margins on house accounts, and other customer margin funds for commodities not subject to U.S. federal regulations, such as London cocoa or sugar.

To ensure that the margin system performs efficiently, each exchange has a clearing organization, which not only reconciles the day's trading activity but also makes sure that brokerage firms have sufficient margin in their accounts to cover their customers' open positions. Just as every buyer or seller of a futures contract must maintain adequate funds in a margin account with the brokerage firm, so must each brokerage firm maintain adequate funds in its margin account with the exchange clearinghouse. (Smaller brokerage houses that are not members of the clearinghouse accomplish this through a firm that is a member.)

Handling margins is an important function of the FCM. Responsibility for placing orders, collecting margin deposits, overseeing the account, making margin calls, and notifying the customer when surplus margin exists usually fall on the AP.

By their regulations, auditing procedures, and financial requirements, FCMs and exchanges make certain that customers are prepared to fulfill their financial commitments in futures and options on futures trading. Regulation of the business conduct and financial soundness of member firms, margin requirements, performance standards for APs, and the segregation of customer margins are not guarantees against customer losses caused by adverse price movements, but they do protect against customer losses resulting from financial failure or improper handling of customer funds.

FURTHER READING

Board of Trade of the City of Chicago Rules and Regulations, Chicago Board of Trade Secretary's Office.

Regulatory Guide for Futures Commission Merchants and Introducing Brokers. Chicago: National Futures Association, 1996.

CHAPTER 5

Clearing Operations: Preserving Market Integrity

A clearinghouse is either a department within a futures exchange or a separate corporation that provides a "financial guarantee" to a trade. Clearinghouses exist to ensure the financial integrity of futures and options contracts traded on futures exchanges. They do this by committing substantial capital as guarantors for futures and options transactions. They perform an essential role in trading operations, including the daily matching of trades (i.e., each long position is matched with a short), collecting and maintaining performance margin requirements, monitoring open risk positions, and settlement of accounts on a daily basis.

In short, the financial integrity of futures contracts draws great strength from the comprehensive and exacting clearing system that has evolved since the late nineteenth century. This chapter gives an overview of the clearing process and covers some of the responsibilities entrusted to the clearinghouses of U.S. futures exchanges.

THE CLEARINGHOUSE GUARANTOR

Clearinghouses, in conjunction with their clearing firms, create a two-tiered guarantee system to protect the integrity of futures and options markets. One tier of the system is that clearinghouses serve as the counterparty to futures and options trades—acting as a buyer to every clearing firm seller and a seller to every clearing firm buyer. Clearing member buyers and sellers of futures and options contracts thus do not create financial obligations to one another, but, rather, to the clearinghouse. (Some clearinghouses guarantee the gross positions of their clearing firms. Others guarantee only the net positions of their clearing firms, charging the clearing firms with the responsibility of guaranteeing their remaining contractual obligations.)

The other tier is that clearing firms extend their own guarantee to buyers and sellers who are not clearing firms. All firms and individuals who do not hold memberships or ownership interests in the clearinghouse (i.e., nonclearing traders) must clear their trades through a clearing firm, which then guarantees these trades to the clearinghouse. Like clearinghouses, clearing firms maintain certain financial requirements that market participants must meet in order to clear their trades through the clearing firm. Also, just as clearing firms create obligations not to each other but to the clearinghouse, nonclearing firm buyers and sellers create obligations not to each other but to the clearing firm that clears their trades.

For instance, a trade in which Smith sells futures to Adams means that Smith's clearing firm is obligated to the clearinghouse to offset (meaning to liquidate a position) before the contract expires or to make delivery. Adams's clearing firm is obligated to the clearinghouse to offset or to take delivery. The clearinghouse acts as the buyer to Smith's clearing firm and the seller to Adams's clearing firm (See Fig. 5.1.). For example:

- Adams buys and Smith sells one T-bond futures contract at 95-00.

- The clearinghouse matches buy and sell orders.

- Adams's clearing firm guarantees Adams's trade, and Smith's clearing firm guarantees Smith's trade.

■ After the trade is matched, Adams and Smith have commitments only to their clearing firms. They have no direct commitment to each other.

Such a clearing system has obvious advantages. Because the trade between Adams and Smith creates obligations to their respective clearing firms, each party is free to buy and sell independently of the other. If this were not the case, buyers and sellers of futures contracts would have to seek out the original trade counterparty to offset their position, hardly an efficient market mechanism.

Just as important, the clearing system anchored by clearinghouses and clearing firms virtually eliminates default risk and greatly simplifies the task of determining counterparty creditworthiness. Adams and Smith do not have to check their counterparty's creditworthiness at all. They only have to know the financial strength of their respective clearing firms and the

F I G U R E   5.1

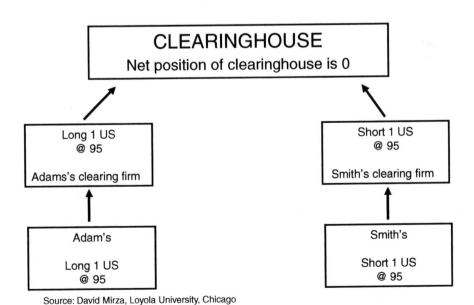

Source: David Mirza, Loyola University, Chicago

exchange clearinghouse. All market participants thus rest easy. Clearing firms will make good on the trades they guarantee, even if the original trade counterparty defaults, just as the exchange clearinghouse will make good on the clearing firm trades it guarantees should a clearing firm itself default.

COMMON CLEARING LINK

In November 2003 the Chicago Board of Trade (CBOT) and the Chicago Mercantile Exchange (CME) implemented a Common Clearing Link whereby the CME would provide clearing and related services for the CBOT. As of this writing this Common Clearing Link clears roughly 85 percent of U.S. futures and futures options trades. The benefits of such a common clearing link between the exchanges are fourfold:

1. Performance bond savings from enhanced portfolio margining is estimated to free up to $1.4 billion in collateral now posted by industry traders.

2. CME's SPAN system will calculate a customer's margin requirements based on the customer's entire portfolio of positions at the two exchanges. For instance a trader who is short the CBOT mini-sized Dow futures can receive margin relief by maintaining a corresponding long position in the CME E-mini S&P futures.

3. A single guarantee fund will be administered for CBOT and CME products that will free up an estimated $400 million in capital that was previously posted by clearing firms.

4. Simplified business practices have resulted from a single set of systems interfaces, including formats, data files, trade messages and reports, and a standardized online interface.

Although the common clearing link represents a new back-office method of clearing trades, the essential process has not changed much. (Additional information about the Common Clearing Link is at the end of this chapter).

THE CLEARING PROCESS

Following is the typical order process:

1. A customer places an order through a brokerage firm.
2. The customer's brokerage firm sends the order to the market, where it is filled.
3. The trade is cleared through a clearing firm. (If the brokerage firm is not a member of a clearinghouse, the trade clears through another firm that is a clearing firm.)
4. The clearing firm transmits the trade to the clearinghouse.
5. The clearinghouse matches the trade, guarantees the trade, and adjusts the clearing firm's account based on the gain or loss from the transaction.

Collecting Trade Data

Trading information is transmitted to an exchange's clearinghouse either by clearing firms or by exchange staff. This information is usually sent via computer from a firm's back-office system or via direct input from a trade-entry system within an hour after a trade occurs. Some exchanges are working together to standardize the method used to relay these trading data.

Trade Matching and Registration

Once the clearinghouse receives completed trade data, computer systems at the clearinghouses compare both sides of a trade, making sure that the price, contracts, and other important trade data match. Unmatched trades are displayed online throughout the trading day so that clearing firms can make corrections. Trades that remain unmatched after the close of the trading day are reconciled at a trade-check session.

Clearinghouse computer systems provide all clearing firms with online and printed verification of all reconciled (matched) trades. Clearinghouses then calculate original margin requirements for each clearing firm's open positions. This registration process is crucial to clearing firms because it is the official record of a day's trading activity.

Daily Settlement of Accounts

The single most distinguishing feature of futures markets, and the most vital procedure for preserving the markets' financial integrity, is the daily settlement of gains and losses. Daily settlement prior to the market's opening the next day confirms that each clearing firm is solvent and can continue to conduct business.

CLEARING MARGINS

Clearinghouses require clearing firms to deposit margin monies based on their own or their customers' positions. These clearing margins act as financial safeguards to ensure that clearing firms perform (post proper margin) on their open futures and options contracts. The clearing margins, set by the clearinghouse risk committee, are distinct from the margins that individual buyers and sellers of futures and options contracts are required to deposit with their brokers.

The original clearing margin is the amount a clearing firm must deposit in support of an order to buy or sell a futures contract. At the Chicago Board of Trade and most other exchanges, a clearing firm's original clearing margin deposits are based on the *net long* (buy) or *net short* (sell) futures position. For example, a clearing firm with a short position of 10 corn futures contracts and a long position of 4 corn futures contracts must deposit margin money on the net short position of 6 corn contracts. (For option contracts, however, margin is required only from the short position.)

Clearing margins may be posted in three primary forms or in combinations of the following: cash, interest-bearing obligations of the federal government, and letters of credit issued by approved banks. Foreign currencies are accepted in some circumstances. The clearing firm does not have access to this money until it is released by the clearinghouse.

Margin levels are set to be consistent with market risks. Naturally, market participants assuming greater price risks are required to post a larger margin. Thus, as a clearing firm's position changes from day to day, so does the required margin. After each trading session, the clearinghouse recomputes the margin requirement for each clearing firm. The clearinghouse provides a margin statement to the clearing firm every evening.

If a net position, or the risk on that position, increases, the clearing firm must deposit additional margin before the market opens the next day. If a net position, or risk, declines, the clearinghouse may return the excess margin money to the clearing firm. Some firms prefer to keep their surplus margin in reserve rather than to draw it back on a daily basis.

In most cases, original margins are sufficient to cover daily maximum price fluctuations. In many cases the clearinghouse collects original margin deposits within 24 hours of a trade (in some instances, within only a few hours of the trade).

In periods of great market volatility or in the case of high-risk accounts, the clearinghouse can call on a clearing firm to deposit additional margin money to cover adverse price changes at any time during a trading session. This call for additional money is known as a *variation margin call*. Within one hour, the member firm must pay the amount called for by wire transfer of funds. This amount is applied to the settlement for the day and does not go into the standing or original margin account.

Variation margin is called twice a day and more often if volatile markets exist. For example, the Board of Trade Clearing

Corporation collected variation margin three or four times on October 19, 1987—the day the stock market fell 508 points. Clearing firms had to make these payments within one hour of the margin call, even if their customers had not deposited additional funds.

In this way, the clearinghouse maintains very tight control over margins as prices fluctuate. This control ensures that sufficient margin money is on deposit at all times—another means of preserving the financial integrity of futures contracts.

In addition to monitoring the clearing firm's positions, clearinghouses monitor the markets as well. The CME/CBOT common clearing operation, for example, uses a sophisticated computer risk-analysis program to monitor the risk of clearing firms and large-volume traders. It evaluates the risk of open positions by calculating the risk a firm is carrying if there is a change in market prices or if there is market volatility.

GUARANTEE FUNDS

In the unlikely event that a clearing firm cannot meet its margin call, clearinghouses guarantee funds payments. Clearinghouses' guarantee funds are pools of money deposited or stock purchases in the clearinghouse. The size of these funds ranges from a few million dollars at some futures exchanges to more than $850 million at the CME/CBOT Common Clearing Link.

Every day, the clearinghouse settles each account on its books. All futures accounts, whether long or short, whether traded during the most recent session or not, are adjusted daily to reflect gains or losses. This debiting and crediting on the basis of price changes (marking-to-market), takes place following the close of each trading day. Clearing firms that are short of funds are required to deposit variation margin. Clearing firms with excess variation margin are paid those excess funds.

The clearinghouse adjusts accounts by calculating the difference between the day's settlement price and the price at which the position was initiated. In the case of options on futures, the clearinghouse receives the full premium from the buyer and passes it on to the seller.

Although the method of determining the settlement price varies, the following methods are the most common. When there is a single price at the close of trading, that price becomes the settlement price. In the flurry of last-minute trading, however, it is common for several separate transactions to be made at different but closely related prices. In this circumstance, averaging the closing range is the most common way to determine the settlement price.

FACILITATING DELIVERY

Another responsibility of clearinghouses is overseeing the delivery process. While all futures positions are either liquidated before a contract expires or delivered against the contract, the vast majority are liquidated through offsetting trades. (In lieu of physical delivery, index-based futures contracts, such as stock index and municipal bond index futures, are settled in cash based on the actual value of the index on the last trading day.) Surprisingly, only 1 to 3 percent of all futures contracts result in delivery of the actual commodity. Still, the fact that buyers and sellers can take or make delivery helps ensure that futures prices reflect the actual cash value of the commodity.

Clearinghouses generally do not make or take delivery of the actual commodity. Rather, they provide the mechanism that enables sellers to make delivery to qualified buyers. (There are exceptions. For example, the Chicago Mercantile Exchange and the MidAmerica Commodity Exchange make or take delivery on currencies and cattle futures.) The delivery process varies somewhat from exchange to exchange, but, in all cases, delivery is possible by completing a series of steps. The Chicago Board of Trade, for example, requires the following three-day delivery process.

Day 1 (Position Day)

The clearing firm representing the seller notifies the clearing service provider that its customer wants to deliver on a futures contract.

Day 2 (Notice Day)

Prior to the market opening on Day 2, the clearing service provider matches the buyer with the oldest reported long position to the delivering seller. The clearing service provider then notifies both parties. The clearing firm representing the seller prepares and sends an invoice to the clearing service provider, which forwards it to the clearing firm representing the buyer. The seller's clearing firm also must prepare a copy of the invoice for the clearing service provider.

Day 3 (Delivery Day)

The buyer's clearing firm presents a certified check for the amount due at the office of the seller's clearing firm. Upon receiving a check from the buyer's clearing firm, the seller's clearing firm gives the delivery instrument (warehouse receipt or shipping certificate) to the buyer's clearing firm. (Treasury securities are delivered via the Federal Reserve wire transfer system.)

PROVIDING MARKET INFORMATION

All clearing organizations record daily trading volume and open interest, which is the total number of futures or options contracts of a given commodity that have not yet been offset by an opposite futures or option transaction nor fulfilled by delivery of the commodity or option exercise. *Trading volume* is simply the number of futures and options contracts traded in a day. Open interest is determined based on the number of futures and options positions for which both long and short remain obligated to meet their delivery or settlement promises—in other words, positions that have yet to be closed out through offset, delivery, settlement, or exchange for physicals (EFPs).

The Commodity Exchange Act, as amended in 1974, requires exchanges to make this information available daily to the general public. In particular, the Commodity Futures Trading Commission uses open interest, trading volume, and large trader reports to compile monthly reports that analyze traders' positions based on account size and whether the trades are used for hedging or speculative purposes. Both daily and monthly open interest and trading volume are reported in newspapers.

CME/CBOT COMMON CLEARING LINK

In November 2003 the CME began providing clearing and related services for certain CBOT products. On January 2, 2004, the CME began providing clearing and related services for all CBOT products under the Common Clearing Link. The link will clear approximately 85 percent of U.S. futures and futures options volume, making the CME Clearing House the largest clearing organization for futures contracts in the world.

The Common Clearing Link brings together two premier financial institutions and provides operating, margin, and capital efficiencies using CME's Clearing House and existing infrastructure and processes. Many people in the futures industry hail this agreement as a milestone of cooperation between two of the world's leading futures exchanges. Following is a summary of the agreement.

Summary of the Agreement

- CME's wholly owned Clearing House clears, settles, and guarantees all CBOT transactions, using the full resources of CME's advanced clearing processes and financial safeguards package. CME's state-of-the-art clearing system, CLEARING 21, processes trades and positions on a real-time basis, providing users with instantaneous information on trades, positions, and risk exposure. CLEARING 21 allows clearing firms to electronically manage their positions, exercise options, manage collateral posted to meet performance bond requirements, and access other online applications.

- The Common Clearing Link created a single, combined clearing cycle, including combined performance bond calculations, collateral, settlement, and financial safeguards.

- The CBOT sets fees, product specifications, and cross-margining treatment for all CBOT products. Net margining still is in effect for CBOT proprietary and customer accounts, while the CME continues to have net margining for proprietary accounts and gross margining for customer accounts. Portfolio margining also is available for customer positions on a net or gross basis.

- The CME's services to the CBOT include post transaction processing, position management, collateral management, and banking functions. Specifically, the CME:

  - Matches and guarantees all pit trades for CBOT products using existing CME match rules

  - Receives and guarantees CBOT electronic trades

  - Combines the CBOT and CME portfolios of a clearing firm, recognizing appropriate risk offsets between markets

  - Establishes a single, combined security deposit pool (guarantee fund)

  - Produces one set of banking instructions

  - Combines and standardizes major business practices—for example, a single back-office interface used for clearing both CME and CBOT products

Customer Benefits

The agreement benefits 54 joint CME/CBOT clearing members, 85 CBOT clearing members, and 80 CME clearing members. These firms enjoy:

- *Capital and margin efficiencies.* CME's SPAN system calculates a customer's margin requirements based on the customer's entire portfolio of positions at both exchanges. This is more efficient than cross-margining the customer's net exposures at two separate clearinghouses.

- *Combined financial safeguards package.* A single guarantee fund is administered for CME and CBOT products. Before the link was implemented, security deposits at the CME totaled about $900 million, which was sufficient collateral to guarantee trades for both CME and CBOT at then-current volume levels. Based upon the amount of security deposits that CBOT members had posted with the Board of Trade Clearing Corporation (BOTCC), this freed up about $200 million in capital.

- *Operational efficiencies for FCMs.* CBOT established a derivatives clearing organization (DCO) under Commodity Futures Trading Commission regulations and outsourced the provision of its clearing processing and guarantee services to the CME's Clearing House. Unlike a common processing outsourcing arrangement, the DCO combines CME and CBOT operations in a manner that delivers maximum benefits to the exchanges' customers and users, by recognizing risk offsets (portfolio margining) among CME and CBOT products, combining guarantee pools, and streamlining banking and collateral costs. Because firms have all their CME and CBOT positions in a single location, all position reporting and open interest calculation is done only once and in the same, consistent manner. With firms' collateral in a single clearinghouse, firms do not have to incur the expenses associated with moving collateral between clearinghouses, thus eliminating the need for costly operational support of a cross-margin arrangement between these exchanges.

- *Cost savings.* Spread credits between CME and CBOT products are recognized by the CME Clearing House in a single portfolio. Spread credits for certain products may be as high as 95 percent.

Industry Benefits

- Reduced contributions to risk capital pools or guarantee funds. Based on existing portfolios, market participants realize an aggregate $1.4 billion reduction in performance bond requirements because of offsetting CME and CBOT positions.

- Reductions in direct clearing-related fees (transaction fees and ancillary fees).

- Operational efficiencies realized by firms able to combine clearing operations for two exchanges into a single back office.

- Simplified business practices—for example, a single set of systems interfaces, including formats for data files, trade messages, and reports; a standardized online interface.

Take, for example the savings on risk capital contributions. The largest 10 contributors to the current CME and The Clearing Corporation risk capital pools save about $120 million in risk capital contributions through Common Clearing Link efficiencies. The percentage of savings for these firms ranges from about 7 percent to more than 33 percent.

Another example is the savings on performance bonds. Table 5.1 and Table 5.2 show the percentage of savings enjoyed

TABLE 5.1

Risk Offset Savings for Stock Index Products

Assuming an 80 percent risk offset on a portfolio containing CME S&P 500 index futures and CBOT Dow Jones Industrial Average futures, and a guarantee fund contribution equal to 5 percent of margin requirements.

Reasonable Hedge Position	Performance Bond without Portfolio Margining	Performance Bond with Portfolio Margining	Risk Offset Savings
Long 2 CME S&P 500 futures	$28,500	$1,425	$27,075
Short 6 CBOT Dow futures	$24,000	$1,200	$22,800
Total performance bond	$52,500	$2,625	$49,875

by the 10 firms with the largest current combined performance bond requirements. These firms save about $730 million in performance bond collateral through Common Clearing Link portfolio margining efficiencies. The average percentage of savings for the group exceeds 21 percent.

TABLE 5.2

Risk Offset Savings for Interest Rate Products

Assuming a 75 percent risk offset on a portfolio containing CBOT 10-year Treasury note futures and CME Eurodollar futures in years five, six, and seven, and a guarantee fund contribution equal to 5 percent of margin requirements.

Reasonable Hedge Position	Performance Bond without Portfolio Margining	Performance Bond with Portfolio Margining	Risk Offset Savings
Long 50 CME ED futures	$40,000	$8,000	$32,000
Short 20 CBOT 10-year note futures	$30,000	$6,000	$24,000
Total performance bond	$70,000	$14,000	$56,000

FURTHER READING

Ensuring Financial Integrity at the Chicago Board of Trade and the Board of Trade Clearing Corporation. Chicago: Chicago Board of Trade, 1995.

MidAmerica Institute, *Margins and Market Integrity: State of the Art Research on the Impact of Margins in Stocks and Futures Markets.* Chicago: Probus Publishing, 1991.

CHAPTER 6

Market Regulation: Preserving Market Integrity

U.S. futures markets have a long history of self-regulation that dates back to the mid-nineteenth century, predating both state and federal regulation. Rules and regulations of the exchanges are designed to support competitive, efficient, liquid markets. Most state and federal regulation, which began shortly after futures trading developed in the United States, serves to enforce self-regulation by the exchanges.

The futures industry is primarily regulated by two organizations: The Commodity Futures Trading Commission (CFTC) and the National Futures Association (NFA). The CFTC is a U.S. federal regulatory agency for futures and options trading. The NFA is an industry-supported, self-regulating organization. This chapter reviews some of the principal rules and trading practices followed on most U.S. exchanges as well as federal and industry regulation of futures trading. Keep in mind that rules may vary among exchanges, partly because of their highly diverse histories and patterns of development. Note, too, that exchange rules and regulations are scrutinized continuously and amended periodically to reflect the needs of market users. The adoption of many new rules and regulations, as well as the amendment of existing ones, requires the approval of the CFTC.

THE NATIONAL FUTURES ASSOCIATION

With the CFTC Act of 1974, Congress authorized the futures industry to create registered futures associations. One such organization is the National Futures Association—an industry-wide, industry-supported, self-regulatory organization for the futures industry.

NFA was formally designated a registered futures association by the CFTC on September 22, 1981, and began operations on October 1, 1982. The NFA oversees commodity professionals who interact with the investing public. The primary responsibilities of the organization are to:

- Enforce ethical standards and customer protection rules
- Screen futures professionals for membership
- Audit and monitor futures professionals for financial and general compliance rules
- Provide for arbitration of futures-related disputes
- Promote consumer and member education concerning the NFA's role in the futures industry

In addition, the Chicago-based association also establishes training standards for members as well as conducts registration and screening of registered members through tests such as the Series 3 commodity exam.

Membership Screening

Membership in the NFA and CFTC registration are both mandatory for futures commission merchants (FCMs), commodity trading advisors (CTAs), commodity pool operators (CPOs), floor brokers, and introducing brokers (IBs) working with customer accounts, as well as floor traders. The CFTC also requires associate membership in the NFA and CFTC registration for most associated persons (APs). Associated persons solicit orders, customers, or customer funds for FCMs, IBs, CTAs, or CPOs. Membership is voluntary for futures exchanges.

Regulation of futures professionals begins with applicant screening. In addition to approving applicants for NFA membership, the NFA is authorized by the CFTC to screen and approve applications for federal registration. Eligibility requirements are strict and specific to ensure high standards of professional conduct and financial responsibility. The NFA staff handles the initial screening process. The NFA membership committee makes the final decision as to whether an applicant will be denied membership or registration.

Proficiency testing is another NFA activity and is required for CFTC registration. FCMs, IBs, CTAs, CPOs, and APs applying for registration must pass the National Commodity Futures Exam (Series 3), which tests their knowledge of futures and options trading and regulations.

Financial and General Compliance

One of the NFA's major functions is to establish, audit, and enforce minimum financial requirements for its FCM and IB members. No such requirements are currently established under NFA rules for other NFA members, such as CPOs and CTAs. General compliance rules require members to maintain complete and timely records and to segregate customer funds and accounts. Advertising and sales practices must be clear and honest and customer orders equitably handled.

The NFA conducts unannounced audits of all its members except those that are members of an exchange. In those cases, audits are conducted by the exchange. NFA audits are all-inclusive and cover every facet of the firm's futures-related business activities. Rule violations may be referred to a business conduct committee for appropriate disciplinary action.

NFA financial requirements are patterned after existing financial standards of futures exchanges, as approved by the CFTC. The NFA's computerized Financial Analysis Auditing Compliance Tracking System (FACTS) maintains financial records of NFA member firms and assists in monitoring their financial conditions. Certain financial matters, such as the setting of margin levels, remain exclusively with the exchanges.

NFA Exemptions

Not all trading professionals are required to become NFA members. Floor brokers and floor traders are subject to exchange regulation and are exempt from NFA membership. Futures exchanges are also exempt from NFA membership because the exchanges are subject to CFTC oversight.

Regulation of FCMs and IBs

FCMs and IBs are the primary interface most self-directed customers use to place orders on the futures exchanges.

The Futures Commission Merchant   The FCM solicits or accepts orders for futures and options contracts and accepts customer money to be used as margin. FCMs can either be clearing or nonclearing firms, and they are required to maintain an adjusted net capital equal to at least $250,000. In order to become a clearing firm, an FCM must satisfy each exchange's capital requirements and abide by the exchange's rules. If an FCM is a nonclearing firm, it must open an "omnibus account" and process all orders through a clearing firm.

The Introducing Broker   The IB solicits or accepts orders for futures and options contracts but does not accept customer money used as margin. IBs can accept customer money in the name of the FCM with which the IB is associated if they have written approval from that FCM. Checks must be deposited on the same day and received into the FCMs "Customer Segregated Funds" account. Once an account is established, the IB places orders through the FCM, who maintains the account. IBs are required to maintain an adjusted net capital equal to at least $30,000.

Regulation of New Customer Accounts

Upon opening a new account, the FCM or IB must ask the customer for specific background information, including name, address, occupation, annual income, net worth, previous trading experience, and age. It is not the responsibility of the FCM or IB to verify the accuracy of this information. If the customer refuses to provide this information, the FCM or IB may still open the account provided there is a written record that the customer refused to provide background information.

FCMs and IBs often enter into a written account agreement with their customers before executing any trades on behalf of the customer. If anyone other than the customer has discretion to trade the account, this must be granted by the customer in writing through a power of attorney signed by the customer. Revocation of this power of attorney must be done in writing or upon the death of the customer.

Regulation of CTAs and CPOs

CTAs and CPOs are the primary source for a customer who wants investment advisors to make trading decisions on their behalf and invest their capital in the futures markets.

The Commodity Trading Advisor   The CTA advises or manages the futures and options accounts of others. CTAs are often compensated based on the profitability of the account and based on a management fee. A CTA may not accept customer funds for margin. Rather, an FCM or IB must open an account under the customer's name and then obtain a letter of discretion/power of attorney from the customer in order for the CTA to trade the account.

Certain people and entities are exempt from registering as CTAs if their trading services are incidental to other business activities. This would include banks, accountants, reporters, and publishers. Additionally, if a person is managing funds for fewer than 15 people during a 12-month period and makes no claim to be a CTA, he or she can trade those customer accounts.

The Commodity Pool Operator   Like a CTA, the CPO manages a portfolio of futures and options positions for customer accounts and is compensated based on the profitability of the account and a management fee. Unlike a CTA, customers who invest with a CPO do not open and control their accounts. Instead, all customer funds are pooled together into a single account, and the investors deposit funds in the pool, rather than through an FCM or IB.

Those exempt from registration requirements include pools under $200,000 in assets with no more than 15 participants, excluding the pool operator, trading advisors, and immediate family members. Also, pool operators who do not receive compensation other than administrative expenses, do not advertise, and operate only one pool can also receive an exemption from NFA registration.

Risk Disclosure Statements

The NFA requires that all members and associate members provide all customers with a standard risk disclosure document, and receive signed confirmation of the documents from the customers, before executing any trades on behalf of those customers. However, if the customers wish to trade options, they must receive an additional options risk disclosure statement.

CPO and CTA Disclosure Documents

Registered CPOs and CTAs must provide each prospective investor with a risk disclosure document, and receive signed confirmation of the document from the investor, prior to accepting funds from that investor. In general, the disclosure documents must provide the following information:

- The business name, type of business, address, phone number, as well as the address of where the accounting records will be kept and information on who will make the trading decisions

- The business background for the last five years of the business and its trading managers, including the names of all employees and their duties
- Any conflict of interest that might exist. Such conflicts include commission arrangements between the CPO/CTA and an FCM/IB or other compensation programs not specifically outlined in the disclosure document
- Actual performance of the investment vehicle (A standard cautionary statement that past results may not indicate future results must accompany performance document records.)
- Minimum amount of funds required for trading
- The types of commodities that will be traded
- The description of the compensation program and any fees or expenses the customer would have to pay
- The extent to which the customer may be held liable for obligations of the investment vehicle in excess of the funds already contributed
- Disclosure of any material criminal or civil actions within the past five years against principals or trading advisors

Promotional Communications with the Public

Communications with the public by FCMs, IBs, CTAs, and CPOs is regulated by the CFTC and the NFA, which prohibit fraud, misrepresentation, and deceit by member firms in solicitation of customers to open accounts. Written communications with the public require approval by a partner or officer in a member firm. No firm may imply that they are endorsed or recommended by the NFA or CFTC. Statements of opinion must be clearly identified as such and must have a reasonable basis in fact. Copies of all promotional materials, along with a record of approval, must be maintained by each member for a period of three years from the last date of use.

Record-Keeping Requirements

NFA members are required to keep detailed customer records in accordance with generally accepted accounting principles for five years. Some of the major records keeping requirements include:

- An FCM must provide customers with monthly statements of all accounts that were active in a given month. Statements for nonactive accounts must be furnished every three months.
- An FCM must provide copies of statements to IBs who introduce customers with both the FCM and the IB keeping customer account forms on file.
- Orders received by FCMs and IBs must be time-stamped. Orders for proprietary accounts and accounts of affiliated persons may not be placed before a customer's order. Orders may not be disclosed unless disclosure is necessary for the execution of the order.
- CTAs must maintain client records in their business office, including customer account forms and written agreements, copies of client transactions, and copies of all written documentation and advertising used to communicate with the customer.
- Records of customer complaints and what was done to manage these complaints must be kept on file by member firms.

Disciplinary Actions

In order to create an environment of integrity in the futures markets, the NFA's regulations and enforcement focus on the antifraud provisions covered in the Commodity Exchange Act (discussed later in this chapter).

The NFA conducts regular audits of its members and aggressively investigates customer complaints. The NFA's compliance director conducts many of these investigations. The director can subpoena documents, and, if violations are found, they are reported to the NFA regional committee that operates where the member resides. If the member is found guilty of conduct inconsistent with NFA guidelines, the membership can be revoked, effectively ending the member's trading career under the NFA's auspices. A decision can be appealed to the appeals committee, which is a subcommittee of the NFA board of directors. Appeals committees' decisions are final, subject to review only by the CFTC.

A full-scope audit is performed on members by the NFA at least once every 24 months, and a limited-scope unannounced audit is also conducted on a regular basis. If violations are found, this triggers further investigation. If serious situations are discovered, the NFA president with approval from the board of directors can initiate a member responsibility action without a hearing, which can require the member firm to immediately cease doing business.

When the disciplinary proceeding is concluded, the regional committee or the appeals committee may impose the following remedies:

- Censure or reprimand
- A fine not to exceed $250,000 per violation
- Limited expulsion or suspension from NFA membership (with a vote of two-thirds of the committee members)
- Issuance of a cease and desist order

While the NFA regulates its members, the CFTC disciplines floor brokers and exchanges and can bring federal judicial actions against any person for violation of the Commodity Exchange Act or any CFTC regulations. Penalties that may be imposed by the CFTC include fines up to $100,000 per violation, suspension or revocation of registration, or a cease and desist order. The NFA forbids its members from conducting futures- or options-related business with suspended NFA members.

Arbitration

Another important function of NFA is to provide a centralized, uniform arbitration system. In most cases, when requested by a customer, arbitration is mandatory for all NFA member firms and their employees, including FCMs, IBs, CPOs, CTAs, and APs. Counterclaims made by members and disputes between NFA members also may be heard by NFA arbitrators. Decisions of the arbitrators are generally final and may not be appealed to the NFA. Alternatives to NFA arbitration include the CFTC's reparation procedure, exchange arbitration, or any other arbitration system mutually agreed to by the member and customer. After a particular method is chosen, no other may be used unless both parties agree. Under NFA compliance rules, any NFA member or employee of a member is subject to disciplinary action for failure to comply with an arbitration decision.

Education

NFA educational efforts are directed to both members and the investing public. The association assists members in complying with NFA rules and CFTC regulations. For the investing public, the NFA produces materials covering such topics as the fundamentals of futures trading and recognizing and avoiding investment fraud.

EXCHANGE REGULATION

Exchange rules and regulations cover many aspects of futures trading—from contract specifications to trading practices to arbitration procedures. Following are some of the more important points, which should serve as a useful guide to exchange self-regulation.

Open Markets

All trades must be made in the open market. This means that all bids and offers must occur in an exchange-approved trading arena—either in the trading pit by open outcry or on an electronic trading system—and be made available to all members present. Exchange for physicals (EFPs), transactions used by hedgers who want to exchange futures for cash positions, are an exception, permitted according to Commodity Futures Trading Commission and specific exchange rules.

Nonclearing and Clearing Members

Nonclearing members must follow certain clearing procedures when trading futures and options on futures contracts. Most important, nonclearing members must clear all trades through a clearing firm. The clearing firm is liable for those trades until the clearing arrangement is officially terminated through procedures specified by the exchange. Immediately following a trade, traders and brokers must report the name of their clearing firm to the trader on the other side of the transaction.

Limits: Quantity and Price Change

Position and daily trading limits help preserve the market's financial integrity and reduce price volatility. A *position limit* is the maximum number of futures or options on futures contracts that a market participant may hold. The CFTC and the exchange in which the contract trades determine this limit. Contract specifications usually list position limits on the long or short positions of a given commodity. Positions at or above specific levels must be reported daily to the CFTC and to the exchange in which the contract trades. Note that position limits apply to both speculative and hedging accounts, although hedgers can expand their position limits by following specific exchange procedures.

Contract specifications also list daily trading limits. Exchanges generally prohibit trading outside an established price range based on the settlement price of the previous business day plus or minus an amount set for each futures contract. For example, if soybeans close at $6.64 per bushel and the normal daily trading limit is 30 cents per bushel, beans can trade within a range of $6.34 and $6.94 on the following business day. (For some futures contracts, the price limit does not apply on or after two business days preceding the first business day of the current month.)

During periods of extreme price volatility, the Chicago Board of Trade has a variable limits provision under which the daily trading limit of a futures contract automatically expands by 50 percent. This provision applies when three or more delivery months of a given commodity in a particular contract year experience limit bid or limit sellers moves on a single day. (*Limit bid:* The market closes at an upward price limit on an unfilled bid. *Limit sellers:* The market closes at a downward price limit on an unfilled offer.) For instance, if the daily trading limit for soybeans is 30 cents per bushel, under the variable limits provision, the daily trading limit on soybeans for the following business day would increase to 45 cents.

Variable limits stay in effect for a minimum of two days. If the market moves limit bid or limit sellers on the second day, the expanded position limits continue for another two days. If the market does not move limit bid or limit sellers on the second day, price limits drop back to their original level. Other exchanges, including the Chicago Mercantile Exchange, also have provisions for expanded daily trading limits in periods of unusual price volatility. These regulations are complex. Consult the rule books of the individual exchanges for specific information.

Offenses

The following acts are considered offenses at most exchanges and will likely result in fines, suspension, or expulsion of offending members or member firms:

- Violating any rule or regulation of the exchange regarding the conduct or business of members or violating any agreement made with the exchange

- Fraud, dishonorable conduct, behavior inconsistent with equitable principles of trade, and default
- Making a fictitious trade or giving an order for the purchase or sale of a futures contract that, when executed, would involve no change in ownership
- Purchases or sales, or offers to buy or sell, that are made to upset market equilibrium and result in prices that do not reflect fair market values
- A false statement made to the board of directors, to a standing or special committee, or on a membership application
- Any act detrimental to the interest or welfare of the exchange, such as reckless and unbusinesslike conduct
- Circulating rumors to manipulate the market and affect prices or giving out false market information
- Manipulating prices or attempting to corner the market
- Trading systematically against the orders or positions of one's customers
- Failing or refusing to submit books or papers to the board of directors or to a standing or special committee when requested or failing to comply with an order of the arbitration committee
- Trading or accepting margins after insolvency
- Trading for the account of a clearing firm, or giving up the name of any clearing firm, without authority
- Attempted extortion

Rules for Trading Behavior

Most exchanges also have rules dealing with trading behavior. The following practices are prohibited:

- Noncompetitive or prearranged trading
- Disclosing an order at any time or divulging, trading against, or taking the other side of any order revealed to a member through a customer relationship

- Trading with yourself
- A member withholding from the open market any order or part of any order for the convenience of another member
- Buying or selling as an accommodation to another trader (such as prearranged trading) at any time; using one order to fill another order or part of an order; buying or selling simultaneously at a prearranged price
- Trading one's own account (at the market price or customer's requested price) before filling customer orders

FCM Responsibility

FCMs and floor brokers may be liable for losses that result from error or mishandling of customer orders. They assume responsibility for the customer account immediately after accepting an order. If an error occurs, the floor broker, FCM, or both are responsible for the loss, depending on who made the error.

Contract Default

Chicago Board of Trade members who default on exchange contracts may be suspended until the contract is performed or the debt is satisfied. If the default is denied, then the member is entitled to arbitration of the claim.

Arbitration

For a long time, the rules and regulations of most exchanges have had defined procedures for arbitration of disputes between members and members and customers. As early as 1859, the Chicago Board of Trade had arbitration committees to settle disputes that were submitted voluntarily. Consult the current rule books of the individual exchanges and current CFTC regulations for specific information about arbitration procedures.

FEDERAL REGULATION

State and federal laws governing the Commodity Futures Trading Commission require that U.S. futures exchanges enforce their own rules and regulations and regulate the conduct of exchange members as well as member firms and their employees. Federal acts throughout the twentieth century—including the Grain Futures Act of 1922; the Commodity Exchange Act of 1936; the Commodity Futures Trading Commission Act of 1974; the various futures trading acts of 1978, 1982, and 1986; and the Futures Trading Practices Act of 1992—have continuously enhanced this obligation, reinforcing the exchanges' efforts to preserve market integrity.

Grain Futures Act of 1922

The farm depression following World War I generated intense speculation in grain futures. In response, in 1921 the U.S. Congress passed the first federal law regulating futures trading, the Futures Trading Act. Shortly thereafter, the Supreme Court declared the law unconstitutional. In 1922, Congress passed the Grain Futures Act based on the interstate commerce clause of the U.S. Constitution.

Under the Grain Futures Act, futures trading in specific commodities could take place only on federally licensed exchanges. This legislation focused on exchange responsibility for preventing market manipulation by its members, member firms, and employees. If an exchange failed to adequately supervise market activity, its license could be revoked.

Commodity Exchange Act of 1936

The U.S. Department of Agriculture (USDA) conducted studies over a period of several years that later led to the introduction of a number of amendments to the 1922 law that were designed to strengthen the government's regulatory powers. In 1936, these revisions and additions to the 1922 law were consolidated in new legislation, the Commodity Exchange Act, which extended regulation from grains and flaxseed to cotton and other agricultural commodities.

The new act created the Commodity Exchange Commission, which was composed of the Secretary of Agriculture, the Secretary of Commerce, and the Attorney General, or their designated representatives.

The commission was responsible for licensing futures exchanges; determining procedures for registering futures commission merchants and floor brokers; protecting customer funds; setting position and trading limits for speculative trading; prohibiting price manipulations, false market information, and illegal trading; and enforcing the Commodity Exchange Act and dealing with violations.

The Commodity Exchange Commission administered the Commodity Exchange Act until 1947, when the Commodity Exchange Authority was established. In addition to administering the act, the Commodity Exchange Authority provided information on futures trading to the general public.

CFTC Act of 1974

During the early 1970s, rising affluence in many of the world's industrially developed countries mingled dangerously with declines in crop production in several major producing nations. What's more, two devaluations of the U.S. dollar made imports of U.S. agricultural goods less expensive and stimulated foreign sales. The result was heavy new demand on reduced supplies of feed grains and vegetable protein. In less than three years, previously ample USDA Commodity Credit Corporation holdings of surplus grain shrunk significantly. By late 1974, it was widely estimated that world feed-grain supplies had dwindled to a month's supply.

As supplies continued to shrink and demand and grain prices rose, the public and members of Congress began to question existing futures market regulation. New pressures also arose to extend regulation to futures markets not covered by the Commodity Exchange Act, such as metals, lumber, and currencies.

In response, the government began a series of hearings in September 1973 on proposed regulatory changes. The result was the Commodity Futures Trading Commission Act of 1974. This new act amended the Commodity Exchange Act and created an independent Commodity Futures Trading Commission (CFTC) to replace the Commodity Exchange Authority of the USDA. Existing Commodity Exchange Authority and Commodity Exchange Commission personnel, records, and appropriations were transferred to the new commission. On April 21, 1975, the CFTC assumed federal regulatory authority over all commodity futures markets.

The agency has five full-time commissioners, appointed by the President with Senate confirmation. They serve staggered, five-year terms, with one designated to serve as chairperson. There are three principal staff divisions: Economic Analysis, Trading and Markets, and Enforcement. Each division director reports to the commission.

Futures Trading Act of 1978

The legislation creating the CFTC contained a sunset provision under which the commission would cease to exist on September 30, 1978, unless it was reauthorized.

Extensive hearings were conducted early that year, resulting in the Futures Trading Act of 1978. That act extended the life of the agency for another four years. CFTC reauthorization continues on a regular basis.

The 1978 Futures Trading Act also expanded the jurisdiction of the CFTC, clarifying some earlier provisions of the Commodity Exchange Act. The amended Commodity Exchange Act gave the CFTC the authority to regulate trading in all futures contracts—those currently trading as well as those that would trade in the future. Prior to 1974, several futures contracts, such as currencies, financial instruments, and metals, were not regulated by the federal government.

CFTC regulation of options on financial futures began in 1981, with the initiation of a pilot program. The success of this program led to the approval of nonagricultural options in 1982. In 1984, the CFTC extended trading in options to agricultural futures as well.

Shad/Johnson Accord

During the 1982 reauthorization of the CFTC, Congress adopted the Shad/Johnson Accord Index Act, developed by CFTC Chairman Johnson and SEC Chairman Shad, to define the jurisdiction of the CFTC and the Securities and Exchange Commission (SEC) over stock indexes. The amendments gave the CFTC exclusive jurisdiction over stock index futures and options on stock index futures contracts. The SEC, on the other hand, has jurisdiction over the trading of options on any security or index of securities or options on foreign currencies traded on a U.S. securities exchange.

Futures Trading Practices Act of 1992

The CFTC was reauthorized again in 1992. The reauthorizing act, the Futures Trading Practices Act, contained a number of important provisions that addressed new futures industry trends and developments. It required exchanges to develop audit trails so that trades could be reconstructed to the nearest minute. Another provision expanded the CFTC registration requirement to include floor traders at exchanges. Floor traders thus joined FCMs, introducing brokers, commodity pool operators, commodity trading advisors, associated persons, and floor brokers among those required to register with the CFTC. (Refer to Chapter 4 for details on CFTC registration requirements.)

The act also gave the Federal Reserve Board margin oversight authority over stock index futures contracts. Before the new law, the exchanges oversaw these requirements. The Federal Reserve has delegated this authority to the CFTC. Now, the Fed and the CFTC monitor stock index futures margin changes to ensure that they do not create undue risks for the nation's financial system. Day-to-day responsibility for setting margins remains with the exchanges, though they must file changes in margins or exchange rules in stock index futures trading with the Fed and the CFTC. The Fed can request a margin change at any time to levels it deems "appropriate to preserve the financial integrity of the contract market or its clearing system."

CFTC Regulation of Exchange Actions

The CFTC's regulatory powers extend to exchange actions and to the review and approval of futures contracts proposed by an exchange. Before approving a new contract for trading, the CFTC must determine that the futures contract is in the public interest—that it serves an economic purpose. In making that assessment, the commission examines how the contract will be used commercially for pricing and hedging.

In fact, one of the first actions the CFTC took in 1975 was to redefine the term *hedge*. The CFTC broadened the definition to permit anticipatory hedging and cross-hedging within certain limits. Anticipatory hedging allows market users to buy or sell a futures contract before they actually own the cash commodity. Cross-hedging enables market users to hedge a cash commodity using a different but related futures contract when there is no futures contract for the cash commodity being hedged and the two markets follow similar price trends. For example, a hedger could use corn futures to hedge barley or soybean meal futures to hedge fish meal.

Exchanges must submit all proposed trading rules and contract terms to the CFTC for approval. When reviewing trading rules and in taking other actions, the CFTC must act in the least anticompetitive way possible. Exchange regulations of major economic significance must be made available to the public and are published in the Federal Register.

Finally, the CFTC reviews exchange actions such as denying membership or access privileges and disciplining members. In reviewing these actions, the CFTC may affirm, modify, or set aside an exchange's decision. The CFTC may also take emergency action in the markets under certain conditions, such as actual or threatened market manipulation or some other event that prevents the markets from reflecting true supply and demand conditions.

CFTC Regulation of Market Participants

The CFTC has broad regulatory powers over floor brokers and floor traders, as well as additional oversight authority over futures commission merchants, associated persons, commodity pool operators, commodity trading advisors, introducing brokers, and other market participants. For example, the commission is authorized to register associated persons and to establish eligibility requirements that may include proficiency tests.

Federal authority to establish minimum financial requirements for futures commission merchants was established with the Commodity Exchange Act of 1936. This same legislation required FCMs to segregate customers' margin deposits from company funds and prohibited using one customer's funds to meet the margin requirements of another customer's account. The CFTC enforces these requirements today. In addition, the 1936 act requires that exchanges have arbitration or claims settlement procedures to handle customer claims against members or their employees. The act stipulates that federal regulators establish procedures as an alternative to exchange arbitration or civil court actions. The CFTC thus provides a reparation procedure for investors to assert claims based on violations of federal commodities law. Claims are heard by an administrative law judge, whose decision can be reviewed by the CFTC. The procedure is flexible, depending on the amount of money involved in the transaction and the consent of the parties.

To facilitate wide dissemination of market information for all market participants, the CFTC also requires that exchanges publish daily trading volume and open interest figures.

FURTHER READING

An Introduction to the National Futures Association. Chicago: National Futures Association, 2005.

Greene, Edward F., *U.S. Regulation of the International Securities and Derivatives Markets,* 7th ed. Chicago: Aspen Publishers, 2004.

CHAPTER 7

Futures' Past: Development of the Marketplace

The groundwork for inventing futures and options was laid long ago by those who faced price risk and had the same need for timely and transparent market information that today's businesses have. Faced with similar needs, these pioneers invented futures and options, built upon the market foundations laid by centuries of commodity merchants, traders, and producers worldwide.

In fact, formalized trading practices such as a fixed time and place for trading, a central marketplace, common barter and currency systems, and the practice of contracting for future delivery all date back to the ancient Greek and Roman markets. The Agora (literally, "marketplace") in Athens was, after all, a commercial market, and the Forum in Rome was initially established as a trading center. At the height of the Roman Empire, such trading centers, called *fora vendalia* (sales markets), served as distribution centers for commodities brought from the farthest reaches of Rome's conquests.

The Visigoths eventually sacked Rome, but the basic principles of the central marketplace survived. During Europe's Dark Ages, when the widespread flow of commerce was disrupted, products were bought and sold in scattered local markets. Eventually, the practice of preannouncing markets to be held at specific times and places reemerged, taking shape as medieval fairs. These regional fairs were organized by merchants, craftsmen, and promoters with the aid of political authorities. *Pieds Poudres,* literally "men of dusty feet," as they were known, traveled from town to town arranging and promoting the fairs.

By the twelfth century, the medieval fairs of England and France were large and complex. Specialization developed, and certain fairs became the focus of trading between, say, English merchants and Flemish, Spanish, French, or Italian merchants. During the thirteenth century, spot, or cash, transactions made for immediate delivery were most common. But the practice of contracting for later delivery of merchandise, with standards of quality established by samples, had begun.

The medieval fairs not only upheld formalized trading practices, but they also contributed key principles of self-regulation and arbitration. In medieval England, a code known as the *Law Merchant* established standards of conduct acceptable to local authorities. In some cases, the standards were minimal, but they formed a basis for common practices in the use of contracts, bills of sale, freight and warehouse receipts, letters of credit, transfer of deeds, and other documents of exchange. Anyone who violated a provision of the Law Merchant could be prohibited from trading by his fellow merchants. This principle of self-regulation, found in English common law and followed in the American colonies, was later adopted by U.S. commodity exchanges.

To arbitrate disputes between buyers and sellers, English merchant associations obtained the right from local and national authorities to administer their own rules of conduct. The associations were able to enforce judgments with assessments of penalties and awards of damages by establishing "the courts of the fair," also known as "the courts of the Pieds Poudres." By the fourteenth century, their jurisdiction superseded that of the local courts.

The regional fairs declined in importance with improved transportation and communication and as modern cities developed. Specialized market centers replaced the fairs in many parts of the world. In Europe, these markets were variously called *bourse, boerse, beurs,* and *bolsa,* after an eighteenth-century innkeeper, Van der Beurs, whose establishment in Bruges, Belgium, became a gathering place for local commerce. At first, the markets were held outdoors, usually in town squares. Later they moved inside to teahouses and inns and, finally, found more permanent locations. (See Fig. 7.1.)

The development of bourses was not limited to Europe. Similar markets were formed in Japan and the United States. Japan's commodity exchanges date back to the eighteenth century and preceded Japanese securities markets by nearly a century and a half.

FIGURE 7.1

Chicago Board of Trade Members Pictured on the Trading Floor during the Early 1900s

Spot, or cash, trading in rice dates from the early part of that century. Forward contracting on the Dojima rice market started as early as 1730. Edible oils, cotton, and precious metals traded as well, but their trading volume was comparatively small.

In Europe and the United States, securities markets usually predated commodity markets. Still, U.S. commodity markets existed as early as 1752, trading domestic produce, textiles, hides, metals, and lumber. Most transactions were cash transactions made for immediate delivery. These early markets greatly enhanced the ease and scope of trading in all sorts of goods.

OLD CHICAGO

The development of modern futures trading began on the Midwestern frontier in the early 1800s and was tied closely to the development of commerce in Chicago and the Midwestern grain trade. Incorporated as a village in 1833, Chicago became a city in 1837 with a population of 4,107. The city's strategic location at the base of the Great Lakes, close to the fertile farmlands of the Midwest, contributed to its rapid growth and development as a grain terminal. Problems of supply and demand and transportation and storage, however, led to a chaotic marketing situation that in turn led to the development of futures markets.

For producers and processors in the early 1800s, supply and demand imbalances were commonplace. Farmers, who brought grain and livestock to regional markets at a certain time each year, often found that the supply of grain and meat far exceeded the immediate needs of millers and packers. These processors, seeing more than adequate supplies, would bid the lowest price. Often, the short-term demand could not absorb the glut of commodities at any price, however low, and grains were dumped in the street for lack of buyers.

The glut of commodities at harvest was only part of the problem. Inevitably, there were years of crop failure and extreme shortages. Even in years of abundant yield, supplies dwindled, prices soared, and people went hungry. Businesses faced bankruptcy because they lacked raw materials to keep their operations going. Farmers, although having sufficient food for themselves, had crops they couldn't sell and therefore lacked the income to pay for needed manufactured products such as tools, building materials, and textiles.

Transportation difficulties and a lack of adequate storage facilities aggravated the problems of seasonal supply and consistent demand. Throughout most of the year, snow and rain made the dirt roads from the farmlands to Chicago impassable. Although roads of wooden boards, called *plank roads,* let farmers bring wagonloads of grain to the city, transportation was very expensive. In the 1840s, if a farmer had to haul a load of wheat 60 miles, he would barely break even. It cost as much to bring the wheat to market as it did to produce it.

Once commodities reached the city, buyers faced the problem of inadequate storage space. Underdeveloped harbor facilities impeded the shipment of grain to eastern markets and the return of needed manufactured goods to the Midwest. In fact, once organized, commodity exchanges became a major force behind legislative efforts to improve rural roads, build inland waterways, and improve and expand storage and harbor facilities.

In response to the intolerable market conditions, farmers and merchants began to contract for forward delivery. *Forward contracting* is a cash transaction in which a buyer and seller agree on price, quality, quantity, and a future delivery date for a commodity. Since nothing in the contract is standardized, each contract term must be negotiated between the buyer and seller.

Forward contracts in corn were first used by river merchants. These merchants received corn from farmers in late fall and early winter but had to store it until the corn reached a low enough moisture level to ship and the river and canal were free of ice. Seeking to reduce the price risk of storing corn through the winter, the river merchants would travel to Chicago and contract with processors for delivery of grain in the spring. In this way, they assured themselves of a buyer as well as a price. The earliest recorded forward contract in corn was made on March 13, 1851. The contract was for 3,000 bushels of corn to be delivered in June at a price of 1 cent per bushel below the price of corn on March 13.

Forward contracts in wheat developed later. For wheat, it was the Chicago merchants and processors who faced the price risk of storing grain. To mitigate that risk, they sold wheat through forward contracts to eastern millers and exporters.

FORWARDS TO FUTURES

In 1848, as the grain trade expanded, 82 merchants gathered above a flour store in Chicago to form the Chicago Board of Trade (CBOT). Their purpose was to promote the commerce of the city and to provide a centralized marketplace where buyers and sellers could meet to exchange commodities.

During the exchange's early years, forward contracts predominated. But forward contracts had their drawbacks. They were not standardized according to quality or delivery time, and merchants and traders often did not fulfill their forward commitments. Market folklore, for instance, tells the story of a farmer who arrived in Chicago with a wagonload of grain only to be told by the buyer that he had no intention of honoring the contract. The unfazed farmer pulled out a shotgun, pointed it at the reneging buyer, and said, "I'm going to unload either the wagon or the shotgun. You choose."

To provide structure and organization to an evolving trade in elevator receipts and forward contracts, the Chicago Board of Trade took steps to formalize grain trading in 1865. The result was standardized agreements called *futures contracts*. The new futures contracts, in contrast to forward contracts, were standardized as to quality, quantity, and time and place of delivery for the commodity traded. (See Fig. 7.2.)

Along with the standardized contracts came a margining system designed to eliminate the problem of buyers and sellers

FIGURE 7.2

During the Early Years of the Chicago Board of Trade, Grain Was Inspected to Determine Its Quality

failing to fulfill their contracts. The system, instituted the same year as futures, required traders to deposit funds with the exchange or an exchange representative to guarantee contract performance.

With these monumental steps, most of the basic principles of futures trading as we know them today were in place. Still, no one could have guessed how this infant industry would change and develop.

The years after the Chicago Board of Trade formalized grain trading were critical to the scope and efficiency of futures trading. Quality and quantity standards developed as a more accurate system of weighing bushels of grain and as inspection procedures began. More trading practices were formalized, contracts were further refined, and rules of conduct and clearing and settlement procedures were established. (See Fig. 7.3.)

Delivery months, for instance, became a standardized feature of futures contracts. Months were chosen, or gradually agreed upon, by grain merchants based on harvesting and transportation conditions. March was a logical choice because the end of winter made transportation possible once again. May became an established delivery month for the cleanup of old-crop oats and wheat (harvested the previous summer). December, the last month that farmers could move corn to market before winter made travel impossible, was selected for marketing new-crop corn (harvested in the fall).

FIGURE 7.3

Clockwise from Upper Left: Chicago Board of Trade Market Reports, Price Boards and Related Market Information, Grain Inspections, and Exchange Trading Floor, circa 1930

Trading also became more efficient as speculators entered the picture. Lawyers, physicians, and others not connected with the grain trade began to speculate on price, buying and selling futures contracts in hopes of making a profit. By purchasing and selling grain that would not otherwise have been traded, speculators made the markets more liquid and helped minimize price fluctuations.

Growth in futures trading increased in the late nineteenth and early twentieth centuries as new exchanges formed and more commodities were traded, including cotton, butter, eggs, coffee, and cocoa. As the United States moved away from an agrarian economy, the number and variety of futures contracts grew. In addition to the traditional agricultural futures, trading developed in precious metals, manufactured or processed products, and nonstorable commodities (e.g., livestock/cattle markets). But the most dramatic growth and successful contracts in the futures industry were yet to come—financial futures.

FINANCIAL REVOLUTION

Beginning in 1971 and continuing throughout the decade, the financial structure of the world underwent tumultuous change. The relative financial stability established by Allied leaders after World War II gave way to dramatic shifts in exchange rates and interest rates and paralyzing economic uncertainty— financial risks that, prior to the 1970s, had been kept under relative control.

Exchange rate relationships were a big part of the problem. Out of the Allied leaders' meeting at the Bretton Woods Conference in 1944 grew the General Agreement on Tariffs and Trade, the International Monetary Fund, the World Bank, and, most significant, a system of fixed exchange rates for the world's benchmark currencies. Yet the fixed exchange rate system established at Bretton Woods failed to consider the changing rates of growth and inflation that different countries would experience.

Static exchange rates simply couldn't govern a dynamic international landscape.

Responding to the relative changes in postwar economies, the Smithsonian Agreement of 1971 devalued the dollar and revalued other major currencies. More important, it increased exchange rate flexibility, allowing currencies to float within prescribed limits. Prescribed limits or not, the genie was out of the bottle. Without the fixed point of reference provided by Bretton Woods and with the continued change in economic relationships, the system could not hold. The dollar was devalued again in 1973, and major currencies began to float against one another.

Exchange rate risk, managed systemically for almost three decades, could now put even well-run firms out of business. Under Bretton Woods, importers knew what they would pay for goods in the domestic currency, just as exporters knew how much they would receive. The system's breakdown introduced uncertainty. Exchange rate volatility meant that no future price for imports or exports could be certain.

The uncertainty didn't stop there. In addition to dramatic international exchange rate changes, U.S. monetary policy underwent a fundamental reorientation over the same time. From 1942 to 1979, the U.S. Federal Reserve measured the success of its monetary policy against interest rate benchmarks, allowing interest rates to fluctuate somewhat but eliminating major swings. In 1979, however, the Fed, under then-chairman Paul Volcker, initiated a fundamental shift in policy. Starting then, the Fed would target money supply rather than interest rates. Freed from Fed control, interest rates could fluctuate dramatically. And fluctuate dramatically they did.

The increase in U.S. government debt over the same period compounded the problems posed by interest rate volatility. From 1970 to 1980, U.S. government debt grew at roughly a 9 percent compounded annual rate, jumping from $380.9 billion to $909.1 billion. Incurring more debt meant auctioning more and more government securities to investors—investors who now faced previously unseen interest rate volatility. The risk in holding bonds, traditionally a "safe" investment, escalated.

The volatility in exchange and interest rates found its way into commodity inputs and all sectors of the world economy. Furthermore, the OPEC oil embargo following the 1973 Arab-Israeli war drove oil prices up dramatically, precipitated extreme domestic shortages in petroleum products, and contributed substantially to the inflationary pressures that marked the 1970s. The management of such financial risks became a critical factor in any firm's success. No longer was the financial world a stable environment, with risk minimized by government control of exchange rates and interest rates. (See Fig. 7.4.)

Like buyers and sellers of grain in old Chicago, businesses in these dramatically different financial markets—exposed to

FIGURE 7.4

Percent Change in Deutsche Mark–U.S. Dollar
Exchange Rate

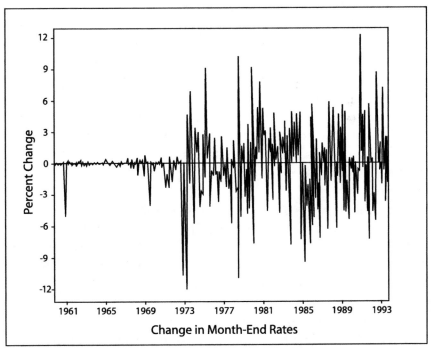

Source: Charles W. Smithson, Clifford W. Smith, Jr., with D. Sykes Wilford, *Managing Financial Risk: A Guide to Derivative Products, Financial Engineering, and Value Maximization.* Chicago: Irwin Professional Publishing, 1995.

new risks—needed risk management help. Since they didn't already have futures, they'd have to invent them.

FINANCIAL INNOVATION

Dramatically increased levels of interest rate and exchange rate risk drew a quick response from innovators at Chicago's futures exchanges, with the Chicago Board of Trade tackling interest rate risk and the Chicago Mercantile Exchange addressing exchange rate risk.

The Chicago Mercantile Exchange began trading futures on the British pound, Canadian dollar, Deutsche mark, Japanese yen, and Swiss franc in 1972, thereby providing access to fixed quantities of foreign currency at specific delivery dates. Foreign currency futures, then a low-cost alternative to the preexisting interbank market, gave companies exposed to exchange rate risk a powerful tool. By buying or selling futures contracts, companies could lock in a price for their imports and exports months ahead of actual delivery.

In 1975, the Chicago Board of Trade began trading contracts based on Government National Mortgage Association (GNMA, or "Ginnie Mae") mortgage-backed certificates. This was a joint effort with members of the mortgage lending industry to help protect against the substantial interest rate risk in long-term mortgage loans. Later, in 1977, the CBOT tackled interest rate risk even more directly with futures contracts on U.S. Treasury bonds.

In the absence of the Federal Reserve's pursuit of interest rate stability, financial institutions became reluctant to make long-term fixed-rate loans. Instead, they shifted the interest rate risk to the borrower. This helped the lenders, but stuck the borrower with the risk. With U.S. Treasury futures, companies and investors exposed to interest rate risk—practically everyone—could lock in lending or financing rates, and thus protect portfolios against interest rate shocks, even create low-cost synthetic debt instruments. Not many years passed before Treasury bond futures surpassed all other futures contracts in terms of trading volume.

With these first financial futures contracts, the floodgates opened. Since their introduction, financial futures trading has grown to include U.S. Treasury notes, stock indexes, fed funds, Eurodollar deposits, municipal securities, and other financial instruments. By 1982, options on futures started trading. Originally called "privileges" and alternately promoted and banned at various times in the history of the Chicago Board of Trade, options essentially give investors and risk managers time to decide. Buyers of options on futures pay a premium for the right, but not the obligation, to buy or sell a futures contract at a specified price. If it's financially advantageous to buy or sell at that price during the life of the option, the option buyer can do so. If not, the buyer lets the option expire unused and his or her loss is limited to the price of the option.

Options on Treasury bond futures began trading in 1982 at the Chicago Board of Trade as part of a government-approved pilot program. The success of this contract opened the way for options on agricultural and other financial futures, beginning with options on soybean and corn futures contracts in 1984 and 1985, respectively. In fact, even before options on futures were introduced, the Chicago Board of Trade formed the Chicago Board Options Exchange, which trades stock options. Unlike the securities exchanges, which also launched option divisions, the Chicago Board Options Exchange adopted Chicago-style trading, in which bids and offers are made in the pits by open outcry.

Perhaps the most remarkable thing about financial futures and options has been their phenomenal growth. While it took a century for agricultural markets to develop, the financial markets sprang up in less than 15 years and surpassed the agricultural markets in many ways. Since the Chicago Board of Trade introduced its first financial futures contract in 1975, the number of financial contracts traded annually at the exchange has soared from a mere 20,125 to nearly 500 million in 2004, or 82 percent of the nearly 600 million contracts traded that year. This

TABLE 7.1

Top 10 U.S. Futures Contracts Traded in 2004

Futures Contract	Contract Symbol	Exchange	2004 Volume
1. Eurodollar	ED	CME	297,584,038
2. Ten-Year U.S. Treasury Note	TY	CBOT	196,119,150
3. E-Mini S&P 500 Index	ES	CME	167,202,962
4. Five-Year U.S. Treasury Note	FV	CBOT	105,469,410
5. E-Mini NASDAQ 100 Index	NQ	CME	77,168,513
6. 30-Year U.S. Treasury Bond	US	CBOT	72,949,053
7. Crude Oil	CL	NYMEX	52,883,200
8. Corn	C	CBOT	24,038,233
9. Mini-sized Dow	YM	CBOT	20,695,848
10. Euro FX	EC	CME	20,456,672

Source: Futures Industry Association, Inc.

same explosive growth has been felt throughout the futures industry. In the United States, financial contracts have consistently dominated exchange trading for the past two decades. In 2004, for example, financial contracts comprised 8 of the 10 most actively traded U.S. futures contracts. Corn is the only futures contract appearing on the 2004 top-ten list that predates the financial revolution. (See Table 7.1.)

INTERNATIONAL GROWTH

Although the United States led the way in creating products to manage risk, every developed and developing nation confronts the same risk management challenges of a global economy. Thus, there has been an explosion in the number of futures exchanges worldwide, which accounts for an ever-growing share of global futures trading.

Beginning in 1982 with the founding of the London International Financial Futures Exchange, or LIFFE (now called

TABLE 7.2

10 Largest Futures Exchanges, Worldwide

	2004 Volume: *Futures and Options on Futures*
1. Chicago Mercantile Exchange	805,341,681
2. Eurex	736,139,535
3. Chicago Board of Trade	599,994,386
4. Euronext LIFFE	387,540,593
5. Mexican Derivatives Exchange	210,390,974
6. Brazilian Mercantile & Futures Exchange	181,805,817
7. New York Mercantile Exchange	161,103,746
8. Dalian Commodity Exchange	88,034,153
9. Tokyo Commodity Exchange	74,511,734
10. London Metal Exchange	71,906,901
Total	3,316,769,520

Note: All volume that was not futures or options on futures was excluded from this report.

Source: Futures Industry Association, Inc.

Euronext LIFFE), futures exchanges have sprung up outside the United States and around the globe. In 2004, non-U.S. exchanges accounted for 7 out of the top 10 largest markets for trading in futures and options on futures. (See Table 7.2.)

Foreign exchanges compete with U.S. exchanges in a number of dimensions, including product offerings, methods of trading, trading hours, and pricing. It is difficult to say which of these dimensions is the single most important, because there is a large degree of interaction between offering viable new products, listing them for trading on a trading platform (open outcry versus electronic trading, for example) suitable for customer needs, having them trade at convenient times, and providing low-cost highly liquid markets.

As the global business environment expands and evolves, new futures industry products and trends will undoubtedly continue to emerge in the United States and around the world.

FURTHER READING

Barrie, Scott, *The Complete Idiot's Guide to Options and Futures.* Indianapolis, IN: Alpha Books, 2002.

Bernstein, Peter, *Against the Gods: The Remarkable Story of Risk.* New York: Wiley & Sons, 1996.

Edwards, Franklin, and Cindy W. Ma, *Futures and Options.* New York: McGraw-Hill, 1992.

Falloon, William, *Market Maker: A Sesquicentennial Look at the Chicago Board of Trade.* Chicago: Chicago Board of Trade, 1998.

Hull, John, *Options, Futures, and Other Derivative Securities,* 5th ed. Englewood Cliffs, NJ: Prentice Hall, 2002.

Kline, Donna, *Fundamentals of the Futures Market.* New York: McGraw-Hill, 2000.

Kolb, Robert W., *Understanding Futures Markets,* 5th ed. Malden, MA: Blackwell Publishers, 1997.

Wasendorf, Russell R., and Thomas A. McCafferty, *All About Commodities: From Inside Out.* New York: McGraw-Hill, 1992.

Market Foundations

Hedging in the Futures Markets: Managing Risk

A primary economic function of futures markets is price risk management, of which the most common method is hedging. *Hedging,* in its simplest form, is the practice of offsetting the price risk inherent in any cash market position by taking an equal but opposite position in the futures market.

A *hedger* is someone who either owns the actual commodity and thus sells futures on that commodity or someone who has a commitment to either deliver or take delivery of a commodity at a fixed price in the future and buys or sells futures to offset price risk before actual delivery occurs. The theory behind hedging is that when the price of the actual commodity changes, the price of the futures changes to a similar degree in the same direction. Hedgers thus use the futures markets to protect their businesses from adverse price changes.

MANAGING PRICE RISK

Every business faces price risk. In agriculture, for instance, a prolonged drought affects a farmer's crop supply as well as the income he or she receives. But the drought also affects the price paid by grain companies for corn, wheat, soybeans, and oats.

Those prices, in turn, directly affect consumer prices for cereals, cooking oils, salad dressings, bread, meat, poultry, and countless other items purchased at the local supermarket.

For manufacturers, an extended labor strike or the embargo of a raw material could result in a diminished supply and eventually a sharp price increase for a specific manufactured product. These economic factors directly affect the price manufacturers and consumers pay for an array of products, ranging from gasoline and home heating oil to jewelry. For a bank or savings and loan, a change in interest rates can affect the rate the institution pays on certificates of deposit as well as the cost of a car loan or home loan. Again, that directly affects consumers, whether they're saving for their children's college education or borrowing to buy a new car or house. There's simply no escaping the varying degrees of price and interest rate fluctuation—risk—in every sector of today's economy. But hedging in the futures markets can minimize the impact of these price changes.

WHO HEDGES WITH FUTURES?

Hedgers are individuals or companies that own or are planning to own a cash commodity—corn, soybeans, wheat, U.S. Treasury bonds, equities, crude oil, etc.—and are concerned that the price of the commodity may change before they either buy or sell it. Virtually anyone who seeks to protect cash market commodities from unwanted price changes can use the futures markets for hedging, provided there's a related futures contract to use.

For example, suppose a soybean processor agrees to sell soybean oil to a food manufacturer six months from now. Both agree on a price today even though the oil will not be delivered or paid for until six months from now. The soybean processor does not yet own the soybeans that will eventually be processed into oil and could lose money on the deal if soybean prices rise before he or she buys them.

To hedge against the risk of rising soybean prices, the processor can be a long hedger by buying (or going long) soybean futures contracts. When the time comes to process soybeans into oil, the soybean processor will buy soybeans at their current cash market price. But, if prices have indeed risen, the futures will also be worth more. The processor will close his or her futures position by selling the futures, and the futures gain will offset all or most of the cash price increase. Thus, the futures hedge will protect the profit on the original sale of oil to the manufacturer.

Hedging works much the same way in the financial markets. For example, with currencies a hedger is trying to protect against fluctuation in currencies either owned by or owed by the individual. Likewise, with interest rates hedgers are seeking to protect themselves against adverse changes in interest rates.

Suppose that two months from now a bank trust officer plans to sell a holding of five-year U.S. Treasury notes to raise cash to pay the trust beneficiaries. Ideally, the bank officer would prefer to sell them just before the payment is due—in two months. But the price of the securities could fall by then. One good way to protect against that eventuality would be to become a short hedger by selling, or going short on, five-year Treasury note (T-note) futures. If Treasury prices decline, the short futures position will gain value and protect the value of the cash holding, because the profits from closing out the futures position will offset the decline in the cash market value of the Treasury notes.

Of course, markets do not always move as expected. Prices could move in the hedger's favor, and the opposite would happen. The loss on the hedger's futures position would more or less offset the gain made in the cash market. Hedgers accept that possibility, even though it may mean forfeiting the opportunity to make a gain in the market. To experienced hedgers, it is more important to protect a basic business investment or regular profit margin rather than risk losing it in pursuit of every last cent of extra profit. Put succinctly by real estate developer Bernard Glassman, hedgers know that, "It is more important to minimize risk than to maximize profit."

SHORT HEDGE OR LONG HEDGE

Depending on their position in the cash market, hedgers will either buy or sell futures. When they sell futures, this is commonly known as a "selling hedge," or "short hedge." When hedgers buy the future, this is known as a "buying hedge," or "long hedge."

An example of a selling hedge is a grain elevator operator who just purchased wheat that he will sell at a later date. The operator is concerned that the cash price of the wheat he just purchased might drop before he sells the actual commodity. The operator would then establish a selling hedge, selling wheat futures to offset this risk.

An example of a buying hedge is a food processor who must purchase wheat three months in the future. The processor is concerned that the cash price of the wheat is going to rise before she buys the actual commodity. The processor would then establish a buying hedge, buying wheat futures to offset the risk of rising prices.

THE RELATIONSHIP BETWEEN CASH AND FUTURES: THE BASIS

It is important that traders and hedgers understand the price relationship between cash and futures. The term *cash* refers to the underlying physical product. Cash corn, for instance, refers to the actual product—kernels of corn. In a typical cash transaction, delivery of the commodity can be immediate or within a specified number of days after the transaction. In the futures market, however, buyers and sellers agree to take or make delivery of a specific commodity or financial instrument at a predetermined place and time in the future. The date of the purchase or sale may be weeks or months away, hence the term *futures.*

Interestingly, the cash price and the futures price are seldom the same. The difference between the cash and futures prices is known as the *basis*.

The Basis

To obtain the basis, the hedger subtracts the futures price from the cash price. What results is known as the basis, which yields either a positive or negative number. If the calculation yields a positive number, where the cash price is higher than the futures price, the basis is said to be "over." Likewise, when the cash price is lower than the futures price, the basis is said to be "under." Hedgers use this over-under terminology to describe the nature of their trade.

For instance, if an elevator operator buys corn from a farmer at $2.68 a bushel on June 5, and the July corn futures contract is at $2.74¼ on the same day, the basis at the local grain elevator would be 6¼ cents under (–6¼ cents) the July contract. If an oil producer is selling crude oil, and the local cash price on June 5 is $19.68 a barrel and the July crude oil futures contract is at $19.66, the basis is 2 cents over (+2 cents) the July futures contract. As these examples illustrate, the basis for physical commodities, such as corn, soybeans, wheat, crude oil, or gold, can be either positive or negative, depending on whether the cash price is higher or lower than the futures price.

Calculating the basis for Treasury bonds and notes requires an extra step. In futures terminology, a bond's basis represents the spread between the bond's cash market price and its delivery price into a futures contract. Therefore, calculating the basis first requires calculating the delivery price. The delivery price is calculated by multiplying the futures price by a conversion factor. Since each bond has a conversion factor determined by its coupon and maturity, the conversion factor allows different bonds to be compared for delivery purposes. (The calculation methodology to arrive at the conversion factor is beyond the scope of this book; however, the CBOT publishes the conversion factors on its Web site.)

Weak or Strong Basis

The basis can and does change. If the basis moves from 8 to 1, or from –5 to –9, hedgers say that the basis has weakened. The trader in general says that it has become less positive or more negative. On the other hand, if the basis moves from 1 to 8, or from –9 to –5, hedgers say that the basis has strengthened. The trader says that it has become more positive or less negative.

A variety of factors can cause the basis to change. If the demand for the cash commodity is strong or the available supply is small, cash market prices could rise relative to futures prices. If there is a large supply of grain and little demand, cash prices could fall relative to futures prices. Other factors that affect the basis of agricultural commodities include:

- Carryover stocks from the previous year
- Expectations of the current year's production
- Supply and demand of comparable substitutes
- Foreign production
- Foreign demand
- Storage costs
- Availability of sufficient storage facilities
- Transportation costs
- Transportation problems
- Insurance costs
- Federal policies
- Seasonal price fluctuations
- The time to expiration of the futures contract

Similarly, several factors affect the basis for financial instruments. These factors include:

- The cost of credit (interest rates)
- Federal Reserve Board monetary policies
- Fiscal policies reflected in the deficit (government spending less tax receipts)
- Time until expiration of the futures contract
- Cost of funding margin requirements
- Coupon of the cash market instrument being hedged against the 6 percent futures contract coupon standard
- Supply of deliverable cash market instruments
- Domestic and foreign demand for cash market instruments
- Inflationary expectations
- General level of business activity
- Seasonal factors, such as estimated quarterly tax payments by corporations and self-employed individuals
- Liquidity of nearby versus distant month contracts

Despite possible changes however, the basis is generally less volatile than either the futures price or the cash price. By adding a futures position to their basic cash business, hedgers replace the risk of price level fluctuation with the lesser risk of a change in the relationship between the cash price and futures price of the commodity—that is, basis risk. In other words, the combination of a futures position with a basic cash business gives the hedger a position in the basis. Long cash and short futures are a long basis position, so that a short hedger is long basis. And short cash and long futures are a short basis position, so that a long hedger is short basis.

Because of a hedger's basis position, a change in the basis during the time of the hedge can influence the results of a transaction. Hedgers must pay close attention to this relationship. Without knowledge of the usual basis and basis patterns for a given commodity, it is impossible for a hedger to make a fully informed decision about whether to accept or reject a given price (cash or futures); whether, when, and in what delivery month to hedge; when to close a hedge; or when and how to turn an unusual basis situation into a possible profit opportunity.

PRICE RELATIONSHIPS: GRAINS

Grain is generally harvested within a few weeks span each year, but only a small portion is actually used at harvest. The rest is stored until it is needed for feeding, processing, or exporting. The expenses of storage—known as the *cost of carry* or *carrying charges*—normally are reflected in futures prices for different delivery months. They include not only the cost of using storage facilities for the grain, but also such costs as insurance on the grain and interest on the invested capital.

The crop marketing year varies slightly with each agricultural commodity, but it tends to begin following harvest and end before the next year's harvest. For example, the marketing year for soybeans begins September 1 and ends August 31. The November futures contract month represents the first major new-crop soybean marketing month; July represents the last major old-crop marketing month. At the beginning of the soybean marketing year, November is considered the *nearby month;* subsequent contract months are referred to as *deferred months.*

Sellers usually require a higher price for deferred contracts in order to cover the carrying charges. Consequently, these carrying charges tend to be reflected in the price of futures contracts. More distant or deferred futures contracts tend to trade at higher prices than do nearby futures contracts. For example, corn futures prices for delivery within the same marketing year are normally stair-stepped upward from one delivery month to the next. If the total cost of storing corn were, say, 4 cents per bushel per month, and if futures prices reflected the full carrying charge, the prices for the different delivery months might look something like this:

December	March	May	July	September
$2.76	$2.88	$2.96	$3.04	$3.12

This example illustrates normal market conditions. In reality, the market usually reflects less than full carrying charges or may even reflect negative carrying charges, which are referred to as an *inverted market*. An inverted market can occur for a variety of reasons, including a strong immediate demand for cash grain or the willingness of elevator owners to store grain for their own accounts at less than the full storage rate.

PRICE RELATIONSHIPS: DEBT INSTRUMENTS

The basis for debt instruments is almost totally dependent on interest rates, so historical basis behavior does not have nearly the same impact on debt instruments as it does in the grain markets. There are repetitive tendencies, however, within the financial markets.

Also, the equity markets during the 7- to 10-day period marking the end of each calendar quarter (March, June, September, and December) are closely watched for changes in equity cash and futures prices. Because portfolio managers' performance is sometimes measured against the quarterly return on the Standard & Poor's 500 Index, managers often adjust their market positions—selling losing positions or buying winning ones—before the end of the quarter and the subsequent release of reports to clients.

In the case of interest rate futures, deferred futures months (those that expire later in the year) are generally priced lower than the nearby futures month (the next contract month that will stop trading). On June 6, 1997, for example, U.S. Treasury bond futures prices exhibited the familiar pattern:

September 1997	December 1997	March 1998	June 1998
111-07	110-26	110-16	110-05

Furthermore, for interest rate futures, cash prices typically exceed adjusted futures prices (futures prices multiplied by the appropriate conversion factor), reflecting a positive cost of carry.

These normal patterns for interest rate futures price spreads and basis are the opposite of the patterns found in normal grain markets. But they are the result of "storage" costs just as with the grain patterns. Like an owner of cash grain, bond owners pay storage. For bonds, storage is made up mostly of interest paid to finance the bond purchase. Unlike the owner of grain, however, bond owners receive income from storing, or owning, the bond—the interest paid by the bond to the bond holder.

Normally, the interest paid by a bond exceeds the interest cost of financing because long-term interest rates exceed short-term financing rates. Because bond holders typically are paid, on net, to own bonds, the deferred futures price for a bond is lower than its nearby futures price. And the basis is positive. For grains the patterns are just the opposite. This difference between financial futures and grain futures patterns reflects the reality that grain owners pay to store their grain until delivery but bond holders are paid to store bonds until delivery.

In short, the cost of carry for Treasury instruments reflects the difference between interest income and financing costs. It includes any interest payments received minus any short-term borrowing costs and transaction costs. Normally, cost of carry is positive—that is, long-term rates paid by bonds or notes exceed short-term borrowing rates. When cost of carry is positive, a cash bond holding produces profit even if its price remains unchanged.

For example, suppose the cost to finance for one month a 12 percent $100,000 U.S. Treasury bond selling at par is 10 percent. Under these circumstances, the investor earns $167 a month by holding the bond.

Annual coupon payment:
    $100,000 × 12% = $12,000

Annual finance cost:
    $100,000 × 10% = $10,000

Annual cost of carry:
    $12,000 − $10,000 = $2,000

Monthly cost of carry:
    $2,000/12 = $167

In this "normal" market environment, the cash instrument is priced at a premium in relation to the futures contract. Since these gains increase as the holding period increases, the nearby futures contract likewise trades at a premium in relation to the deferred futures. On the other hand, if the cost of carry is negative, investors lose money holding the investment until delivery. To compensate for this negative cost of carry, investors trade the cash instrument at a discount in relation to the futures contract. And since carrying costs rise as the holding period increases, the futures price of the nearby contract month trades at a discount in relation to the deferred contract month.

For example, suppose the cost of financing the security above rises to 14 percent. In this instance, the cost of carry is negative, and the investor loses $167 a month carrying the bond until delivery.

Annual coupon payment:
    $100,000 × 12% = $12,000

Annual finance cost:
    $100,000 × 14% = $14,000

Annual cost of carry:
    $12,000 − $14,000 = ($2,000)

Monthly cost of carry:
($2,000)/12 = ($167)

The key to debt market conditions—and whether "normal" cost of carry conditions are present—is the shape of the yield curve. That's because the yield curve reflects the cost of carry—the relationship between long-term and short-term interest rates. The yield curve is a chart or graph that visually depicts yield to maturity for debt instruments of different maturities but with the same rating. *Yield to maturity* is the rate of return an investor theoretically receives if an interest-bearing instrument is held until its maturity date and all coupon income can be reinvested at that rate. U.S. government debt instruments—Treasury bills, notes, and bonds—are most often used because all government debt carries the same credit rating and offers investors maturities ranging from days up to 30 years.

The yield curve is positive when long-term rates are higher than short-term rates. In such an environment, investors are willing to accept a lower yield on short-term investments and are compensated at a higher rate for lending their money over an extended time. (See Fig. 8.1.)

When short-term rates are higher than rates on long-term investments, however, the yield curve is inverted. An inverted, or negative, yield curve typically occurs during inflationary periods, when heavy credit demand pushes short-term rates higher than long-term rates. (See Fig. 8.2.)

When the yield curve has a normal shape, that is, when long-term rates exceed short-term financing rates, bond owners are paid interest, on net, to own bonds. The nearby futures price exceeds the deferred futures price to reflect this positive cost of carry, just as the cash price exceeds the adjusted futures price. When the yield curve inverts, that is, when short-term financing rates exceed long-term rates, bond owners pay interest, on net, to own bonds, and futures price relationships become like those in normal grain markets, with nearby futures less than deferred futures and the futures price exceeding the cash price.

F I G U R E   8.1

Positive Yield Curve

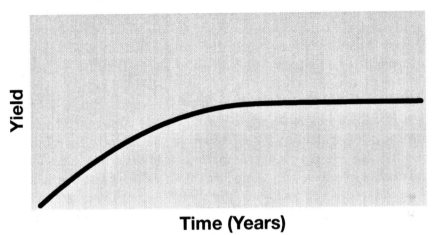

Time (Years)

F I G U R E   8.2

Negative Yield Curve

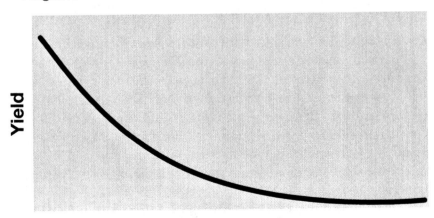

Time (Years)

DELIVERY: CASH AND FUTURES LINK

Hedging works primarily because changes in futures prices generally track with changes in cash prices. The delivery process forges the cash-futures link. So strong is that link that the futures price equals the cash price at expiration at the futures delivery location.

Futures contracts for most physical commodities, such as grains, require market participants holding contracts at expiration to either take or make delivery of the underlying commodity. It's this responsibility to make or take delivery that forces futures prices to reflect the actual cash value of the commodity. As with other contractual obligations, futures market participants must complete predetermined delivery steps within a specified time to comply with the terms of the futures agreement. For example, the Chicago Board of Trade corn contract specifies that the deliverable grade is No. 2 yellow or permitted substitutions at differentials established by the exchange. Delivery of financial instruments also must satisfy established criteria. A particular U.S. Treasury bond is eligible for delivery against the T-bond futures contract if there is time remaining to maturity, or time remaining to call if callable, of at least 15 years as of the first day of the delivery month.

Note, however, that although Treasury futures allow delivery of a range of issues, one issue will be more economical than the others to deliver against the futures contract. Futures market participants call that issue the *cheapest to deliver* (CTD). Because anyone trading bond futures can assume that a seller will deliver the most economical instrument, Treasury contracts tend to trade to the price of the CTD. In addition to following the credit markets in general, financial hedgers must know which issue is cheapest to deliver at any point in time and at what interest rate levels that issue is likely to change to a different bond or note.

Identifying the CTD bond or note relative to a particular futures contract involves doing a fairly complex computation for each cash bond eligible for delivery. While there is no shortcut for the computation, many data vendors track the CTD for their subscribers.

Not all futures contracts require physical delivery. Futures contracts that track indexes, such as stock or bond index futures contracts and such physical contracts as feeder cattle, are cash-settled. Cash-settled futures contracts are specifically designed to converge with the value of the underlying index at expiration—ensuring that delivery month pricing remains correlated to the underlying index.

Whether futures are settled by cash or physical delivery, cash and futures prices are linked by a market practice called *arbitrage,* in which arbitrageurs simultaneously buy and sell similar commodities in different markets to take advantage of a price discrepancy. Arbitrage also extends the link to times prior to delivery. In fact, only about 3 percent of all futures contracts actually see delivery. Instead, most are offset before they expire. To offset a futures position, hedgers take a second futures position that is opposite their initial transaction. For instance, if a hedger established an open position by selling, or going short, five July wheat contracts, that hedger can offset the position by buying, or going long, five July wheat contracts. In other words, most futures traders use the futures market as a pricing mechanism. Few actually deliver or take delivery of the commodity.

Yet continuous market forces, applied by arbitrage traders, ensure that pricing relationships between the cash and futures markets remain in line. These reliable price relationships enable hedgers to use the futures market as an effective pricing mechanism. When cash prices are higher than the futures prices (after carrying costs are netted out), or vice versa, active traders generally buy the lower-priced, or "cheaper," instrument and sell the higher-priced, or "dearer," instrument. Because many traders attempt to capitalize on these price distortions, their actions have the net effect of forcing prices back into line, quickly minimizing price disparities.

This trading practice is crucial to preserving a reliable relationship between the cash and futures markets. Indeed, arbitrage ensures that the basis approaches zero by the time the contract expires. Without this activity, it would be impossible for hedgers to transfer their unwanted risk, because the futures contract might have little, if any, price correlation to the cash market.

EXCHANGE FOR PHYSICAL

In addition to making or taking delivery of a commodity, hedgers can enter into an exchange for physicals (EFP) transaction. Also known as "against actuals" or "versus cash," EFPs generally are used by two hedgers who want to "exchange" futures for cash positions. EFPs are the only type of futures transaction allowed to take place outside the trading pit and are permitted according to specific exchange and Commodity Futures Trading Commission rules.

For instance, suppose a grain exporter commits to a forward sale of grain and simultaneously hedges with a futures purchase. On the day he must acquire the grain for shipment, he makes a cash bid to an elevator operator expressed in terms of basis. The elevator operator also has hedged, but with a short futures position to protect against a possible decline in value of the stored grain. Both the exporter and elevator operator agree to the basis terms.

The elevator operator (short hedger) delivers the actual cash grain to the exporter (long hedger) in exchange for a long futures position. That long position offsets the elevator operator's initial short futures position, thus ending the hedge. The grain exporter, in turn, acquires the actual grain needed for shipment and assumes a short position, which automatically offsets his initial long futures position. The price of the cash grain contracted between the elevator operator and grain exporter is determined by the agreed-upon basis plus the price at which the futures contracts were exchanged. For example, if December corn futures were exchanged at $2.50 and the basis is 10 cents under (−10 cents), then the cash price agreed to in the EFP would be $2.40.

EFPs involving financial instruments, usually fixed-income instruments, frequently occur. Institutions with opposite cash-futures positions find it profitable and convenient to use U.S. Treasury bonds, notes, or bills in EFP transactions.

Exchange for physicals is important to commercial users because if both the long and short hedgers were required to liquidate their futures positions by open outcry auction in the pit, they might have to do so at different prices. This would mean that the effectiveness of the agreed-upon basis for both buyer and seller would be lost. Consequently, some cash commodity dealers who trade the basis often specify when trading the cash market commodity that they will exchange only against futures.

THE IMPERFECT HEDGE

In theory when a hedger sells a corresponding future, it is intended to lock in the price/profit of the hedger. However, in reality the future and the cash commodity don't always perform exactly as expected. This creates an *imperfect hedge.*

It is important to realize that a hedge may not precisely eliminate all price risk. This results from a host of factors. For example, changes in the economic climate can cause changes in the basis (as discussed earlier). Some other leading factors that can contribute to an imperfect hedge often center around the standardized nature of the futures contract and the often unstandardized nature of the hedger's needs. A few examples follow.

Delivery Months   One source of price disparity between the cash market and the futures market occurs when the standardized delivery months of a futures contract do not match the actual delivery month of the cash commodity. For instance, let's say that on June 15 the price of cash wheat is $3.02½ and that the price of the September futures is $3.14¼. The farmer is looking to sell her crop in late August, so she decides to hedge with the September futures. When the time to sell in August arrives, the cash is now selling at $3.08½ and the price of the September future is selling at $3.26¼. The farmer made $0.06 on the increase in the price of the cash commodity yet lost $0.12 on the futures contract. Because the cash and the future moved to different degrees, the hedge cost the farmer $0.06 per bushel. The reasons for this delivery month price shift can vary. In the case of the grain market, selling pressure of a harvest may influence the immediate price of the cash to a greater degree than that of the distant futures contract.

Contract Size   Often the standardized size of a futures contract does not match the exact needs of the hedger. For instance, let's say a U.S. manufacturer plans to purchase a product from a Swiss company three months in the future. The purchase price is 1,050,000 Swiss francs, and the U.S. manufacturer would like to limit the upside price risk of a rising franc by buying the franc future at current levels. However, the contract size of each Swiss franc futures contract is 125,000 francs. In this instance, if the manufacturer hedged using eight futures contracts (1,000,000 francs), that would leave a portion of the contract value (50,000 francs) unhedged, thus creating an imperfect hedge.

Product Specifications   Sometimes the standardized product specifications of a futures contract do not exactly match the needs of the hedger. For instance, the Chicago Board of Trade corn contract specifies delivery of No. 2 yellow corn. However, if a farmer has produced No. 3 grade corn, the price fluctuation between grades may be different, thereby creating another imperfect hedge.

While hedging may not be perfect, it works to a large degree and performs a most important function—enabling businesspeople to manage future price risk and predict profit with relative accuracy.

BASIC HEDGING STRATEGIES

Hedging with futures requires a two-step process. Depending on a hedger's cash market risk exposure, the hedger will either buy or sell futures initially. Next, the hedger must offset that opening position before the futures contract expires by taking a second position opposite the initial one. The position in both the opening and closing trades must involve the same commodity, number of contracts, and delivery month.

The following examples illustrate both long and short hedges. For ease of explanation, basis is not taken into consideration in the following strategies. There is one exception—the short soybean hedge. As shown in that example, a change in basis affects a hedger's ultimate price. Because of this, traders must include basis analysis in any real-life hedge transaction. The examples also do not include commission or transaction costs.

Short Hedging to Protect against Falling Soybean Prices

Using futures, farmers can take advantage of seasonal price patterns to establish prices for their crops long before harvest. Soybean and corn cash prices typically peak in June or July and are lowest at harvest, which runs through October and November. A short futures hedge can help capture the better early summer prices. But to take full advantage of the possibilities, farmers must have solid understanding of the relevant basis pattern.

Suppose that in June a farmer expects to harvest at least 10,000 bushels of soybeans in September. The new-crop November futures contract is trading at $6.25, and the current cash quotation is 25 cents under the November contract, or $6.00. The farmer could lock in that price with a forward contract. But, by consulting this basis, he sees that the current basis of 25 cents under is weaker than the historical harvest level and that the basis normally strengthens by about 10 cents by the end of October. The farmer thus sees the potential for gain if the basis becomes less negative between June and the time he sells his cash beans. With that in mind, the farmer might prefer to hedge the 10,000 bushels with futures. That would allow him to lock in the futures price in June but wait to lock in the cash price when the basis improves.

Essentially, the farmer wants to short hedge. To establish the hedge, and his basis position,* in early June the farmer sells two November soybean contracts at $6.25. (Farmers seldom hedge their entire expected production because they can't know exactly how many bushels they will produce until harvest. In this example, the farmer expects to produce more than 10,000 bushels, but the 10,000 figure preserves a safety margin.)

By late September, with the soybeans harvested, cash and November futures prices have both fallen, but the basis has strengthened from 25 under to 16 under the November price. When the farmer sells his soybeans to the local elevator operator for $5.85 a bushel, he lifts his hedge by buying back his two futures contracts at $6.01. The futures gain of 24 cents a bushel gives the farmer a net selling price of $6.09 a bushel—9 cents a bushel better than the June price because of the basis gain. (See Table 8.1.)

September cash sale price	$5.85 per bushel
Futures gain	$0.24 per bushel
Net sale price	$6.09 per bushel

Had the farmer not hedged, he would have received only $5.85 a bushel for his beans—the September cash price. That's 24 cents less than he received by hedging with futures. Had the farmer hedged in June with a forward contract, locking in a $6.00 per bushel cash sale price, he would have done somewhat better by not hedging, but he would not have participated in the

---

* Cash plus short futures are a long basis position.

TABLE 8.1

Short Hedge on Soybeans

	Cash	Futures	Basis
June	New-crop beans at $6.00 per bushel	Sell two November futures at $6.25 per bushel	−25 cents
September	Sell 10,000 bushels of beans at $5.85 per bushel	Buy two November futures at $6.01 per bushel	−16 cents
Results	Cash sale loss: −15 cents per bushel	Futures gain: +24 cents per bushel	+9 cents

basis gain offered by his short hedge and the long basis position in the futures market.

Note that the farmer cannot exactly predict the basis. Had the basis become more instead of less negative, the farmer's net selling price would have been lower than he would have received by locking in a $6.00 cash sale in June with a forward contract. But basis does tend to adhere to a normal pattern in most crop years. Thus, a short hedge combined with careful basis study can provide the means for establishing a price for a crop when the farmer sees an advantage in doing so.

Long Hedge to Establish the Price of Silver

Suppose a film manufacturer wants to establish a ceiling price for the 20,000 troy ounces of silver he plans to purchase during December and January. Anticipating a price increase, he would like to take advantage of the current cash price of $5.20 per troy ounce but does not want to buy the silver right now. Thus, on June 15, with silver futures for December delivery trading at $5.70 per troy ounce, the manufacturer decides to purchase 20 December silver futures contracts. Each contract represents 1,000 troy ounces of silver.

Several months elapse, and silver prices continuing to rise. The manufacturer decides to purchase silver in the cash market at $9 and closes his futures position by selling 20 December silver contracts at $9.45. (See Table 8.2.)

TABLE 8.2

Long Hedge on Silver

	Cash	Futures
June	Needs 20,000 ounces of silver in December; silver at $5.20 per troy ounce	Buys 20 December silver futures at $5.70 per troy ounce
November	Acquires 20,000 ounces of silver at $9 per troy ounce	Sells 20 December silver futures at $9.45 per troy ounce
Result	$3.80 price increase	$3.75 per troy ounce gain

November cash purchase price	$9.00 per troy ounce
Futures gain	<u>$3.75 per troy ounce</u>
Net purchase price	$5.25 per troy ounce

In this instance, the futures gain of $3.75 per troy ounce cushioned the cash price increase, which resulted in an additional cost of only 5 cents per troy ounce from what the film manufacturer initially expected to pay. By hedging, the manufacturer paid only $5.25 per troy ounce as opposed to the $9 per ounce he would have had to pay if he had not hedged in the futures market—and was able to delay his actual purchase of the silver until the more convenient November time.

Long Hedge Using Treasury Note Futures

Institutional investors frequently use the futures markets to reduce their exposure to the risk of fluctuating interest rates. For instance, suppose the investment manager of an insurance company wants to take advantage of the high yield offered on U.S. Treasury notes in May. Yet the company's cash inflows are weak because of unexpected policy payouts and low new policy sales. The company expects cash flows to return to normal by September.

In May, long-term September Treasury note futures are trading at 84-12, and the cash notes are priced at 99-16. The portfolio manager wants to purchase the 8 percent T-notes that mature on May 15, 2005. She calculates that a weighted hedge requires 103 September T-note futures and buys them at 84-12 in May.

During the next couple of months, interest rates decline, thereby raising the cash market value of the T-notes to 101-04. The price of T-note futures rises to 86-00. (See Table 8.3.)

August cash purchase price	$10,112,500
Futures gain	$ 167,375
Net purchase price	$9,945,125

Had the investment manager not established a long hedge, it would have cost her an additional $162,500 to purchase the Treasury notes in the cash market at August prices. Using T-note futures to hedge the purchase price, the investment manager not only avoided that additional cost, but also generated a modest profit of $4,875, which reduced the effective purchase price. Of course, such profit, which is neither intended nor typical, is incidental to the defensive steps the portfolio manager took. Long hedgers simply seek to lock in a favorable purchase price prior to their actual cash purchase.

Note, too, that since futures hedging helps lock in a price, hedging prevents gains if prices move in a favorable direction. If T-note futures and cash prices had fallen, to 81-00 and 96-04, respectively, instead of rising, the investment manager would

TABLE 8.3

Long Hedge on Treasury Note Futures

	Cash	Futures
May	T-notes at 99-16, $9,950,000 total	Buys 103 September T-note futures at 84-12, $8,690,625 total
August	T-notes at 101-04, $10,112,500 total	Sells 103 September T-note futures at 86-00, $8,858,000 total
Result	$162,500 price increase	$167,375 gain

have lost money on her futures position, offsetting any potential gains in the cash market. Experienced hedgers, however, are willing to forfeit such a possibility in exchange for price protection. (See Table 8.4.)

Even though the investment manager may have lost $347,625 on her futures position, the purchase price of the T-notes in the cash market is $337,500 lower than she anticipated. She reminds herself that a few weeks ago when she initiated the hedge, she was satisfied with a purchase price of 99-16 on her cash bonds. In fact, the price hedgers pay for protection is the inability to take advantage of a price move after a hedge has been established.

It's hedges like those discussed here that demonstrate the extraordinary economic value of futures. Hedging is an indispensable risk management tool for institutional investors and businesspeople throughout the world economy, and the futures markets offer vehicles for managing price and interest rate risk. Because there is always some price risk in buying, selling, or holding a commodity for any length of time—whether grains, metals, or money itself—it is important that businesspeople and investors in all economic sectors take advantage of the opportunities available to protect their profit margins against unwanted and unforeseen price fluctuation. The futures markets provide a cost-effective means for providing that protection.

TABLE 8.4

Forfeiting Gains for Price Protection

	Cash	Futures
May	T-notes at 99-16, $9,950,000 total	Buys 103 September T-note contracts at 84-12, $8,690,625 total
August	T-notes at 96-04, $9,612,500 total	Sells 103 September T-note contracts at 81-00, $8,343,000 total
Result	$337,500	($347,625)

FURTHER READING

Burghardt, Galen D., and Terrence M. Belton, *The Treasury Bond Basis: An In-Depth Analysis for Hedgers, Speculators and Arbitrageurs.* Chicago: Probus Publishing, 1994.

Burghardt, Galen D., Terrence M. Belton, Morton Lane, Geoffrey Luce, and Richard McVey, *Eurodollar Futures and Options: Controlling Money Market Risk.* Chicago: Probus Publishing, 1992.

DeRosa, David F., *Managing Foreign Exchange Risk.* Chicago: Probus Publishing, 1991.

Figlewski, Stephen, et al., *Hedging with Financial Futures for Institutional Investors: From Theory to Practice.* Cambridge, MA: Ballinger Publishing, 1985.

Nielsen, Lars Tyge, *Pricing and Hedging of Derivative Securities.* Oxford, England: Oxford University Press, 1999.

Stephens, John, *The Business of Hedging.* Upper Saddle River, NJ: Financial Times/Prentice Hall, 2001.

CHAPTER 9

Speculating in the Futures Markets: Providing Liquidity

Futures markets facilitate the transfer of price risk between hedgers and speculators. Hedgers look to the futures market for protection against that risk. Speculators provide the protection by assuming the price risk that exists constantly for producers, users, and inventory holders of commodities or financial instruments.

Why assume risk when life is already so full of risk? Speculators assume the risk because they're interested more in opportunity than in security. They know that risk is the other side of the opportunity coin, and they'll take on price risk in the hope of making a profit. Their motto: buy low, sell high.

In taking on price risk, speculators demonstrate a key market principle—namely, that competitive markets are win-win, that pursuing one's own self-interest can balance productively with others pursuing their self-interests. Specifically, by taking and holding the other side of a hedger's trade, speculators add capital to the market and limit the risk of a hedger's exposure to price fluctuations.

Speculators also add liquidity. (*Liquidity* is a characteristic of a security or commodity market with enough units outstanding to allow large transactions without a substantial change in price.) Without market risk takers, short hedgers could trade only with long hedgers. Finding a hedger with exactly the opposite position would be a time-consuming and costly process. Speculators bridge the gap between long and short hedgers, thus adding depth and immediacy to the market.

In addition to assuming risk and providing liquidity, speculators stabilize the market by dampening extreme price moves. For example, by purchasing futures when the price seems too low, speculators increase demand. And increasing demand raises prices. Similarly, speculative selling in an overbought market puts downward pressure on prices. In this way, speculative activity softens the extreme price moves that might otherwise occur.

Speculators also enhance the price discovery role of futures markets by bringing additional information to the marketplace. By gathering and analyzing data to judge whether a market price is too low or too high, as well as to formulate expectations on market direction, speculators add critical information to the marketplace, which, in turn, enhances the price discovery function of futures markets.

The speculator's vital economic function has not gone unnoticed. No less a commentator than Supreme Court Justice Oliver Wendell Holmes wrote, "In a modern market contracts are not confined to sales for immediate delivery. People will endeavor to forecast the future and to make agreements according to their prophecy. Speculation of this kind by competent men is the self-adjustment of society to the probable."

Indeed, adjusting to the probable is the speculator's main game. A speculator's potential trading profits are directly proportional to his or her skill in analyzing data and forecasting price movement. Speculators thus scrutinize any factors that affect price. They note how the price of grain, for example, changes along with supply and demand, how plentiful supplies at harvest usually mean a low price for grain. They note how adverse weather conditions during the growing season or an unexpected increase in export demand, both of which decrease grain supplies, drive prices up. And they note how financial instruments fluctuate in price because of changes in interest rates and various economic and political factors.

Of course, speculators rarely have an interest in owning the cash commodity or financial instrument that underlies a futures contract. Whether long or short, speculators can offset their positions and never have to make or take delivery of the actual commodity. Typically, they buy contracts when prices seem too low in order to profit by making an offsetting sale at a higher price. They sell contracts when prices seem too high in order to profit by making an offsetting purchase at a lower price. Unlike some markets, futures markets make it easy to enter the market by either buying or selling futures contracts. The speculator's decision as to whether to buy or sell first depends solely on the speculator's market expectations.

SPECULATIVE TYPES

The market classifies speculators in several ways. The simplest, and most direct, is to refer to speculators as long or short. Speculators who are *long futures* have purchased one or more futures contracts; speculators who are *short futures* have sold one or more futures contracts.

Speculators also may be classified by the size of their positions, as designated by the Commodity Futures Trading Commission (CFTC). After they reach a specific number of open contracts, speculators' positions must be reported periodically to the CFTC. These speculators are classified as *large position holders*. They include professional traders who hold memberships on futures exchanges and public speculators who actively trade through commission houses. Public speculators who carry smaller positions are not required to report their positions.

Another method of categorizing speculators is by the price forecasting methods they use. Fundamental analysts look at supply and demand factors. Technical analysts use charts to plot price, volume, and open interest movement in current and recent years. (Chapter 10 discusses price forecasting methods in more detail.) Still another way to classify speculators is by their trading methods. A *position trader,* for example, initiates a futures or options position and then holds it over a period of days, weeks, or months. A *day trader,* on the other hand, holds market positions only during the course of a trading session and rarely carries a position overnight. Most day traders are futures exchange members who execute their transactions in the trading pits.

Scalpers are professional traders who trade for themselves in the pits. Their technique is to trade in minimum price fluctuations, taking small profits and losses on a heavy volume of trades. As a group, scalpers' willingness to buy at the bid price and sell at the asking, or offer, price creates the largest amount of total speculative liquidity. Like day traders, scalpers rarely hold positions overnight.

Finally, speculators can be *spreaders.* Spreaders focus on the shifting price relationships between different delivery months of the same commodity, between the prices of the same commodity traded on different exchanges, between the prices of different but related futures contracts, or between cash and futures prices of the same commodity. In each case, normal relationships exist from month to month that reflect usual market situations. When those price relationships deviate from their usual patterns, spreaders sell the overpriced market and buy the underpriced market. Their actions serve an important economic function by pulling prices back to a more normal relationship. (Chapter 11 discusses spreading in more detail.)

WHAT SPECULATORS MUST KNOW

Speculating in any market requires careful work. Justice Holmes, you may recall, praises the speculative efforts of "competent" persons, not just any market participant.

Trading in the futures markets requires considerable attention. One major reason is *leverage,* which is the ability to control large dollar amounts of a commodity with a comparative small amount of capital. Leverage, inherent in futures trading, is an important part of futures markets. Leverage enables speculators to control the full value of a futures contract with relatively little capital. As such, it magnifies both gains and losses in the futures market.

For example, if a trader buys one soybean contract (5,000 bushels) at $6.50 per bushel ($32,500 for the contract), the required margin might be $1,400 (approximately 4 percent of the contract value, or about 28 cents per bushel). This capital requirement is not a down payment for the futures contract; it is a security deposit to ensure contract performance.

If the market moves just 5 cents per bushel higher, the speculator's margin account will be credited with a gain of $250. Of course, if the market moves 5 cents per bushel lower, the speculator will lose $250 and be required to deposit additional margin. In either case, that's less than 1 percent of the contract's *notional value*—the dollar amount a contract value represents—but almost 20 percent of the margin posted by the speculator in order to trade. (Alternately, the notional value of the CBOT T-bond contract is $100,000.) In fact, in this example, the market needs to increase by only 28 cents per bushel to double the speculator's trading account—or decrease by 28 cents per bushel to wipe it out.

Leverage thus works like any valuable tool. Good artisans use it to get more work done with less effort. Amateurs simply frustrate and injure themselves. That's one important reason why speculators must develop a trading strategy or a plan to guide their market activity. Although such strategies must fit the individual, systematic approaches to the market save speculators from much grief.

First, successful speculators know their futures contracts. To make sound judgments about price movement, they know that they must have adequate knowledge about the contracts they are trading and limit the number of contracts they follow. This is true whether they're using fundamental analysis, technical analysis, or a combination of both trading techniques. Even experienced traders can have difficulty following more than three futures contracts at a time.

Second, successful speculators have a profit objective and maximum loss in mind before they trade. They combine price forecasts with a realistic and potentially profitable trading strategy. What's more, the profit potential is large in relation to the risk involved. They identify specific profit objectives as well as the maximum loss they are willing to sustain. Personal preferences determine the acceptable minimum levels for profits and maximum levels for losses.

Third, successful speculators determine their risk capital. After setting the profit objective and loss limit, they determine the amount of money they're willing to risk. To maximize returns, they limit the amount of money they will risk on a single trade. Also, they limit open positions to as many as they can adequately follow and reserve some capital for additional opportunities.

Successful speculators also typically make additions to an initial position only after the initial position proves correct—that is, when it shows a profit. Additional investments are made in amounts less than the initial position. Successful and unsuccessful positions alike are liquidated based on the original trading plan and not based on greed or fear. Still, successful speculators know that market conditions can change in an instant and so maintain some degree of flexibility in making these trading decisions.

The desirability of a trade—potential profits versus risks—depends on a speculator's experience and preferences. Determining profit objectives and loss limits, additions to the original position, and when to close a position also depend on personal preference and experience. Successful price forecasting and trading are ultimately influenced by individual temperament and objectivity, as well as by the analysis and trading plan that the speculator developed.

In addition to a systematic approach, many successful speculators follow a number of useful guidelines. A few of the many follow:

- Before initiating a futures position, successful speculators carefully analyze that market. They avoid quick actions based on rumors and tips.

- Successful speculators generally execute orders close to the best possible prices. Rarely are they able to buy at the lowest market price or sell at the highest. As Joseph Kennedy said of his selling stocks prior to the 1929 crash, "Only a fool holds out for top dollar."

- They speculate when the potential profit is great relative to the risk involved.

- Successful speculators limit losses and let profits run. They are prepared to accept numerous small losses, since a limited number of highly profitable trades can quickly offset losing trades.

- Successful speculators follow a well-developed trading plan that limits the amount of money risked on any single trade and maintains reserve capital.

Guidelines, of course, can tell only so much of the story. Speculating, perhaps even more than most activities, involves much learning by doing. The following examples offer some sense of how some position traders might have fared by speculating during pivotal market events.

Long Corn in 1975

The 1975 corn futures market offers a good example of how a variety of fundamental and technical factors can affect corn prices. Speculators facing such markets need to keep abreast of the most current market conditions, changing events, and shifting market attitudes.

On June 30, 1975, the December '75 corn futures contract marked a new seasonal low of $2.32½ per bushel. A *seasonal low* (or *high*) is the lowest (or highest) price a particular futures contract has traded at since it opened. Among the bearish fundamental factors was an excellent outlook for the new crop. In fact, a subsequent U.S. Department of Agriculture (USDA) crop report indicated that farmers had planted 1.8 million more acres of corn than had been estimated in the March 1 planting intentions report. What's more, weather conditions had been ideal for field work, planting, and early corn growth, and export sales had been slow. Even domestic demand for corn was down because of lower livestock numbers.

By all signs, the fundamental situation appeared bearish, with the supply prospect increasing and the demand outlook deteriorating. Both situations implied an increased carryover supply at the end of the crop year.

Yet despite this prevailing bearish sentiment, the technical indicators gradually began to show a change in the price of corn. Within six trading sessions after the market's new seasonal low, the December contract advanced by more than 25 cents per bushel to $2.58 on July 9. In the process, prices exceeded the highs of the previous month. This price rise also occurred with increasing trading volume, a positive technical indicator.

At about the same time, the fundamental supply and demand picture began to change. On July 10, the USDA estimated the crop to be 6.05 billion bushels below previous expectations, which had ranged as high as 6.5 billion to 7 billion bushels. Temperatures continued above normal in the second half of June and into July for the Corn Belt and the southeastern United States. These above-normal temperatures during the critical tasseling stage for corn raised concerns that U.S. corn production could be lower than normal. Furthermore, unconfirmed reports began to filter into the marketplace suggesting that Russian crop conditions were also deteriorating because of record high temperatures and below-normal precipitation.

After carefully reviewing and analyzing these factors and after considering that the majority opinion was quite bearish just the week before, one speculator decided to initiate a long corn futures position. So, at the market opening on July 11, the speculator bought one December corn futures contract at $2.55. Although the speculator assumed that prices would continue moving up and planned to sell his position at around $2.85, he entered a protective 10-cent stop-loss order to sell at $2.45 in the event that his timing or market judgment proved wrong.

Later that day, corn futures prices advanced sharply, closing at $2.64¼, reflecting reports of Russian ocean-freight bookings and further reports of hot, dry weather in the United States and abroad. After the market close, the CFTC released the June 30 report on Commitments of Traders, which showed that the average speculator had a large net short position. This was generally the result of the bearish opinion that had prevailed just 11 days earlier.

On Monday, July 14, there was further buying and short-covering (buying futures to offset short futures positions), and the December contract reached $2.69. At that point, the speculator already had a potential profit of 14 cents per bushel. But since the uptrend was expected to continue, he held on to the position. The most aggressive traders that day, however, were sellers, acting on the thought that the 36½-cent advance in only two weeks was probably sufficient to discount the still minor concern over domestic and Russian crop supplies.

On that day, July 14, the market closed at $2.59½. During the balance of the week, prices fluctuated between a high of $2.71 and a low of $2.54¼ and finally closed on Friday, July 18, at $2.55¼. This closing price was only a quarter of a cent above the speculator's purchase price. His profit opportunity appeared to have been lost.

Although discouraged at having possibly missed the chance to profit, the speculator reviewed the fundamental situation and the technical indicators and decided to stick with his basic plan. By the next Friday, the December contract closed at $2.70¼, after an earlier high of $2.74¾. At $2.74¾, the speculator had a potential gain of nearly 20 cents per bushel. Once again, the speculator reviewed the multitude of technical and fundamental information and decided to stay with his initial trading plan.

More adverse crop news was reported over the weekend. This led to *limit-up moves* (the maximum advance or decline from the previous day's settlement price permitted for a contract in one trading session by the rules of an exchange) Monday and Tuesday that pushed the December price to $2.90¼. Although the speculator's initial plan was to sell at around $2.85, the market action, the severity of the crop news, and the weather forecast caused him to revise his basic plan. He raised his profit objective by another 30 cents per bushel to $3.15 and placed a new protective stop-loss order to sell at $2.65 to lock in at least an 8- to 10-cent profit should the market reverse itself. Subsequently, the December contract sold down to $2.75½, but still held above his stop.

Based on the recent news and the basic uptrend, the speculator again decided to hold the position. Later, the market advanced and closed on August 8 at $3. On the following Friday, August 15, the market closed at $3.18¾, after reaching a high of $3.25. The speculator again revised his profit objective because he was more and more impressed with the market's strength and the substantial uptrend. In addition, there was very bullish news coming from Iowa, Nebraska, and Russia regarding the deteriorating condition of the crops. Also, the hog and cattle markets were making new highs, which suggested that domestic feed demand would improve as farmers increased livestock production.

Once again, the speculator raised his profit objective by 30 cents per bushel to $3.45 and raised his stop-loss order by another 20 cents to sell at $2.85. He felt this stop would probably assure him of at least his original profit objective of 30 cents per bushel.

The following week, prices again rose, and the December contract reached $3.30¼ on August 21. Somewhat surprisingly, however, the market reacted sharply late in the session and closed at about 4 cents lower on a day with the heaviest trading volume since the uptrend had begun in early July. Though not conclusive, this negative technical signal suggested that the trader needed to make a critical review of the market's technical and fundamental factors. As a result, the speculator raised his sell stop-loss order to the previous low of that week, $3.10. A penetration of that price level, following the high-volume reversal that occurred on August 21, would suggest that the uptrend might be over. The following week, prices did decline as the weather pattern changed, and the speculator's position was stopped out on that Wednesday's market opening at $3.08 per bushel. Following is a summary of the action:

July 11   Bought one December corn contract at $2.55
                 per bushel

August 27   Sell-stop order executed at $3.08 per bushel

Result   Gained $0.53 per bushel, or $2,650 on one
                 contract

In the example, the speculator did not buy at the bottom or sell at the top of the market. That rarely happens. Considering his risk-reward ratio, however, he made the decision to buy when he recognized a clearly developing uptrend and took his profit when the market seemed to suggest that his position had reached its potential.

Long Bonds in the 1987 Crash

This example is based on events surrounding the stock market crash on October 19, 1987. It highlights the importance of analyzing the economic factors and conditions that both directly and indirectly affect futures markets. Note that the time frame and trading opportunities summarized in this example may not be representative of most market conditions because of the unusually wide price swings that occurred following the 1987 crash.

A speculator had been studying the bond and equities markets since the beginning of 1987. For the first three months, bond prices were relatively stable. By late March, however, bond prices began to fall as interest rates rose. Several interrelated factors appeared to be affecting this trend:

- *A weak U.S. dollar.* There was widespread fear among investors that a weak dollar would produce greater inflation and higher interest rates (lower bond prices).

- *A worsening U.S. trade deficit.* This occurred despite efforts to spur U.S. exports and decrease imports through a weaker dollar.

- *The threat of tighter monetary policy.* The Federal Reserve appeared ready to tighten monetary policy because of weakness in the dollar and market worries about inflation.

During the summer, bond prices continued to drop, and the market sentiment remained primarily bearish. Despite the bearish mentality and expectations of higher interest rates, several noted economists predicted a market turnaround. These economists believed the bond market was in the process of establishing a major bottom. Prices had been falling for nearly two years and reached a two-year low on Friday, October 2, 1987, before closing up for the day. In fact, bond prices actually closed up for that week. It had been a month since bond prices had closed higher for the week (Monday through Friday) and over three months since the bond market had closed higher from one Friday to the next. These technical indicators seemed to be pointing to a bond market rally.

In addition, some economists focused on the state of the stock market, claiming that the market was overbought and stocks were overvalued. They predicted an end to the five-year bull market that had tripled stock prices.

Taking all these factors into consideration, one speculator believed the bear market in bonds was about to end or at least take a breather. He was worried about the highly overvalued stock market and believed a major break was about to occur—a break that would send investors fleeing to bonds. On October 12, the speculator decided to take a long futures position in bonds and bought two December T-bond futures contracts at 79-08, or $79,250 per contract.*

Events throughout the week led to a drop in bond prices. The huge trade deficit number released on October 14 especially affected bonds, and the December T-bond contract closed down for the week at 77-30—a loss of 1-10, or $1,312.50, on the posi-

---

* T-bond futures contracts are quoted in 32nds, but the prices generally are written as follows: 79-08 = 79$\frac{8}{32}$. The minimum price fluctuation for one Chicago Board of Trade T-bond futures, with a contract value of $100,000, is $\frac{1}{32}$ of a percent. A $\frac{1}{32}$ of a percent change on a $100,000 contract equals $31.25.

tion. Yet the speculator continued to maintain the opinion that the market was bullish and stayed with the long bonds.

Over the weekend, investors began to lose confidence in the U.S. stock market. Comments made by then–U.S. Treasury Secretary James Baker—who threatened to let the dollar drop—made foreign investors nervous. There was worldwide uncertainty and fear regarding the status of the U.S. economy. By Sunday night, European and Japanese investors had begun selling stocks heavily.

When the markets opened Monday, October 19, panic had already set in. There was selling pressure from foreign investors and portfolio insurers as everyone tried to get out of stocks and into other investment vehicles. The Dow Jones Industrial Average plunged a record 508 points that day, and cash bond prices, in response to falling stock prices and selling pressures that had begun on the New York Stock Exchange, rallied 2 points immediately following the futures market close at 2 p.m. The speculator's decision to stay long bonds turned out to be a good one.

The immediate result of the stock market crash was heightened uncertainty over the future direction of interest rates, the value of the dollar, and the health of the economy. Many economists and market analysts began predicting a recession, possibly even a depression, for 1988.

To ensure the liquidity of the financial system and avert the collapse of securities firms, the Federal Reserve decided to suspend its tight monetary policy. By acting as the ultimate supplier of funds, the Fed flooded the banking system with dollars by purchasing government securities and thus driving down interest rates. Bond prices rallied significantly as interest rates fell, and investors began pouring money into fixed-income securities.

In a substantial flight-to-quality, investors transferred their dollars from stocks to bonds as they sought a safe harbor for their funds. Within just one week's time, the December T-bond futures contract rose by about 11 percent, rocketing from a 77-30 close on October 16 to 86-18 by the close of trading on October 23.

At this point, had he chosen to offset his position, the speculator would pocket a $14,625 profit. Yet after reviewing the current market, the speculator decided to stick with his position. The market expected the Fed to continue its easy monetary policy (lower interest rates) to ensure market liquidity, and economists continued to predict a recession for 1988.

Throughout the next few weeks, bond prices continued to climb, reaching a high of 90-15 by the week of November 2. During the two weeks that followed, though, the December T-bond contract more or less stabilized, fluctuating between 88-00 and 89-00. The speculator kept a close watch on market conditions, especially the dollar, economic growth, and the Fed's monetary policy. By mid-November, fears of a recession in 1988 were beginning to subside. The impact of the crash on the overall economy was not clear, and the economy was stronger than expected. Some experts again began to worry about the possibility of inflation and the higher interest rates that would be needed to contain it.

Toward the end of November, bond prices began to fall. On November 27, the December T-bond contract closed down for the week at 87-02. Throughout the following week, prices ranged from a high of 88-13 to a low of 86-15. Considering the mixed economic statistics following the crash, the various predictions of recession or inflation for 1988, and the recent downtrend in prices, the speculator reviewed his position and decided it was time to close it out. Following the opening of trading on December 7, the speculator offset his position by selling two December T-bond futures contracts at 87-20. The profit on the position was $8,375 per contract, or $16,750. Following is a summary of the action:

October 12   Bought two December T-bond contracts at 79-08

December 7   Sold two December T-bond contracts at 87-20

Result   Gained 8-12, or $8,375 per contract, $16,750 on the position

Short Crude Oil in 2004

The crude oil futures market of late 2004 provides another example of how traders must follow and interpret complex fundamental and technical factors in order to execute successful trading strategies. When crude oil prices first broke through the $40 per barrel level in the second quarter of 2004, there were immediate concerns that record high oil prices would hamper the U.S. economy.

Nevertheless, crude oil futures prices continued to edge up, with the spot month closing at $44.41 on the New York Mercantile Exchange (NYMEX) on August 5, 2004. General market sentiment leaned toward even higher prices, although market fundamentals did not fully support this opinion. The Organization of the Petroleum Exporting Countries, or OPEC, supplied about 40 percent of total world oil production and purportedly was pumping oil as fast as it could. In fact, oil supplies were exceeding demand by roughly 2 million barrels per day.

Global demand, however, was also strong. In addition to meeting the needs of the United States and other major importers, oil producers were facing surging demand from China and India, where strong economic growth had fueled an equally strong appetite for oil. No one expected demand to decline any time soon.

Still, many analysts claimed that supply solidly exceeded demand and that other factors beyond market fundamentals were driving the market. Chief among them was a built-in risk premium. Traders simply felt that too many variables could act to impede supply, which prompted a general unwillingness to let oil prices decline. With most of the world's oil sitting in the Middle East, where the U.S.-led occupation of Iraq had added to general tensions in the region, there were ongoing concerns about terrorist attacks on major oil facilities.

Political unrest was also brewing in Venezuela, the third largest oil-producing nation in the world. In Russia, the giant oil company Yukos was battling with the Russian government over taxes, thus adding to oil production concerns. Traders were also edgy about the pending national election in the United States, which increased concerns about the threat of terrorist activities in the coming weeks.

Of course the oil markets had always contended with volatile conditions. This time, however, it was generally believed that the market lacked most of the cushions that typically buffered such problems, including spare production and refining capacity and spare inventories. Technical indicators also pointed to higher price supports, with a floor of $40 per barrel expected for some time to come.

With the summer driving season coming to a close, prices did moderate during the second half of August. However, September's arrival brought a series of hurricanes that devastated Florida and other parts of the Gulf, prompting oil production delays in the region. Over the course of the next six weeks, crude oil prices rose by nearly $15 per barrel, closing at an unprecedented $55.17 per barrel on October 22, 2004.

A trader watching this sequence of events believed that the recent run-up in prices did not have long-term support. Saudi Arabia had recently announced plans to increase production by a half-million barrels a day, a move expected to be followed by other OPEC countries. This eased some concerns over spare production capacity. In the trader's opinion, market participants were too fixated on production disruptions. Heavy participation by hedge funds and other large speculators also supported his belief that the crude oil market was overbought, showing signs similar to the Internet technology stock market bubble of 2000.

On October 27, the market exhibited its largest recent trading range, from $52.10 to $55.62 per barrel, closing at $52.46. Deciding that this signaled a change in market sentiment, the trader opened a short position of two December contracts at $52.75 per barrel on the following day. For the next two weeks, crude oil prices continued to edge downward.

Then on November 11 and 12, the market held to a tighter trading range, closing at $47.42 and $47.32, respectively. The trader was concerned that the market would bottom out soon and that prices would begin to edge up. The next day, however, brought another solid price decline, with crude oil trading as low as $45.25 per barrel. Prices remained in the $45.24 to $47.45 range for the next four days, prompting the trader to take his profits and unwind his short position. On November 18, he bought two December crude oil contracts at $46.35, netting a profit on his position of $12,800. Following is a summary of the action:

October 28	Sold two December crude oil contracts at $52.75 per barrel
November 18	Bought two December crude oil contracts at $46.35 per barrel
Result	Gained $6.40 per barrel, or $6,400 per contract, $12,800 on the position

Note that this gain—in fact, the gain realized in all these examples—does not include commission or transaction costs. Note, too, that in all these scenarios, the speculators realized a profit. Yet if they had been incorrect in their price forecasts or overlooked one or more changing market conditions, all positions could easily have resulted in a loss. This is why speculators must keep a close watch on the market and develop a trading plan before initiating a futures position.

FURTHER READING

Bernstein, Jake, *The Complete Day Trader: Trading Systems, Strategies, Timing Indicators, and Analytical Methods*. New York: McGraw-Hill, 2000.

Eng, William F., *Trading Rules: Strategies for Success*. Chicago: Dearborn, 1990.

Kleinman, George, *Trading Commodities and Financial Futures: A Step-by-Step Guide to Mastering the Markets*. London: Financial Times/Prentice Hall, 2004.

Luft, Carl F., *Understanding and Trading Futures.* Chicago: Irwin Professional Publishing, 1990.

Powers, Mark, *Starting Out in Futures Trading.* New York: McGraw-Hill, 2001.

Schwager, Jack D., *The New Market Wizards: Conversations with America's Top Traders.* New York: HarperBusiness, 1994.

Teweles, Richard J., and Frank J. Jones, *The Futures Game: Who Wins, Who Loses, & Why.* New York: McGraw-Hill, 1998.

CHAPTER 10

Price Analysis: Technical and Fundamental Approaches

Market analysts use two basic techniques to forecast price movement in the futures markets: fundamental analysis and technical analysis. Purists of each respective technique tend to use their approach exclusively. However, many traders combine fundamental and technical approaches, since both technical and fundamental factors affect price. Forecasting price movement based on the technical approach requires study of historical price movement and current market activity. The fundamental approach, on the other hand, requires the study of supply and demand factors that affect the price of a commodity or financial instrument.

THE TECHNICAL APPROACH

Technical traders try to anticipate future market movement by studying past price patterns. They use historical prices, trading volume, open interest, and other trading data relative to current pricing. The concept behind technical trading is that *the market-place* considers all the information at its disposal, including fundamental information (discussed later in this chapter), and then determines fair value through a process of price discovery. When prices reach certain historical levels where a surge of buying or selling has historically taken place, known as support or resistance, respectively, a technical trader might anticipate prices to rise or fall.

Bar Charts

Perhaps the oldest method of technical analysis is known as *charting*. All major charts (bar charts, point-and-figure charts, candlestick charts, and line charts) are readily available; a number of Internet sites provide ready-made charts for a fee. The charts shown throughout this chapter are for illustrative purposes only and provide some idea of what technical traders (often referred to as *market technicians*) look for.

The most commonly used chart is the *bar chart*. In a bar chart, the vertical axis represents price; the horizontal axis represents time. For daily bar charts, a vertical line that connects the lowest and highest price of the day represents each trading day. A horizontal bar that crosses the vertical line indicates the day's closing price. Some bar charts indicate the opening price with a horizontal bar marked to the left and the closing price with a horizontal bar marked to the right of the vertical axis. (See Fig. 10.1.)

Bar charts can be created to reflect a variety of time frames. For instance, if traders had a very short-term outlook, they

FIGURE 10.1

Standard Bar Pricing with Open, High, Low, and Close

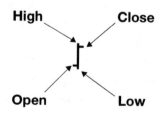

FIGURE 10.2

Daily Chart Moving in Downtrend

10-Year US Treasury Note Price (EOD) ($UST)

$UST Daily   23-Aug-2005 O:110.89 H:111.30 L:110.89 C:111.18 V:0.00 Chg:+0.12

might choose a five-minute or hourly chart. For a longer-term perspective, traders might look at a daily, weekly, or monthly chart. In fact, many technical traders view the markets from a variety of time frames in order to gain a picture of the market from a short- and long-term perspective. Figure 10.2 is a daily bar chart; Figure 10.3 is a weekly chart. As you can see, they present very different views of the markets—the daily chart indicates a downtrend while the weekly chart indicates sideways movement.

Candlestick, Point-and-Figure, and Line Charts

A variety of charting methods exists in addition to bar charts. Some of the most used include candlestick, line, and point-and-figure charts.

With a *candlestick chart,* a narrow line, known as the "shadow," shows the day's price range. A wider body differenti-

FIGURE 10.3

Weekly Chart Moving Sideways

10-Year US Treasury Note Price (EOD) ($UST)

ates between the open and close of the market. If the close is higher than the open, the body of the candle is often left unfilled or white. (See Fig. 10.4.) If the close is below the open, the body is often filled in with either black or red.

Point-and-figure charts are unique in that in that they illustrate all trading as one continuous path and ignore time. As with

FIGURE 10.4

Standard Candlestick with Open, High, Low, and Close

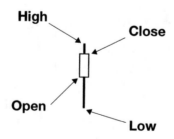

F I G U R E   10.5

Point-and-Figure Chart Formations

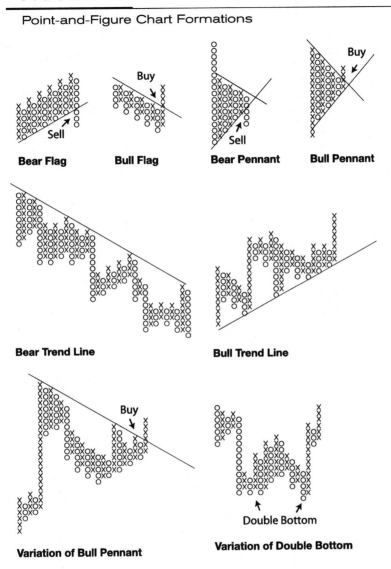

bar charts, the vertical axis of the point-and-figure chart represents price; however, there is no time reference along the horizontal axis.

The point-and-figure technician uses an *x* to indicate an
uptick and an *o* for a downtick. Generally, point-and-figure technicians set their price objective by counting the x's and o's of the
specific chart formation. The point-and-figure technician theo-
rizes that the amount of price movement at a given level is
important in forecasting prices, which is quite similar to the
logic of support and resistance in bar charting (described in
more detail below).

Point-and-figure charts are used to track intraday price
moves or long-term trends. As with bar charts, there are several formations revealed in point-and-figure charts, shown in
Figure 10.5.

Unlike a candle or bar chart, a *line chart* considers only the
open and close of a particular time period. By connecting the var-

FIGURE 10.6

Line Chart

ious opens and closes, a line chart provides a different view of the market from the view provided by comparative methods. Technicians sometimes like line charts because they eliminate the "noise" caused by intraperiod price gyrations and focus only on the open and close of the market. (See Fig. 10.6.)

Support and Resistance

By charting, technicians can see different trends or formations that tend to recur over time. Analysts use this information to predict future price movement. Chief among these recurring formations are support and resistance.

Technicians use specific terms to describe different market conditions. For example, sometimes a price decline ends because of buying pressure. Or perhaps a market rallies and then falls back to a previous price range. Technical traders describe this as *support* and *resistance,* respectively. *Support* is a place on a chart where recurring buying is sufficient to halt a price decline. *Resistance* on a chart indicates a price range where selling pressure is strong enough to stop a market advance. (See Fig. 10.7.)

After a trading range has been established for a month or two of sideways price movement, prices tend to meet support at the lower end of the range and resistance at the upper end of the range. If prices break out of a specific support or resistance area, some technicians use this information to make buying and selling decisions.

Uptrends and Downtrends

In addition to support and resistance, technical traders may also refer to price trends. An *uptrend* is a sequence of higher highs and higher lows. Conversely a *downtrend* is a sequence of lower lows and lower highs. Some technicians consider the trend intact until the previous low (or high) is broken. Other technicians will draw an uptrend (or downtrend) line connecting the lows (or

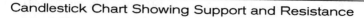

FIGURE 10.7

Candlestick Chart Showing Support and Resistance

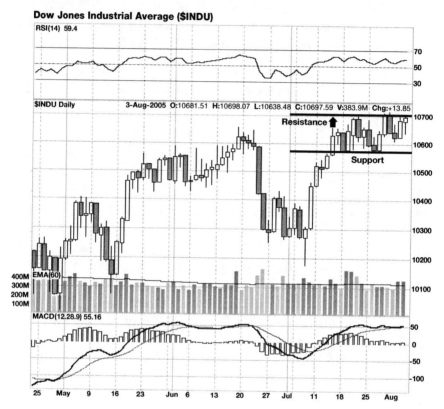

Dow Jones Industrial Average ($INDU)

highs), and the trend is considered intact until this line is broken. (Fig. 10.8 illustrates a downtrend.)

Price Channels, Triangles, Flags (Pennants), and Wedges

Sometimes the lines connecting highs and lows run almost parallel to a trend line. This type of price movement creates what is known as a *price channel*. If the price breaks a major trend

FIGURE 10.8

Line Chart Showing Downtrend

Dow Jones Industrial Average ($INDU)

line, it might indicate market movement in the direction of the penetration.

Like price channels, *triangles* in many forms recur in price charts and are used to indicate related uptrend or downtrend lines. There are three triangle patterns: the ascending triangle, the symmetrical triangle, and the descending triangle.

The *ascending triangle* can point to a breakout on the upside of the triangular area. Conversely, the *descending triangle* can point to a breakout on the downside of the triangular area. The *symmetrical triangle* is considered the least dependable of the three and forecasts that a substantial move out of price congestion may take place. The symmetrical triangle is often a formation in which a breakout favors the continuation of the previous price trend.

Considered more significant than the triangle patterns are the flag formation (also known as the *pennant formation*), and

FIGURE 10.9

Pennant and Flag Formations

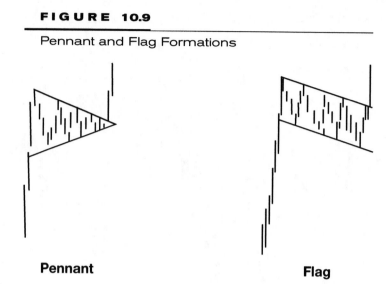

Pennant   **Flag**

the wedge formation. The *flag formation* is formed when a substantial upward move is followed by a downward price drift, which creates the appearance of a limp flag on a pole. After the flag is formed, the upmove is abruptly resumed. (See Fig. 10.9.)

The ascending *wedge formation* is a series of price-up days that fail to accelerate. The irony of the wedge is that even though prices are rising, the upside movement is usually not significant compared to the initial days of the formation. To the trained technician, this is a negative pattern that could reverse to the downside.

Topping and Bottoming Patterns

One of the most important decisions a trader has to make is determining a major top in a rising market or a major bottom in a declining market. Here are the most common chart indicators:

- Head-and-shoulders or inverted head-and-shoulders
- Double tops and double bottoms
- Rounded tops and rounded bottoms
- Gaps

Head-and-Shoulders Formation   The head-and-shoulders formation is considered one of the most reliable patterns for indicating a major reversal in the market. This formation consists of four phases: the left shoulder, the head, the right shoulder, and a penetration of the neckline. The head-and-shoulders formation is complete only when the neckline penetration occurs with a close below the neckline. Some theorists believe that once prices break through the neckline, the distance from the top of the head to the neckline signals the extent of the movement away from the neckline. The head-and-shoulders formation occurs in a rising market; its opposite, the inverted head-and-shoulders, occurs in a declining market.

Double Tops and Bottoms   Double tops and double bottoms are exactly what their names suggest, appearing as an M or W on a technician's chart. Double tops and bottoms have a tendency to indicate major market moves. These formations are usually considered complete when prices move past the first reaction point following the first top or bottom. (See Fig. 10.10.)

Gaps   Gaps occur between trading sessions when the price at the start of one session is higher than the highest price or lower

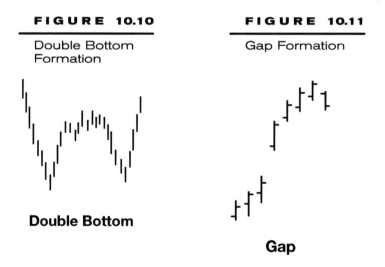

FIGURE 10.10

Double Bottom Formation

Double Bottom

FIGURE 10.11

Gap Formation

Gap

than the lowest price of the preceding session. (See Fig. 10.11.) There are several types of gaps, including the common gap, the breakaway gap, the runaway gap, and the exhaustion gap.

The common gap formation can appear at any time and has no particular significance. Frequently the gap is filled in during later trading. The *breakaway gap* occurs when prices jump beyond a trading range, leaving an area in the chart where no trading took place. A breakaway gap is useful for predicting the end of a consolidation phase of the market and can signal a dynamic move. A *runaway gap* appears when a trend accelerates and is quite typical of a strong bull or bear market. The *exhaustion gap* occurs after a relatively long period of steadily rising or falling prices. Technicians theorize that the exhaustion gap signals the imminent end of a trend.

Moving Averages

Probably one of the best-known approaches to trading analysis is the *moving average,* an average of a series of prices. Technicians can calculate moving averages for various periods of time, such as 20-day, 50-day, and 200-day moving averages. A moving average is often displayed as a smooth line running horizontally across a graph. The horizontal axis represents the trading day, whereas the vertical axis represents the price. One advantage to using the moving average is that it tends to smooth out some of the price irregularities that can occur in the market.

Deciding which average to use depends on several elements. For example, technicians have to determine how sensitive they want the average to be relative to the market. The more closely a trader wants the average to reflect turning points in a trend, the fewer the number of days that should be averaged. On the other hand, the more days that are incorporated in the average, the less effect short-term market factors will have on the average price. Figure 10.12 is a bar chart that illustrates a moving average.

Moving averages are used on a number of technical fronts. For instance, if a market is trading over the 200-day moving average, the longer-term trend of the market is said to be up.

FIGURE 10.12

Bar Chart Showing Moving Average

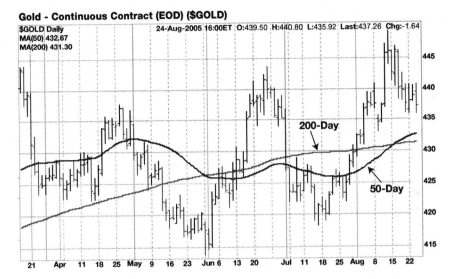

Gold - Continuous Contract (EOD) ($GOLD)

Likewise, if the market is trading below a key moving average, the trend of the market is said to be down. Moving averages also serve as points of support or resistance at which buyers or sellers take the market higher or lower.

Traders could create a chart of moving averages themselves by calculating the average of the open and close or high and low for each day for a given period of time. However, most traders rely on software or Internet charting services to calculate moving averages.

Oscillators

An *oscillator* is a technical indicator that allows a trader to measure overbought or oversold conditions. Some of the more commonly used oscillators include the relative strength index (RSI) and the moving average convergence divergence (MACD).

The *RSI* is a momentum oscillator that compares the magnitude of recent gains to the magnitude of recent losses and turns that information into a number that ranges from 0 to 100. Not to be confused with relative strength charts that compare one stock to another, the RSI indicates an overbought market when it moves over 70 and an oversold market when it moves below 30. (See Fig. 10.13, top.) RSI is also used to identify divergences in the market. When a market reaches new price highs but the RSI does not, this is said to be a negative divergence, and it is a potential red flag.

The *MACD* is considered one of the simplest and most reliable indicators. MACD uses moving averages to turn into a momentum oscillator by subtracting the longer moving average from the shorter moving average. The result is a line that oscillates above and below zero. When the lines of the indicator cross, it is said to yield a buy signal. Like the RSI, the MACD is also used to identify market divergence. (See Fig. 10.13, bottom.)

FIGURE 10.13

Candlestick Chart with RSI and MACD

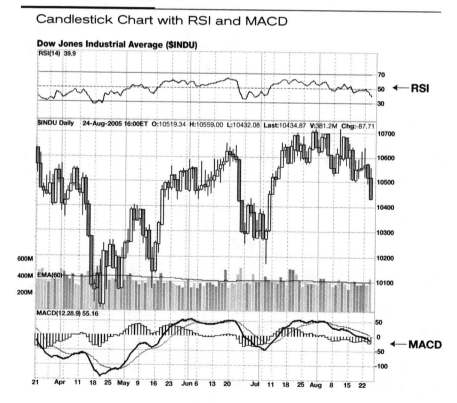

Trading Volume and Open Interest

In addition to charting and moving averages, a technician may use other techniques to assist in predicting future price movements. These include volume and open interest.

Trading volume is the total number of contracts traded for a given period. Each contract represents both a long and a short position. Technical traders hypothesize that changes in volume are associated with price movements in the same direction. For example, a gradual increase in volume during a downtrend often indicates a continuation and acceleration of the price decline, while increasing volume during an uptrend signals a further rise in prices. Rapidly accelerating volume after a substantial price move, however, often signals the approach of a major high or low and an impending price reversal.

Open interest refers to the number of contracts that has been entered into but not yet liquidated by delivery or offset. As with volume figures, each open interest contract represents both a long and short position. Some technicians use open interest figures to get a handle on future price movement. As with volume, a rise in open interest could signal a continuation of a recent price trend, while a decline in open interest could signal a weakening of the trend.

Opinion of Market Participants

Technical traders have access to a variety of trading pattern information. Every other Friday, the Commodity Futures Trading Commission publishes the Commitment of Traders Report. This report contains a breakdown of open interest for reportable and nonreportable traders in all futures as of the close of the prior Tuesday. The report shows the total number of open positions held by large-volume traders, speculators, and hedgers, as well as those held by market participants with smaller positions.

Some technicians tend to study these reports carefully, noting in particular any unusual changes in various trading patterns that may indicate differences of opinion between large commercial, institutional, and speculative interests and smaller speculators and hedgers. Traders who hold larger positions are better capitalized and thus are viewed as making the market more stable. Likewise, traders who hold smaller positions are often viewed as making the market unstable. A tipping of the balance in one direction or another would provide the trader with clues to future market direction.

Traders sometimes apply similar market composition reasoning to the market analysts who have advisory services and to those who trade options. The theory of contrary opinion holds that when more than 80 percent of analysts are bullish, it implies that their followers have taken long positions, thus leaving fewer potential additional buyers to absorb any selling that develops. Conversely, if 80 percent are bearish, very few sellers would be able to absorb any buying that develops.

Traders also view the *put/call ratio* as a contrary indicator. The put/call ratio measures the volume of puts relative to calls. The theory of contrary opinion holds that when call volume reaches high levels relative to puts, a market top might be indicated. Similarly, high volume in puts relative to calls might indicate a bottom.

Cyclical Theories

Cyclical theories are another area of interest to technical traders. They are based on the premise that in nature certain phenomena have cycles. Analysts follow this principle in forecasting price. The Elliot Wave Principle and Fibonacci Numbers are examples of cyclical theories that are regularly used by technical traders.

Market Profile

The Chicago Board of Trade's Market Profile is an information service that helps technical traders analyze price trends. Traders often utilize the Market Profile to measure the strength of support and resistance. The *Market Profile* consists of a time and sales quotation ticker and the Liquidity Data Bank. The time and sales ticker is an online graphic service that transmits price and time information throughout the day to subscribers. The second half of the system is the Liquidity Data Bank, which summarizes the entire day's trading activity, including volume and a breakdown to the nearest 30 minutes of when specific trades were made.

Why Technical Analysis?

When comparing technical to fundamental approaches, many technicians believe that it is simply impossible to know and understand every factor that might affect supply and demand and that at times a trader will overlook something that could substantially affect the market. Further, technicians believe that the marketplace in its price discovery process analyzes all fundamental information. Therefore, price movements are the most important factor in the marketplace, and because such price movement is the foundation upon which most technical indicators are based, it is a sufficient method to analyze the markets. There is another, more practical reason as to why technical analysis tends to work. It is a self-fulfilling prophecy: many major market participants use technical indicators, which tends to propel buying or selling at particular technical levels.

Whatever your thoughts on the subject, many traders combine the use of technical analysis with a fundamental approach.

THE FUNDAMENTAL APPROACH

Traders who use fundamental analysis watch the economic factors that affect supply and demand as they attempt to forecast prices and develop profitable trading strategies. They often analyze government reports and other economic indicators to help forecast future price movement. Fundamental analysts operate on the principle that any economic factor that decreases the supply of or increases the demand for a commodity or financial instrument tends to raise prices. Conversely, any factor that increases the supply of or decreases the demand for a commodity or financial instrument tends to lower prices.

For instance, a corn trader using a fundamental approach would analyze a crop report to help understand supply and demand. If the report indicated that supply might tighten or that demand might increase, the corn trader might then presume that corn prices could rise in the future. Take the changes in corn's supply and demand that occurred in 1983, when the price of corn fluctuated greatly. The United States had a huge supply of corn in storage following a bumper crop in 1982. Many market participants expected farmers to plant another large corn crop in 1983. In fact, the expectation of a potential corn glut drove prices to record lows. To curtail additional surpluses, President Reagan announced the Payment-In-Kind (PIK) acreage reduction program in January 1983. Later that year, drought and hot weather brought corn production down, lowering potential supplies even more.

These factors led both farmers and traders to believe that corn prices would skyrocket. Yet potential buyers of corn, anticipating rising prices, chose to reduce the amount of corn they would need by cutting livestock numbers, using other grains as feed, and substituting or decreasing the amount of corn sweetener used in prepared foods and beverages. As demand for corn dropped, so did prices.

Agricultural Markets

The 1983 market involved nearly all the basic fundamental factors that can affect agricultural commodities—carryover, politics, weather, yield, and other feed grain usage.

Carryover stocks of agricultural commodities are among the most critically watched factors by fundamental analysts. *Carryover* is the amount of grain or oilseeds that remains at the end of a marketing year. The size of the carryover affects the strength or weakness of the commodity's price in the near and distant future.

Carryover indicates the tightness of supply. A tight supply means higher prices, while ample supply forces prices down. Projections of ending stock prices rise or fall based on the level of projected demand and production. With the exception of some nonstorable commodities such as livestock, fundamental analysts keep a constant watch on stock levels as price indicators. Even with livestock, the inventory of breeding animals, the livestock on feed, and the number of livestock brought to slaughter help to forecast meat production.

In using carryover figures to forecast price movement, however, traders must also consider other factors. The size of the upcoming crop, for example, may be more important in predicting prices than the current carryover is.

Measuring the production of agricultural commodities such as corn involves a combination of acreage and yield, with yield per acre dictated by weather and the latest farm technology. *Yield* is the amount of grain harvested per acre planted, and it directly affects the attitude and action of buyers in the marketplace. This attitude determines how high or low prices will move.

Monitoring the production of agricultural commodities requires that the fundamental analyst watch the regularly scheduled government and private reports on farm production in the United States and abroad. Numerous U.S. Department of Agriculture (USDA) reports exist for all types of agricultural products, from livestock to orange juice. The information for these reports is gathered by each state and compiled in Washington, D.C. Because traders place such importance on these national figures, safeguards are taken to ensure that the statistics are released at precisely the scheduled time.

Corn and wheat reports are issued monthly. The reports early in the calendar year show the number of bushels produced the previous year. Later reports indicate the number of acres farmers are expected to plant. Information released through the summer months details the size of the crop and, at the end of the year, the harvested crops.

Weather uncertainty can cause more anxiety in the marketplace than all other fundamentals combined. Traders monitor the amount of moisture, the time of frost, and the temperature during the growing season and its impact on growing conditions to gauge how crop production is affected around the world. Weather conditions also influence livestock production. During periods of drought, livestock producers are forced to reduce livestock numbers because of the high cost of feed. This causes a glut of meat and lowers prices in the short term. In the long term, however, meat prices rise because of the shortage of livestock after the drought-related slaughter. Furthermore, during winter months, blizzards can close roads, hence temporarily delaying livestock shipments to market.

In addition to carryover yield and weather, there are other significant economic conditions that affect commodity prices. There is a relationship between the livestock and grain markets. For instance, affluent consumers are more likely to eat red meat, which, in turn, influences the demand for livestock. A rise in livestock numbers increases consumption of feed, which contains large amounts of corn. This eventually decreases the supply of corn. On the other hand, the less money available to consumers, the less spent on more expensive foods like red meat.

Livestock feeders also make a larger profit when grain prices are low, which encourages the number of livestock to increase. Yet when the livestock supply becomes too large, livestock prices drop. Feeders are forced to cut their herds, which leads to lower grain usage and, eventually, lower grain prices.

Another important variable the fundamental analyst monitors is the pattern of consumption for a commodity. Take the breakdown of U.S. corn usage. Livestock and poultry feed represents approximately 50 to 55 percent of use; exports represent

20 to 25 percent; and food, industry, and seed uses account for another 15 to 20 percent.

Similarly, the ability to substitute one commodity for another in a product can have a great effect on demand and, subsequently, on price. For instance, when soybeans are scarce and prices are relatively high, livestock producers may substitute cottonseed meal as a feed additive, or vegetable oil manufacturers may use coconut or palm oil as a base rather than soybean oil. Of course, each substitute has specific qualities, and one may be more appropriate to use than another.

Government policies regarding agricultural production also can influence the prices of commodities both domestically and worldwide. In the United States, for example, the government has offered special acreage reduction programs to farmers to cut the number of acres of specific crops planted. This lowers production and, eventually, reduces supply; lower supply generally leads to higher prices.

Other U.S. programs of particular importance to the supply of various commodities include feed grain and loan programs, as well as the management of stocks accumulated from defaulted loans. Other countries or organizations such as the European Union offer similar programs to farmers in an effort to control production and prices, although the current political trend in both the United States and abroad is to reduce government programs and move toward more market-oriented policies.

Fundamental analysts also watch worldwide competition, particularly to assess supply factors. The United States is a major producer of several agricultural commodities, including soybeans, corn, and wheat. These crops and others are also grown in many other countries throughout the world. For example, Australia and Canada produce large quantities of wheat for export. The former Soviet countries are also major wheat producers, and at times they import large quantities. Brazil and Argentina have been expanding their export markets for some time, especially in soybeans.

Fundamental analysts closely monitor the growing conditions in countries that are either large exporters or importers of agricultural commodities. Both devastating weather conditions and optimum growing environments can greatly affect production and, thus, the supply and price of crops. Other long-term factors influencing the supply of and demand for agricultural commodities include seasonal usage trends; the number of potential producers of a commodity and their capacity to produce that commodity; international trade; foreign exchange rates; and general economic conditions, such as interest rates, unemployment rates, inflation, and disposable income.

Financial Markets

Fundamental price analysis in the financial markets involves forecasting the supply of and demand for credit and the price of fixed-income securities. The fundamental analyst must simultaneously evaluate economic factors, political forces, and investor attitudes.

The Federal Reserve Board is responsible for U.S. monetary policy. Because the Federal Reserve influences the money supply, its policies and actions have a great impact on credit and interest rate levels. In a slow economy, the Fed can lower the discount rate, lower its fed funds rate target, or buy Treasury securities in open market operations to infuse cash into the economy and stimulate spending. During inflationary times, the Fed does just the opposite—raising the discount rate, increasing its fed funds target, or selling Treasury securities to take money out of the system and reduce borrowing.

The demand for money comes from four major financing areas: business financing, consumer and personal financing, mortgage financing, and government financing. In an expanding economy, the combined credit needs of these sectors tend to put upward pressure on interest rates. Theoretically, interest rates rise to the level that brings demand for funds into balance with the supply of funds. On the other hand, in periods of sluggish economic activity, interest rates fall, thus helping to stimulate borrowing.

Private and government issuers of debt instruments compete for available capital by adjusting the interest rates they pay to lenders and investors. Among the financial instruments affected by these influences are long-term U.S. Treasury bonds, long- and intermediate-term U.S. Treasury notes, short-term U.S. Treasury bills, foreign currency, precious metals, stocks, corporate and municipal bonds, and prime commercial paper or time deposits of various maturities.

The task of the fundamental analyst is to sort through the volume of financial information, pinpoint the significant factors, and accurately weigh their effect on the supply and demand for credit. Economic reports released by the U.S. government help in that regard. The elements that make up these reports can be grouped into three categories of indicators: leading, concurrent, and lagging.

Leading indicators signal the state of the economy for the coming months. They imply potential changes in the business cycle and, as a result, provide the analyst with an early indication of interest rate trends. The Conference Board has combined a number of these statistical elements into a single index called the Leading Indicator Index. This index includes:

- Average workweek of production workers in manufacturing
- Initial claims for unemployment insurance
- Orders for consumer goods and materials
- Percentage of companies reporting slower deliveries
- Change in manufacturers' unfilled orders for durable goods
- Plant and equipment orders
- New building permits
- Materials prices
- Index of consumer expectations

- Stock market prices
- Money supply

A value change in one of the index's components is often an early signal of a production or investment change within the economy. An increase in demand for goods requires additional labor, which, more than likely, would be seen first in the lengthening of the manufacturing workweek. Eventually, there would be an increase in the number of manufacturing workers hired. Similarly, when demand for goods falls, a cut in work hours precedes layoffs. Traders usually react immediately to these indicators as they are released throughout the month, and this results in short-term price volatility.

Concurrent and lagging indicators show the general direction of the economy and confirm or deny a trend implied by the leading indicators. The market adjusts quickly as investors react to these economic signals. Key concurrent and lagging monthly indicators include:

- *Employment.*   Released at the start of the month, employment reports show the change in employment for the preceding month and current economic activity.
- *Trade balance.*   The trade balance reveals the difference between imports and exports of merchandise over time. It can indicate the strength of the dollar, which the market follows closely as an indicator of potential foreign purchases of securities.
- *Domestic car sales.*   The number of cars sold during the previous month is a good measure of consumer confidence and overall economic activity.
- *Retail sales.*   The retail sales report summarizes the value of credit and cash retail purchases and serves as a good indicator of consumer confidence and overall economic activity.
- *Producer Price Index (PPI).*   PPI shows the cost of resources needed to produce manufactured goods during

the previous month. It lists the rate of inflation for raw materials.

- *Business inventories.*   Business inventories reflect the demand for short-term credit by businesses. As inventories build, they are usually financed through bank loans or commercial paper. Therefore, increases or decreases in inventory usually signal changes in the demand for short-term credit. Inventory levels also generally indicate the duration and intensity of business slowdowns or speedups. If inventories are high when a slowdown begins, economists usually expect a longer and more severe recession because factories then run at reduced levels until inventories are sold off. High inventories also may act as short-term support for interest rates. When inventories are high and the economy is in a business slowdown, demand for credit to finance inventories can keep interest rates higher longer than normal. Low inventories going into an upturn in the business cycle can result in a short inflation spurt and a quick acceleration of business activity. Rebuilding inventories creates jobs and ultimately causes consumer demand to increase. This demand often cannot be met by existing inventories, so economic activity increases and factories open.

- *Housing starts.*   Housing starts show the demand for long-term mortgage money and short-term construction loans. They also indicate the number and type of mortgage-backed securities that the market will need in the near future.

- *Industrial production.*   Industrial production figures give the level of factory output in the previous month and show the level of intensity for economic recessions and booms.

- *Personal income.*   Personal income reflects consumers' buying power and weighs potential demand for goods and services.

- *Gross domestic product (GDP).*   GDP reports the value of all final goods and services produced by an economy over a particular time period, normally a year.

- *Consumer Price Index (CPI).*   CPI measures inflation and is a key factor in bond prices, as investors usually demand a real rate of return for government bonds over the long term. Traders watch these numbers closely, since they often indicate future changes in long-term bond and money market rates.

These indicators are reported in daily newspapers, on TV, and on the Internet as information is released. Market experts, however, make forecasts of the data prior to the actual release, and the market generally begins to react before the news is announced, which means that pricing is influenced by expectations rather than by reality. In fact, a market aphorism counsels, "Buy the rumor, sell the fact."

No one indicator permanently dominates, and "the most important" indicators replace one another as key factors in the market. Sometimes the market will concentrate on one or two elements and ignore others for a time. It is the job of the fundamental analyst to identify the factors currently of most concern to the market.

For example, during most of 1982, many market analysts watched money supply and ignored other indicators. Money supply is the amount of money in the economy and consists primarily of currency in circulation plus checkable deposits in banks. The consensus was that the Federal Reserve was going to dominate the market and make policy decisions based on money growth and inflation rates. Yet, later that year and in early 1983, money supply and inflation were downplayed, as other economic indicators showed that the economy was in a general slide, and the Fed indicated that it was going to pay less attention to money supply in its policy making.

In late 1990 and early 1991, many market analysts watched precious metals and oil prices, as everyone was speculating on what effects the Gulf War would have on the markets. A year later, the war was over, and analysts had turned their attention to the economy. Traders kept close tabs on housing starts, durable goods, nonfarm payroll, and employment, as well as CPI and PPI, as indicators of how the economy was doing. Others were again looking at money supply.

Market analysts still watch employment, CPI, and PPI closely. Perhaps to an even greater extent, the financial markets scrutinize information from the Federal Reserve, the Fed chairman, and Fed board members for indications of future Fed policy. The Federal Reserve system itself provides information for analyzing the economy and predicting Fed activity. Weekly reports contain information on:

- The money supply growth on a one-week lag basis
- Loan demand
- The average rates for fed funds
- Dealers' positions in Treasury issues
- The condition of the accounts

Federal Reserve Bank

The Fed reports the level of reserves that banks must maintain at the central bank, which provides information about transactions that affect the fed funds rate. The fed funds rate is the interest rate banks charge one another for borrowing and lending excess reserves. The financial markets scrutinize the fed funds rate and view it as a good indicator of short-term Fed policy.

Other Fed reports give the total amount of commercial paper and industrial loans outstanding at financial and nonfinancial institutions, showing overall credit demand and which sectors of the economy are demanding it; the minutes of the Federal Reserve Open Market Committee monthly meeting; and the results of the Fed's regional survey of economic strength in various Fed bank districts, called the "Beige Book," which is scrutinized by analysts for inflationary pressures.

Using Fundamental Analysis

According to price theory, the point where supply and demand intersect represents an equilibrium or market price. Fundamental analysis attempts to pinpoint and recognize the major factors in the market and predict their effect on the equilibrium price of a commodity. Profit opportunities exist when a fundamental analyst can project how these factors will affect both the short-term and long-term equilibrium price. Supply-and-demand indicators may vary greatly from one commodity to another, but the process of fundamental analysis is similar for all products.

Still, the information fundamental analysts need to forecast prices in agricultural and financial markets is vast and complex. Many fundamental analysts collect the information on their own, but services are also available that provide this information.

Fundamental analysts must exercise good judgment since each piece of information they feed into the computer must be weighted for its particular significance. Such subjective evaluations are a necessary part of using economic models as price forecasting tools.

A CAUTIONARY NOTE

Regardless of which method or combination of methods traders use for price analysis, they must recognize that none is foolproof. The price discovery process in futures markets represents the collective wisdom of all market participants trying to estimate futures prices, and this is not an exact science.

FURTHER READING

Murphy, John J., *Intermarket Analysis: Profiting from Global Market Relationships.* New York: Wiley, 2004.

Murphy, John J., *Technical Analysis of the Futures Markets: A Comprehensive Guide to Trading Methods and Applications.* New York: Prentice Hall, 1986.

Niermira, Michael P., and Gerald F. Zukowski, *Trading the Fundamentals: The Trader's Complete Guide to Interpreting Economic Indicators and Monetary Policy.* New York: McGraw Hill, 1998.

Pring, Martin J., *Technical Analysis Explained: The Successful Investor's Guide to Spotting Investment Trends and Turning Points.* New York: McGraw Hill, 2002.

Shaleen, Kenneth H., *Volume and Open Interest.* Chicago: Irwin 1996.

Steidlmayer, J. Peter, *Steidlmayer on Markets: Trading with Market Profile.* New York: Wiley, 2002.

CHAPTER 11

Spreading: From Butterflies to the Crush

A *spread trade* is the simultaneous purchase and sale of two different futures contracts of a related commodity. For instance, a trader who purchased the CBOT March mini-sized gold contract and then sold the September mini-sized silver contract would have initiated a spread trade.

Unlike traders who look at absolute price levels and initiate outright positions in one contract, spread traders form opinions on how the price relationship between two contracts is likely to change. If market prices move as expected, spread traders can liquidate the spread and profit from the change in the price relationships between the contracts.

This chapter examines some of the underlying economic factors that account for the normal price relationships between different futures contracts. It also includes a few examples of spreading and explains some of the more common agricultural financial spreads.

Traders find spreads attractive for two primary reasons: reduction in risk and margin benefits.

WHY USE SPREADS:
LOWER POTENTIAL RISK

Spreads generally are considered less risky than outright positions. For the most part, this is primarily because prices of two different futures contracts for the same commodity exhibit a strong tendency to move in the same direction. Spread trading also offers some protection against losses caused by unexpected or extreme price volatility. This "protection" exists because gains from one side of the spread are more or less offset by losses from the other side. The short side of a futures spread, for example, might generate a loss resulting from a price increase, but the long side should produce a profit, which will offset much of this loss.

Although spread trading is generally considered less risky than outright position trading, this is not always the case. For example, intercommodity spreads, such as long wheat and short corn, may not always be less risky than an outright position. Wheat prices might unexpectedly decrease and corn prices might increase during the life of the spread, thus creating a loss on both legs of the spread that is larger than an outright position in one futures contract.

WHY USE SPREADS: MARGIN BENEFITS

Because spreads for the most part carry less risk than an outright position, spread margin rates are generally lower. Lower margin rates enable traders to diversify their portfolios with a smaller amount of capital. However, another caveat: spread margins may not be always be lower than outright positions. For instance, spread margins are higher for intermarket spreads, in which traders spread the same futures contracts at two different futures exchanges that do not have cross-margining agreements. Separate clearinghouses may not recognize other market positions in determining margin requirements.

ECONOMIC BENEFITS OF SPREAD TRADING

From the exchange's perspective, the economic contributions of spreading are twofold. Spreading provides market liquidity through increased volume. But perhaps more importantly, spreading corrects distortions in price relationships. Because of this corrective influence, all market participants, spreaders or not, must have at least some understanding of spread relationships.

Types of Spreads

There are several types of spreads. We give a brief overview of each spread here and then examine the more significant spreads in detail later in this chapter.

- *Interdelivery spreads,* also known as *calendar spreads,* are those with the same commodity on the same exchange in different contract months. As an example, buying the March mini-sized Dow future and selling the June mini-sized Dow contract all at the CBOT would be considered an *intramarket* spread.

- *Intermarket spreads* involve the same commodity on different exchanges. For example, long March CBOT mini-sized gold and short March COMEX gold.

- *Intercommodity product spreads* involve the purchase of a raw material and the sale of a derived process product(s), or vice versa. For instance, one common such spread is known as the "crush." This is the purchase of July soybeans and then the sale of soybean oil and soybean meal. There are different versions of this type of product spread, such as the "crack," which involves selling heating oil and gasoline and buying crude oil.

Quoting Spreads

The term *spread* actually refers to the difference in price between two related contracts. For example, if a trader purchased the September S&P Index contract at 1169 and sold the December contract for 1170, he would have established a spread with a one-point difference between the two contracts. Spreads are thus quoted as the price difference between two related contracts. To calculate an agricultural spread such as the July/November soybean spread, traders subtract the price of the November contract from the price of the July contract. Generally, this difference will result in a positive number, as agricultural commodity prices are typically lowest at harvest and trend higher during the marketing year as storage, interest, and insurance costs accumulate. As a result, July soybeans (old-crop beans) are usually priced higher than November soybeans (new-crop beans).

Placing a Spread Order

If a trader buys the higher leg of a spread, she expects the difference between the two contracts to widen. Conversely, if a trader sells the higher leg of a spread, she expects the difference between the contract months to narrow. When a trader "buys the spread," she buys the higher leg and sells the lower leg; when a trader "sells the spread," she sells the higher leg. This holds true in both a normal (carrying-charge) market and an inverted (discount) market.

Spread orders are commonly placed as limit orders, but they can also be placed as market orders and stop orders. For instance, a common limit order spread might read as follows: Sell September S&P futures and buy August S&P futures for a premium of three points or lower to the buy side.

Spread Strategies

Spread traders form opinions on the likelihood of different scenarios taking place, and they put on spreads to capitalize on the expected price relationship changes. For example, for July soybeans to gain on November soybeans, one of four possible market scenarios must occur:

- In a bull market, July soybeans rise more than November soybeans rise.
- In a bear market, July soybeans fall less than November soybeans fall.
- July soybeans remain unchanged, while November soybeans fall.
- July soybeans rise, while November soybeans remain unchanged.

AGRICULTURAL MARKET SPREADS

The three basic types of spreads used in the agricultural markets are the interdelivery spread, the intermarket spread, and the intercommodity spread. General definitions and explanations are provided above. The following discussions expand on these definitions and explanations as they relate specifically to the agricultural market.

Interdelivery Spreads

An *interdelivery spread,* one of the most commonly used spreads, lets spread traders take advantage of abnormal price differences between two delivery months of a single futures market. Traders describe interdelivery spreads as either bull or bear spreads. In an agricultural (ag) bull spread, a trader buys the nearby month and sells the deferred, expecting the nearby to gain on the deferred. An ag bear spread is just the opposite: a trader sells the nearby month and buys the deferred, expecting the deferred to gain on the nearby. The nearby futures month refers to the contract month closest to expiration, while a deferred futures month is any contract month further from expiration. (Note that in a metals bull spread, traders sell the nearby month and buy the deferred—just the opposite of an ag bull spread. That's because in the ag markets, an increase in the cash price typically raises the nearby month more than it raises the deferred month. In the metals market, an increase in price typically raises the deferred month price by more.)

Among storable commodities, such as grains and metals, carrying charges have the greatest impact on the underlying futures prices of different delivery months. Carrying charges represent the costs of storage and insurance for wheat, corn, soybean, or oats. In 1993, the Chicago Board of Trade approved grain elevators, which averaged 3.9 to 4.5 cents per bushel per month in 1993. A set amount of cents per month for interest is more difficult to state because interest rates are typically a variable component of carrying charges.

Theoretically, in a normal futures market—reflecting adequate supplies of the underlying cash commodity and sufficient storage capacity—the price of the nearby futures month and the price of the deferred futures month have a definite relationship. That is, the deferred futures price is usually higher than the nearby futures price by approximately the amount of the cost of carrying the commodity from the nearby to the deferred month. Each futures delivery month price is typically higher than that of the previous month by the amount of the cost to store, insure, and finance the commodity from month to month.

For example, in the case of corn priced at $2.50 per bushel with a base cost for storage and insurance of 4.5 cents per bushel per month and an interest rate of 10 percent, the carrying charge is 6.58 cents per bushel per month:

$$\frac{(\$2.50 \times 10\%)}{12} + \$0.045 = \$0.0658/\text{bu/mon}$$

Thus, the theoretical spreads of futures prices at full carry are:

December	March	May	July
$2.50	$2.69¾	$2.83	$2.96¼

These prices reflect the corn crop year that begins on September 1 and ends on August 31. Consequently, December is considered the first new-crop futures delivery month, and July is considered the last month. Futures prices stand to be at their seasonal low right after harvest—October and November for corn. In a normal market, then, December futures should be priced lower than the deferred contract months since carrying charges accumulate as the marketing year progresses.

Remember that these full-carry markets are theoretical. In practice, interdelivery futures price spreads only rarely reflect the full cost of carry that results from changing market conditions.

Take, for example, actual corn spreads at the Chicago Board of Trade from mid-November 1982. With the nearby December corn futures selling at $2.34½ per bushel and a prime rate of 11½ percent, the monthly carrying cost was about 7 cents.

December	March 1983	May	July	September
$2.34½	$2.45	$2.51½	$2.56¼	2.60

These spreads are far from full carry. Many different market variables could have affected the spread during the delivery months, including expectations about the amount of corn planted by farmers during the next crop year; corn demand for animal feed, food, seed, and industrial users; carryover expectations (remaining supplies of corn carried from one crop year to the next); the expected rate of inflation; interest rate fluctuations; and the availability of storage.

In fact, some markets may not reflect carrying charges at all. During periods in which a commodity is in short supply, the nearby futures contract can trade at a premium in relation to the deferred futures. Such a market is called an *inverted market*. The inversion represents, in effect, a negative return for holding inventories.

One of the most common interdelivery spreads is the intercrop, or old-crop/new-crop spread. It involves buying futures in one crop year and selling futures in another crop year. Since prices are usually lowest at harvest, new-crop futures tend to be priced lower than futures from the previous crop year.

Traders must consider a number of factors, however, when they establish an old-crop/new-crop spread. First, traders should look at the price relationship—not the absolute price levels—between the two contracts and determine how they think the spread will change. Then traders must ask:

- How large are remaining supplies (carryover) from the last harvest?

- What is the outlook for the size of the next harvest?

- How does the rate of usage compare to previous forecasts?

- How strong is future demand expected to be?

Answering these questions helps traders determine how a spread will change over time. If traders expect old-crop prices to rise relative to new-crop prices, they can buy the old-crop month and simultaneously sell the new-crop month. If, on the other hand, they expect new-crop prices to gain relative to old-crop prices, they can buy the new-crop month and simultaneously sell the old-crop month. In any case, both sides of the spread are usually executed in one step, not two.

The July/December corn spread is a common intercrop spread. July represents the old-crop month; December represents the new-crop month. Traders calculate the spread by subtracting the December futures price from the July futures price (July minus December).

For example, say a spread trader in May 1986 expected July prices to decline relative to December (that is, for the spread to become less positive) because no new export business developed in the time after the Chernobyl nuclear accident. On May 28, the trader simultaneously sold one July 1986 corn futures contract at $2.37 and bought one December 1986 corn futures contract at $1.95, thus initiating a bear intercrop spread. The spread on May 28 was 42 cents ($2.37 − $1.95).

On July 2, the trader offset both positions and closed out the spread, buying one July 1986 corn futures contract at $2.05, for a gain of 32 cents ($2.37 – $2.05), and selling one December 1986 corn futures contract at $1.82, for a loss of 13 cents ($1.95 – $1.82). The spread thus did become less positive, moving from 42 cents to 23 cents, for a net gain of 19 cents per bushel ($0.42 – $0.23). Notice that this equals the 32-cent gain on the July contract less the 13-cent loss on the December contract. Since one futures contract equals 5,000 bushels, this spread trade produced a $950 gain ($0.19 × 5,000 bushels) for the trader.

	July Futures	December Futures	Spread
May 28	Sold one July corn at $2.37 per bushel	Bought one December corn at $1.95 per bushel	$0.42
July 2	Bought one July corn $2.05 per bushel	Sold one December corn at $1.82 per bushel	$0.23
Result	$0.32 gain per bushel	$0.13 loss per bushel	$0.19

Intermarket Spreads

Some commodities trade on not just one, but several exchanges. Futures trading in wheat, for instance, occurs at the Chicago Board of Trade, the Kansas City Board of Trade, and the Minneapolis Grain Exchange. Traders who take intermarket spreads attempt to take advantage of changing price relationships within these various markets. For example, a trader might take a long position in Kansas City wheat futures against a short position in Chicago Board of Trade wheat futures.

These price differences often reflect specific geographic factors that the intermarket spreader must analyze. Transportation costs, for instance, are one important factor. Wheat prices are generally lowest in the primary producing areas, and prices increase by at least the cost of transportation elsewhere.

The value of the class and grade of wheat deliverable on each exchange also influences price differentials. While the different exchanges generally allow delivery of several classes of wheat (premiums and discounts), each market tends to reflect the prices of a particular wheat class. For example, Chicago Board of Trade wheat futures prices tend to reflect the price of soft, red, winter wheat, while Kansas City wheat futures reflect the price of hard, red, winter wheat. So each market reflects the type of wheat grown nearby. Spread traders must also realize that different wheat classes tend to vary in price, depending on their use.

Market participants interested in spreading watch the relationship between these two markets. When the price relationship becomes abnormal, spreaders buy the underpriced contract and sell the overpriced contract. This occurred in October 1986, when Chicago wheat futures traded 40 cents higher than Kansas City wheat futures. The price discrepancy corresponded to a shortage of soft winter wheat in the cash market, which was caused by a poor crop coupled with heavy participation of wheat producers in government programs. In this market situation, spreaders bought Kansas City wheat futures and sold Chicago Board of Trade wheat futures. When the price relationship reflected more normal market conditions, spreaders closed their spreads by selling Kansas City wheat and buying Chicago wheat.

Opportunities also exist for spreading between U.S. futures markets and foreign futures exchanges. Some common international spread positions include New York versus London sugar, cocoa, or copper; and gold spreads between New York, London, and Chicago.

Intercommodity Spreads

An *intercommodity spread* is a spread between two different but related commodities. The two commodities can either be used interchangeably or have common supply and demand characteristics. Although it is not necessary to spread the same months in both commodities, it is a common practice to do so.

One popular intercommodity spread, the wheat/corn spread, involves buying (or selling) one or more wheat futures contracts and selling (or buying) one or more corn futures contracts of the same delivery month. The wheat/corn spread is quoted as wheat over corn—that is, wheat minus corn. Since wheat prices are generally higher that corn prices, the spread is usually positive.

Changes in the wheat/corn spread are often seasonal. The wheat/corn spread tends to become less positive some time in May/June/July, following the winter wheat harvest, when wheat prices are low and corn prices are high. On the other hand, a trader might expect the spread to become more positive in September/October/November, during the corn harvest, when corn prices are low and wheat prices are high.

Given the existence of a "normal" spread relationship between wheat and corn, traders can take advantage of abnormal relationships in the spread as those relationships return to normal. Conversely, traders can also seize opportunities when they anticipate abnormal spread relationships developing from normal ones.

Suppose a trader anticipates a normal spread, with wheat falling faster relative to corn until summer, and then wheat gaining on corn in the fall. On June 29, the trader buys one wheat futures contract at $3.75 per bushel and sells one corn futures contract at $3.02½ per bushel in anticipation of the spread becoming more positive. The spread difference is 72½ cents a bushel ($3.75 − $3.02½).

On November 2, the trader offsets the position by selling one wheat futures contract at $4.01 per bushel and buying one corn futures contract at $2.49 per bushel, for a difference of $1.52 per bushel ($4.01 − $2.49). The spread moved from 72½ cents to $1.52, and the trader profited accordingly, actually gaining on both legs of the spread. The total gain on the position was 79½ cents per bushel ($1.52 − $0.72½) or $3,975 per spread ($0.79½ × 5,000 bushels).

	Wheat Futures	Corn Futures	Spread
June 29	Bought one December wheat at $3.75 per bushel	Sold one December corn at $3.02½ per bushel	$0.72½
November 2	Sold one December wheat at $4.01 per bushel	Bought one December corn at $2.49 per bushel	$1.53
Result	$0.26 gain per bushel	$0.53½ gain per bushel	$0.79½

A special type of intercommodity spread is the spread between a commodity and its products. The most common example, the spread between soybeans and its two by products—soybean meal and soybean oil—is knows as the *crush spread*. By buying soybean futures and selling soybean oil and soybean meal futures, soybean processing firms often "put on the crush" to hedge the purchase price of soybeans and the selling price of soybean oil and soybean meal.

Specifically, these processing firms use the crush spread to minimize the financial risk of sudden increases in soybean costs or declining values of finished soybean oil and meal. To make a profit from soybean processing, processors must buy beans at a lower cost than the combined sales income from the finished oil and meal. The difference, or profit margins, is called the *gross processing margin* (GPM). Application of the GPM to the soybean, soybean oil, and soybean meal futures markets makes it possible for processors to buy soybean futures in order to hedge later purchases of cash soybeans and, at the same time, sell soybean oil and meal futures to hedge later sales of meal and oil.

Given a favorable price relationship between soybean futures and soybean oil and meal futures, processors buy soybean futures and simultaneously sell soybean oil and meal futures. They hold the long soybean portion of the hedge until they actually buy the required cash soybeans.

Suppose, as a processor feared, the price of soybeans rises in the cash market. The processor remains relatively unaffected because the futures price of soybeans also increases in response to the same economic factors. The processor buys soybeans in the cash market and offsets the long soybean futures position—at a higher price—by selling an equal number of soybean futures contracts. The gain on the futures position approximately offsets the increased cost of the raw material.

The processor holds the short side of the crush hedge—the sale of soybean oil and meal futures—until he or she is ready to sell the finished oil and meal. If the cash market prices of soybean oil and meal decline, the futures price probably will decline as well. Thus, even if the processor received less income from a cash market sale of the oil and meal, the gain the processor can realize in the futures market roughly offsets this cash market loss.

This crush spread hedge works in the same way and for the same reasons as do all well-placed hedges—because of the tendency of cash and futures prices, which are influenced by the same economic factors, to move in the same direction. But the crush spread is a uniquely effective hedge because if affords soybean processors protection in three related markets.

The crush spread's opposite, a *reverse crush,* works well too. This spreading opportunity results from distortions in normal price patterns; that is, when the cost of soybeans exceeds the combined sales value of soybean oil and meal. The resulting unfavorable gross processing margin makes it unprofitable for soybean processors to manufacture meal and oil.

When the GPM drops below a profitable level, soybean processors may slow down or even stop manufacturing operations and at the same time possibly initiate reverse crush spreads—selling soybean futures and buying oil and meal futures. Other market participants would likely move to seize the same spreading opportunity, and the concerted market pressure of reduced soybean meal and oil manufacturing and reverse crush spreads in the futures market will gradually return price relationships to a more normal level.

FINANCIAL MARKET SPREADS

Spread relationships exist among any number of financial futures contracts and vary in reaction to and in anticipation of changes in economic circumstances. Just as in the agricultural markets, when traders expect financial market price relationships to shift, they initiate spread trades to take advantage of these transitions.

In the financial markets, the three primary types of spreads are interdelivery spreads, intermarket spreads, and intercommodity spreads. General definitions and explanations for these terms are provided earlier in the chapter. The following discussions expand on these definitions and explanations as they relate specifically to the financial market.

Interdelivery Spreads

Interdelivery spreads involve buying and simultaneously selling different delivery months of the same futures contract on the same exchange. For example, spread traders might sell (or buy) December T-bonds and buy (or sell) March T-bonds.

A primary motivator in establishing interdelivery spreads in the financial markets is the implication of *carry*. Chapters 8 and 14 discuss carry and the financial markets in more detail. The following examples provide simple sketches of some of the interdelivery spreads commonly used by financial futures traders.

In a financial bull spread, for instance, traders go long the nearby contract month and short the deferred contract month. If prices increase, a bull spread profits if the nearby month rises faster than does the deferred month. Conversely, if prices fall, the spread profits if the nearby month falls more slowly than the deferred month.

Suppose a trader has been watching the T-bond futures market for several months. She knows that most market analysts call for higher interest rates in December, anticipating an increased demand for seasonal credit. Still, analysts expect this demand to be temporary; it should not affect interest rates past year-end. For this reason, the price of March T-bond futures has remained relatively unchanged at 110-16, while December T-bond futures have dropped from 111-25 to 111-08 by mid-October.

A bear spread is just the opposite of a bull spread. Traders short the nearby contract month and go long the deferred contract month. If prices rise, the spread profits if the nearby month increases at a slower rate than the deferred month. If prices decline, the spread profits if the nearby falls at a faster rate than does the deferred.

	December Futures	March Futures	Spread
October 16	Bought 10 December T-bonds at 111-08	Sold 10 March T-bonds at 110-16	00-24
December 3	Sold 10 December T-bonds at 111-18	Bought 10 March T-bonds at 110-20	00-30
Result	00-10, or ¹⁰⁄₃₂, gain	00-04 or ⁴⁄₃₂, loss	00-06

A variation on the interdelivery spread is the butterfly spread. *Butterfly spreads* involve putting on two interdelivery spreads in opposite directions, with the center position being common to both spreads. For example, a trader might go long three March T-bonds and short six June T-bonds and long three September T-bonds. Or he might go short three March T-bonds, long six June T-bonds, and short three September T-bonds.

Note that butterflies are actually two joined interdelivery spreads. The first example, for instance, is long March T-bonds and short June T-bonds, short June T-bonds and long September T-bonds. In other words, the butterfly spread combines a bull spread (long March bonds and short June bonds) with a bear spread (short June bonds and long September bonds). The second example, on the other hand, combines a bear spread (short March bonds and long June bonds) with a bull spread (long June bonds and short September bonds).

Traders establish butterfly spreads when they believe that the price of the middle contract is out of line with the contract months on each side. They also use them to take advantage of changes in the shape of the yield curve, using contracts with different maturities but with the same delivery month. For example, a yield curve butterfly spread might include December 2-year T-notes, December 5-year T-notes, and December 10-year T-notes.

Intermarket Spreads

Intermarket spreading involves taking opposite positions simultaneously in two similar markets at two different exchanges. Common intermarket spreads include LIFFE bunds/DTB bunds, the CBOT Dow Jones Industrial Average/S&P 500, and CBOT 10-year T-note/DTB German Government bond futures. The following presents a stock index intermarket spread.

All stock indexes reflect general market risk at somewhat different variabilities. They therefore tend to move in the same direction over time but do so at differing rates. Spreaders base their trading on the strength of one contract relative to another, rather than on overall market direction. One equity index contract is strong relative to another if it advances faster during a market rally or declines slower in a bear market.

For example, if traders anticipate the Dow Jones Industrial Average will be strong relative to the somewhat broader S&P 500 Index, they'll buy CBOT DJIA futures and sell CME S&P 500 futures. The traders profit if the Dow advances faster that the S&P in a bull market or declines slower in a bear market.

Stock index futures contracts perform differently in certain phases of the market because of the nature of the underlying stocks. The S&P 500, for example, is a blue-chip-oriented composite of 500 large U.S. companies. The Dow is even more concentrated, consisting of only 30 of the nation's largest and strongest companies from the economy's various market sectors—the bluest of the blue chips.

Historically, blue-chip stocks like those in the S&P and the Dow tend to lead the rest of the market in the early stages of a bull market although one may move more strongly depending on specific market fundamentals. As the bull market matures, investors often buy more affordable secondary and over-the-counter issues. So blue-chip buying levels off, while activity in secondary issues continues to increase.

For example, suppose a trader forecasts a bull stock market, but expects the Dow stocks to gain on the broader market, which is reflected in the S&P 500. The trader's expectation is largely caused by increased buying by overseas investors, who tend to prefer the most liquid securities possible, and an anticipated run-up in the price of IBM, a prominent Dow stock.

Traders usually construct stock index spread trades by

ratioing the contracts to match total contract values (the dollar multiplier times the index point level.) On October 1, the trader buys three CBOT DJIA futures contracts at 7672 and sells one S&P 500 futures contract at 885. By November 2 the market moves higher, and he closes his position by selling three CBOT DJIA contracts at 7880 and buying one S&P contract at 901. The 208-point gain on the CBOT DJIA futures at $10 a point times the three contracts, gives the trader a $6,240 gain. That's $2,240 more than the 16-point loss on the S&P Futures, which at $250 a point came to $4,000.

	CBOT DJIA Futures	S&P Futures
October 1	Buy three December Dow at 7672	Sell one December S&P 500 at 885
November 2	Sell three December Dow at 7880	Buy one December S&P 500 at 901
Result	208-point, or $6,240, gain (208 × $10 × 3)	16-point, or $4,000, loss (16 × $250 × 1)

Intercommodity Spreads

Traders normally use intercommodity spreads to take advantage of price relationships between two different but closely related futures markets. For example, traders might spread CBOT municipal bond index futures and CBOT T-bond futures (commonly called the *MOB spread*—munis over bonds) or 10-year T-note futures and 30-year T-bond futures (called the *NOB spread*—notes over bonds). MOB and NOB spreads are two of the most actively traded intercommodity spreads among financial instruments. Other commonly traded intercommodity spreads include the TED spread (Treasury bills over Eurodollars), the FOB (5-year T-notes over bonds), the FITE (5-year T-notes over 10-year T-notes), and a variety of different 2-year T-note spreads against 5-year T-notes, 10-year T-notes, and T-bonds.

The MOB spread takes advantage of price differences between municipal bond index futures and Treasury bond futures. When traders expect municipal bonds to gain on government bonds, the strategy consists of buying muni-bond futures and selling T-bond futures, called "buying the MOB." Conversely, traders who believe that government bonds will gain on municipal bonds sell muni-bond futures and buy T-bond futures, called "selling the MOB."

Suppose a spread trader has been observing a general rally in the long-term debt markets. Muni issuance, however, has been picking up significantly. The trader expects an oversupply of munis to depress prices, while the Treasury market continues its strong rally. With December muni futures at 117-18 and December T-bond futures at 110-15, the spreader sells one muni contract and buys one bond contract. As expected, both contracts rally, but T-bonds rise faster than do munis. The trader then offsets the position, selling one T-bond contract at 114-10 and buying one muni contract at 119-29, for a gain of 1-16 or $^{48}\!/_{32}$ on the spread. At $31.25 a tick, that's a gain of $1,500 ($48 \times \$31.25 \times 1$).

	Muni Bond Futures	T-Bond Futures	Spread
Now	Sell one December muni contract at 117-18	Buy one December T-bond at 110-15	07-03
Later	Buy one December muni contract at 119-29	Sell one December T-bond at 114-10	05-19
Result	02-11 loss	03-27 gain	01-16

The NOB refers to the spread between 10-year T-note futures and T-bond futures. The spread is quoted as notes over bonds—T-notes minus T-bonds. NOB spread strategies take advantage of the different price sensitivities of 10-year notes and T-bonds to changes in interest rates. Typically, bond prices are more sensitive to interest rate shifts than are note prices. Depending on interest rate expectations, traders either buy or sell the NOB. Spreaders buy the NOB, buying T-note futures and selling T-bond futures, to take advantage of an equal increase in yields along the yield curve. Because an increase in interest rates will have a greater impact on the price of T-bond futures than on the price of 10-year T-note futures, a parallel shift up in the yield curve will make the NOB spread more positive. To take advantage of an equal decline in yields along the yield curve, with the NOB spread becoming more negative, traders sell the NOB, selling T-note futures and buying T-bond futures.

For example, suppose that in April a trader anticipates the general level of interest rates to rise by about 20 basis points (0.2 percent) over the course of the next few weeks for Treasury instruments of all maturities. Since the trader knows longer-term securities are more price-sensitive than shorter-term maturities, she buys the NOB spread to profit from the greater price sensitivity of T-bond futures relative to 10-year T-notes. With June 10-year T-note futures at 112-30 and June T-bonds at 112-22, the trader buys the NOB spread at 00-08 (10-year T-notes minus T-bonds), buying ten 10-year T-note futures contracts and selling ten T-bond contracts.

By late May, interest rates rise by 20 basis points, as expected. The NOB spread became more positive because the increase in interest rates had a greater impact on the price of T-bond futures than on the price of T-note futures. The trader offsets the spread, selling ten 10-year T-note contracts at 111-04 and buying ten T-bond contracts at 110-08, for a gain of $20/_{32}$ on the spread. At $31.25 a tick, that's a gain of $6,250 on the ten contracts (20 × $31.25 × 10). Because an equal increase in the level of interest rates had an unequal impact on the prices of T-bond and 10-year T-note futures, the trader profited from the long NOB spread position.

	10-Year T-Note Futures	T-Bond Futures	Spread
April 11	Bought 10 June notes at 112-30	Sold 10 June bonds at 112-22	00-08
May 28	Sold 10 June notes at 111-04	Bought 10 June bonds at 110-08	00-28
Result	01-26, or $58/_{32}$, loss	02-14, or $78/_{32}$, gain	00-20

Keep in mind that the information and examples presented in this chapter merely introduce the concept of spreading. This

chapter provides a basic explanation of how spreads are established, the advantages of spread trading, and some idea of the
price relationships between various futures contracts.

FURTHER READING

Bernstein, Jake, *How to Profit from Seasonal Commodity Spreads: A Complete Guide.* New York: Wiley & Sons, 1983.

Schap, Keith, *The Complete Guide to Spread Trading.* New York: McGraw Hill, 2005.

Smith, Courtney, *Futures Spread Trading: The Complete Guide.* Greenville, SC: Traders Press, 1999.

CHAPTER 12

Options on Futures: More Trading Dimensions

Options on futures contracts add a new dimension to risk management and speculative trading. Options on futures contracts were introduced in October 1982 when the Chicago Board of Trade, as part of a government pilot program, began trading options on Treasury bond futures. The ultimate success of this program led the way for trading other options on agricultural and financial futures contracts.

Trading in options is not new. Options traditionally have been used with underlying cash securities, such as stocks, as well as with physicals, such as precious metals and real estate. Trading over-the-counter options on shares of common stock took place long before the creation in exchange trading in options.

OPTION BASICS

An option provides time to choose. The buyer of an option acquires the right, but not the obligation, to buy or sell an underlying commodity (whether a physical commodity, security, or futures contract) under specific conditions in exchange for the payment of a premium. Within the futures industry, the underlying instrument is a futures contract. Regardless of how much the market swings, the most an option buyer can lose is the option premium. He deposits the premium with his broker, and this money goes to the option seller.

Selling Option Premium

Unlike the option buyer, when traders establish a position by selling an option, they have the obligation to make or take delivery if that option expires "in the money." Whereas option buyers have a defined risk—the most they can lose on a trade is the cost of the option—the option seller is accepting an undefined risk. In the case of either a call or put, the option buyer (option holder) must pay the option seller (option writer) a premium. The premium is determined during trading on an exchange and depends on market conditions, such as supply, demand, volatility, and other economic and market variables.

Calls and Puts

There are two types of options: calls and puts. A *call option* gives the buyer the right, but not the obligation, to purchase a particular futures contract at a specific price. A *put option* gives the buyer the right, but not the obligation, to sell a particular futures contract at a specific price.

The price at which the buyer of a call has the right to purchase a futures contract and the buyer of a put has the right to sell a futures contract is known as the *strike price* or *exercise price.*

In options trading, it is important to understand that trading in call options is completely different from trading in put options. For every call buyer, there is a call seller; for every put buyer, there is a put seller.

If someone purchases a call option, he can offset the position by selling the same call option contract. Conversely, if someone purchases a put option, he can offset the position by selling the same put option. The same is true for an option seller. If an option seller wants to offset his short position, he buys back an option at the same strike price and expiration date—a specific day preceding the futures contract delivery month.

Exercising Options

Both buyers and sellers may offset an open option position any time prior to its expiration. However, only option buyers may exercise the contract, that is, acquire a futures position at the option strike price. "American" style options can be exercised on any trading day up to and including the last day an option is being traded, which is usually the day before the actual expiration day of the option. European options can be exercised only on the expiration date.

Once the buyer of a put or call exercises the option, the exchange at which the contract is traded records an open futures position for the designated contract month at the strike price in the accounts of the buyer and the seller. Table 12.1 illustrates the positions assigned to an option buyer and seller after an option is exercised.

Options Classes

Options are commonly grouped into three primary classifications: type, class, and series. The type of an option is its classification as either a put or call. The class of an option refers to the underlying contract. As an example, all mini-sized Dow call con-

TABLE 12.1

Futures Positions after Options Exercise

	Call Option	Put Option
Buyer assumes	Long futures position	Short futures position
Seller assumes	Short futures position	Long futures position

tracts, regardless of expiration date and exercise price, are the same class. A series of options means all option contracts of the same class with the same exercise price and expiration date. An example of an options series is a CBOT gold December 450 call.

Margin and Marking-to-Market

Because of the limited and known risk, option buyers are not required to maintain margin accounts. However, buyers pay sellers the full premium in the option. Option sellers, on the other hand, face risks similar to those faced by participants in the futures market and thus have margin requirements similar to those for futures.

For example, since the seller of a call is assigned a short futures position if the option is exercised, his risk is the same as someone who initially sold a futures contract. Because no one can predict exactly how the market will move, the option seller posts margin to demonstrate his ability to meet any potential contractual obligations.

Following the conclusion of each trading session, each seller's option position is marked-to-market to reflect the gains or losses from that particular trading session. If there is a significant adverse price move, the seller may have to post additional margin before the start of the next day's trading to maintain the open position.

Furthermore, option margins are set by the exchange at which the contract is traded at a level high enough to guarantee the financial integrity of the marketplace without unduly increasing the cost of participation to the investor. During conditions of high price volatility, futures exchanges raise margins; as price volatility decreases, these margins are lowered.

OPTION PRICING

Even though the marketplace is the ultimate determinant of how much an option is worth, there are some basic guidelines traders use to calculate option premiums. In general, an *option premium* is the sum of intrinsic value and time value. This amount is influenced by volatility, the difference between the strike price and the underlying price, and time to maturity.

Intrinsic Value

Intrinsic value is the difference, if any, between the market price of the underlying commodity and the strike price of an option. A call option has intrinsic value if its strike price is below the futures price. A put option has intrinsic value if its strike price is above the futures price. Any option that has intrinsic value is referred to as being "in-the-money."

For example, a corn call option with a $2.50 strike price gives the holder the right to purchase corn futures at $2.50 a bushel. If corn futures are trading at $3 a bushel and a trader exercises his $2.50 call, he realizes a 50-cent profit ($3 – $2.50). A call option with a strike price less than the current futures price is said to be in-the-money.

A corn put option with a $3.25 strike price, on the other hand, gives the holder the right to sell corn futures at $3.25. If corn futures are trading at $3 a bushel and an option holder exercises his $3.25 put, he realizes a 25-cent profit ($3.25 – $3). A put option with a strike price greater than the current futures price is said to be in-the-money.

A call option with a strike price above the current market price is said to be "out-of-the-money." For instance, if an option buyer holds a $3.50 corn call option, he has the right to buy a corn futures contract at $3.50. But, if the futures price is $3, he would be better off buying a corn futures contract at the lower price of $3 a bushel rather than exercising his option to buy at $3.50.

A put option with a strike price below the current market price is also said to be out-of-the-money. If an option buyer holds a $2.50 corn put, he has the right to sell a corn futures contract at $2.50. But, if corn futures are at $3, his put option is not worth

214

PART TWO   MARKET FOUNDATIONS

TABLE 12.2

Calculating Intrinsic Value

	Call Option	Put Option
In-the-money	Futures > strike	Futures < strike
At-the-money	Futures = strike	Futures = strike
Out-of-the-money	Futures < strike	Futures > strike

exercising, since he can sell a corn futures contract for a higher price in the futures market.

When the strike price of any put or call option equals the current market price, the option is said to be "at-the-money." With corn futures at $3 a bushel, a $3 call or a $3 put option is said to be at-the-money.

A summary of the intrinsic value of different put and call options is provided in Table 12.2.

Time Value

The second major component of an option premium is time value. *Time value* is the amount of the premium associated with the option relative to time to expiration and distinct from intrinsic value or volatility. Of course, since there are sellers as well as buyers in the market, time value also reflects the price that sellers are willing to accept for writing an option.

In general, the more time remaining until expiration on an option, the greater the time value. That is because the right to purchase or sell something is more valuable to a market participant if he has a year to decide what to do with the option rather than just six months. Conversely, an option buyer is asking the seller to face the risk of exercise (that is, the action taken by the holder of a call option, if he wishes to purchase the underlying futures contract, or by the holder of a put option, if he wishes to sell the underlying futures contract), and a year's worth of risk costs more than six months' worth. (See Fig. 12.1.)

FIGURE 12.1

Time Decay
As the chart illustrates, when an at-the-money option approaches expiration, its time value erodes faster (all else being equal) because there is less time for the option to move in-the-money. At expiration, an option has no time value; its only value, if any, is its intrinsic value. One option pricing derivative, theta, measures the rate at which an option value decreases with the passage of time, that is, the slope in the time decay chart. Many traders use theta when selling options to gauge their potential profit or when buying options to measure their exposure to time decay.

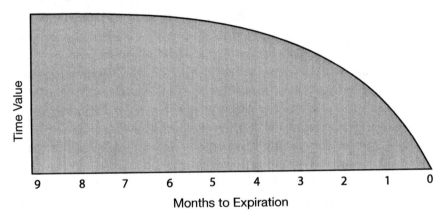

Months to Expiration

Some parallels can be drawn between the time value of an option premium and the premium charged for a casualty insurance policy. The longer the term of the insurance policy, the greater the probability a claim will be made by the policyholder, thus, the greater the risk assumed by the insurance company. To compensate for this increased risk, the insurer will charge a greater premium. The same is true with options on futures—the longer the term until option expiration, the greater the risk to the option seller, hence, the higher the option premium.

Volatility

Volatility of the underlying commodity is one of the more important factors affecting the value of the option premium. *Volatility* measures the change in price of a contract over a given time period. It is often expressed as a percentage and computed as the annualized standard deviation of percentage changes in daily prices.

While there are several mathematical models that compute volatility, the basic theory behind its influence on price is simple. Volatile prices of the underlying futures contract increase the probability that an option will move in-the-money, thereby increasing the option premium. The more volatile the price of the underlying commodity, the greater the chance of an adverse price move; thus, buyers are willing to pay more, and option sellers facing the risk of exercise require higher premiums.

For instance, if silver futures are trading for $6 an ounce and remain at that price for a year, there is little risk in selling a $6.50 call option. But if silver futures trade between $6.00 and $7.00 an ounce during the same week, there is a greater risk that the $6.50 call will run in-the-money. The option seller must be paid for taking on the risk the option buyer requests, so the option premium should be greater than the same call in a less volatile market.

The Greeks

Option prices are often determined by a series of factors, including what are commonly known as "the Greeks": delta, gamma, theta, and vega. The Greeks are essentially sensitivity measures associated with an option premium.

Delta measures how much an option premium changes, given a unit change in the underlying futures. For instance, when the underlying future moves 2 points, an option with a 50 delta will generally have a price move of 50 percent of the underlying. Delta is often described as the probability that the option will be in-the-money at expiration. So an option with a 50 delta has a 50 percent chance of closing in the money.

Gamma measures how fast delta changes and is defined as the change in delta, given a unit change in the underlying futures price. The higher the gamma of an option, the higher the rate of change in the option's price. Generally speaking, out-of-the-money options have low gammas and thus experience relatively small rates of price change. Conversely, in-the-money options have high gammas and thus experience relative larger price movements. The longer the life of an option, the smaller the gamma and thus the lower the rate of change in the price.

Theta calculates the premium deterioration of an option. Theta is inversely related to the amount of time left in an option. The longer the term of the option, the less the premium deterioration. The shorter the term of the option, the higher the depreciation.

Vega is a measure of the net change in an option premium given a 1-point change in volatility.

Option Pricing Models

There are many option pricing models that take different variables—intrinsic value, time remaining to expiration, and volatility—into account (as well as other factors such as short-term interest rates) in calculating the theoretical value of an option. These theoretical values may or may not correspond to the actual market values in the marketplace, but are used by traders to make trading decisions.

One of the most prominent option pricing models was introduced by Fischer Black and Myron Scholes in 1973. Different option pricing models also calculate the value of delta, gamma, vega, and other pricing sensitivities. (While it is beyond the scope of this text to describe how the Black-Scholes or any other option pricing model works, several texts that cover this topic in depth are listed on our Web site located at www.cbotguide.com.)

OPTION STRATEGIES

Options are used in all market environments—bullish, slightly bullish, bearish, slightly bearish, and neutral. In no way can all of them be covered in this chapter, but, in reviewing those that are discussed, the reader will gain a basic appreciation of why call and put options are bought and sold daily.

Buying Calls: Protection against Higher Prices

Since a call gives the buyer the right to buy a futures contract at a fixed price, a call option buyer believes futures prices will rise by at least enough to cover the premium he paid. In some situations, a trader might buy a call to establish a price ceiling for the future purchase of a cash commodity or to protect a short futures position.

For example, a treasurer of an investment firm anticipates having funds available at a later date to purchase U.S. Treasury bonds. However, the treasurer is worried that between now and the time she purchases the bonds, interest rates may decline, raising bond prices. She would like to have temporary insurance against a sudden price increase, but she also wants to avoid paying too much if bond prices decline. To achieve both price protection and an opportunity to purchase bonds at a lower price, the treasurer decides to buy a call option.

Suppose in May the price of a specific cash Treasury bond is 87-00. The treasurer purchases a September 86-00 for $2,000. By August, interest rates on long-term Treasury bonds have declined and the price of the cash bond is 96-00. The September 86-00 call is priced at $10,100. She decides to offset her position by selling the September 86-00 call.

By selling back her call option for $10,100, the treasurer makes an $8,100 gain ($10,100 − $2,000) and offsets most of the increased cost in the price of T-bonds.

	Cash	Options
May	Price of T-bonds is 87-00	Buys September 86-00 call option for $2,000
August	Price of T-bonds is 96-00	Sells September 86-00 call option for $10,100
Result	$9,000 loss (or 9-00 loss)	$8,100 gain

A major advantage of this strategy is that the treasurer established an interest rate floor, but not a ceiling. Had interest rates increased instead of decreased, the treasurer could have purchased T-bonds at a lower price and either let the option expire or offset her option position to earn any remaining time value. The only cost for this price protection was the option premium.

Buying Puts: Protection against Lower Prices

Bearing in mind that a put is an option to sell a futures contract at a fixed price, a put option buyer expects futures prices to decline by enough to cover the premium. In many cases, a market participant might buy a put to establish a minimum price for the future sale of a cash commodity or to protect a long futures position.

Assume a feed manufacturer expects soybean meal prices to rise, so he contracts ahead for all his soybean meal needs during the spring and summer months. Prices do trend higher for a short time, but after hitting $165 per ton in mid-April, it appears that prices could drop sharply.

Fearing that competitors might pass along any cost savings to their customers and gain market share, the manufacturer buys an August $160 soybean meal put option for $4.40. By mid-June, soybean meal prices have fallen to $148, so the manufacturer sells back the put for $12.50 and makes a profit of $8.10 per ton.

The feed manufacturer uses the $8.10 per ton profit from the put to keep his selling price for feed competitive. If soybean meal prices moved higher, the manufacturer could have let the put option expire or offset his option position to earn any remaining time value. The only cost for this price protection was the option premium.

	Cash	Options
Mid-April	Soybean meal price is $165	Buys August $160 put option for $4.40
Mid-June	Soybean meal price is $148	Sells August $160 put option for $12.50
Result	$17 loss	$8.10 gain

Selling Options to Earn Premium

The primary reason for a trader to sell either a call or put option is to earn the option premium. Generally, individuals who anticipate either little price movement or a slight decrease in prices sell options. However, some sophisticated strategies do involve the directional selling of option premiums to profit from market moves. In any case, most option sellers hope the underlying futures price will not rise to a level that will cause the option to be exercised and result in a loss greater than the premium received. (See Table 12.3.)

For example, at a time when the futures price is 76-00 for Treasury bonds, an investor collects a premium of $3,000 by selling a six-month, at-the-money call. Since an at-the-money call, by definition, has no intrinsic value, the $3,000 premium is entirely time value. If the futures price at expiration is at or below 76-00, the option will expire as worthless—with neither intrinsic value nor time value—and the investor's return will be the original $3,000 premium.

If the futures price at expiration is above 76-00, the option seller stands to realize some net return at expiration as long as the intrinsic value of the option is less than the premium received when the option was sold. Assume the futures price has risen to 78-00 by expiration. The option buyer exercises the call, and the option seller incurs a $2,000 loss on the short futures position. However, since the initial premium received by the options was $3,000, the seller's net gain is $1,000.

As stated earlier in this chapter, an option seller wishing to

TABLE 12.3

Market Expectations for Option Buyers and Sellers

	Call Option	Put Option
Buyer	Bullish	Bearish
Seller	Neutral to slightly bearish	Neutral to slightly bullish

liquidate a position prior to exercise or expiration can make an offsetting option purchase at the prevailing premium. To whatever extent the erosion of the option's time value has reduced the cost of the offsetting purchase, the seller still realizes a net profit.

What if, three months after the investor sold the 76-00 call, the futures price is still 76-00, but the option's time value has declined to $2,000? By making an offsetting purchase at this price, the option seller realizes a net gain of $1,000. This purchase eliminates any further possibility of the option being exercised.*

Option Spread Strategies

As the previous examples illustrate, there are a variety of ways options can be used to achieve either price protection or profits. While some option strategies can be as simple as either buying or selling one option, option strategies can become quite complicated and incorporate a combination of long and short options and/or futures and cash positions. Many of the more complicated option strategies fall under the category of spreads.

An *option spread* is the simultaneous purchase and sale of one or more options contracts, futures, and/or cash positions. Since the prices of two different contracts for the same or related instruments have a tendency to move up or down together, spread trading can offer protection against losses that arise from unexpected or extreme price volatility.

This occurs because losses from one side of a spread are more or less offset by gains from the other side of the spread. For example, if the short (sold) side of a spread results in a loss resulting from a price increase, the long (bought) side should

---

* An option can be exercised by the option buyer any time before expiration. Although gains on in-the-money options are often realized through offsetting option sales and the majority of exercises do not occur until at or near expiration, early exercise remains the prerogative of every option buyer.

produce a profit, offsetting much of the loss. While option strategies allow traders to limit the amount of risk they are carrying, other reasons for establishing option spreads are to capitalize on a market environment in which one option is overvalued or undervalued in relation to another, to hedge, or to enhance the return on investments.

Market participants have a variety of different option strategies at their fingertips to use in reaching their market objectives. These strategies can take into account different strike prices, futures prices, and expiration dates.

Vertical Spreads   *Vertical spreads,* sometimes referred to as *money spreads,* offer traders limited return with limited risk. These spreads involve buying and selling puts or calls of the same expiration month but with different strike prices. The spreads are divided into spreads for bull markets and spreads for bear markets. Bull spreads are used when the trader expects a rising market, while bear spreads are used when the trader expects a declining market. The four major types of vertical spreads follow:

- *Bull call spread.* Buying a call at one strike price and simultaneously selling a call at a higher strike price.

- *Bull put spread.* Buying a put at one strike price and simultaneously selling a put at a higher strike price.

- *Bear call spread.* Selling a call at one strike price and simultaneously buying a call at a higher strike price.

- *Bear put spread.* Selling a put at one strike price and simultaneously buying a put with a higher strike price.

A bull call spread can be used to provide moderate price protection. For example, with the price of soybean oil at 17.2 cents a pound, a trader executes a bull call spread by purchasing a December 17-cent soybean oil call option for 0.96 cent a pound and simultaneously selling a December 18-cent soybean oil call option for 0.535 cent a pound.

By early September, soybean oil prices have risen to 17.8 cents, so he closes out the spread. He sells back the 17-cent call option for 1.285 cents, for a profit of 0.325 cent, and buys back the 18-cent call option for 0.55 cent, for a loss of 0.015 cent. When the results from both legs of the spread are combined, the hedger has a net gain of 0.31 cent a pound.

	Cash	**Options**
Late June	Soybean oil price is 17.2 cents	Buys December 17-cent call for 0.96 cent; sells December 18-cent call for 0.535 cent
Early September	Soybean oil price is 17.8 cents	Sells December 17-cent call for 1.285 cents; buys December 18-cent call for 0.55 cent
Result	0.6-cent loss	0.325-cent gain on Dec 17-cent call option; 0.015-cent loss on December 18-cent call; 0.31-cent net gain on spread

Horizontal Spreads   *Horizontal spreads,* also known as *calendar spreads,* offer traders the opportunity to profit from different time decay patterns associated with options of different maturities. Therefore, horizontal spreads involve the purchase of either a call or put option and the simultaneous sale of the same type of option with typically the same strike price but with a different expiration month. Because time value in a near-term option decays more rapidly than time value in a more distant option, a near-term option is often sold at the same time a distant option is bought.

Horizontal spreads using calls often are employed when the long-term price expectation is stable to bullish, while horizontal spreads using puts often are employed when the long-term price expectation is stable to bearish.

Conversions and Reverse Conversions

With a *conversion,* the trader buys a futures contract, buys a put option, and sells a call option. The put and call options have the same strike price and the same expiration month. The futures contract price is usually as close as possible to the options' strike price. If the futures price is above the call strike price before expiration, the short call is exercised against the trader, which automatically offsets his or her long futures position; the long put option expires unexercised.

If the futures price falls below the put strike price before expiration, the long put option is exercised by the trader, which automatically offsets his or her long futures position; the short call option expires unexercised.

Conversions can be used to take advantage of price discrepancies. For example, assume a 90-day $3 wheat put option is underpriced by a quarter of a cent at 10¼ cents, while a 90-day $3 wheat call option is correctly priced at 10½ cents, with the underlying futures at $3.

The trader establishes the conversion by buying wheat futures at $3, buying the at-the-money put for 10¼ cents, and selling the at-the-money call for 10½ cents. In this market scenario, the trader is guaranteed a profit of a quarter of a cent per bushel, or $12.50 on the position (¼ cent per bushel × 5,000 bushels per contract). The profit is produced because the position generates a net credit of $12.50 at initiation and is always worth zero when the position is closed out at the expiration of the options.* The net credit at initiation comes from selling the call for a quarter of a cent more than the price paid for the put.† The zero value of the

TABLE 12.4

Initiating the Conversion

Position	Calculation	Revenue (Cost)
Long one $3 put	10¼ cents per bushel × 5,000 bushels	($512.50)
Short one $3 call	10½ cents per bushel × 5,000 bushels	$525.00
Long one futures at $3	No revenue (cost) at initiation	$0
Net revenue (cost)		$12.50

* There may be variation requirements that must be met prior to expiration.
† Net credit = (premium received – premium paid) 0; net debit = (premium received – premium paid) 0.

position at expiration occurs regardless of which way the futures price moves. If the futures price falls, the profit on the long put is offset by a loss on the long futures. If the futures price rises, the gain on the long futures is offset by a loss on the short call. The calculations in Tables 12.4 and 12.5a–c illustrate.

In this example, the conversion was initiated at a net revenue of $12.50 and was closed for a net cost of zero. So the value of the conversion (revenue less cost) was $12.50. Alter-

TABLE 12.5

Closing the Conversion

a. If the futures price decreases to $2.50 at expiration

Position	Calculation	Revenue (Cost)
Exercise the $3 put, get short futures	($3.00 – $2.50) × 5,000 bushels	$2,500
$3 call expires out-of-the-money	No revenue (cost)	$0
Long futures is offset by put's exercise	($2.50 – $3.00) × 5,000 bushels	($2,500)
Net revenue (cost)		$0

b. If the futures price remains at $3 at expiration

Position	Calculation	Revenue (Cost)
Exercise the $3 put, get short futures	($3.00 – $3.00) × 5,000 bushels	$0
$3 call expires at-the-money	No revenue (cost)	$0
Long futures is offset by put's exercise	($3.00 – $3.00) × 5,000 bushels	$0
Net revenue (cost)		$0

c. If the futures price increases to $3.50 at expiration

Position	Calculation	Revenue (Cost)
Abandon $3 put, out-of-the-money	No revenue (cost)	$0
Assigned on $3 call, get short futures	($3.00 – $3.50) × 5,000 bushels	($2,500)
Long futures offset by assignment on short call	($3.50 – $3.00) × 5,000 bushels	$2,500
Net revenue (cost)		$0

natively, the return on a conversion can be calculated more directly as:

$$\text{Return on conversion} = (\text{call premium} - \text{put premium})$$
$$- (\text{futures price} - \text{strike price})$$

In a reverse conversion, or *reversal,* the trader sells an underlying futures contract, sells a put, and buys a call.

The put and call options have the same strike price and the same expiration month. The futures price is usually as close as possible to the options' strike price. If the futures price is above the strike price by the time of expiration (which automatically offsets the short futures position), the trader exercises the long call option; the short put option expires unexercised. If the futures price falls below the strike price by the time of expiration, the short put option is exercised against the trader, which automatically offsets the short futures position; the long call option expires unexercised.

FURTHER READING

McMillian, Lawrence G., *Options as a Strategic Investment.* New York: Prentice Hall, 2001.

Natenberg, Sheldon, *Option Volatility and Pricing: Advanced Trading Strategies and Techniques.* New York: McGraw-Hill, 1994.

Saliba, Anthony, *Options Workbook.* Chicago: Dearborn Trade, 2002.

PART THREE

Underlying Markets

CHAPTER 13

Agricultural Markets: Grains, Oilseeds, Livestock

Today, financial market activity that trades in stocks, bonds, currencies, and other instruments drives the majority of trading volume at the world's futures exchanges. But none of this activity is nearly so historically linked to the development and character of futures markets as is the long-standing activity of the agricultural markets. When commodities are mentioned, most people are inclined to think of the corn, soybean, and pork belly futures that are traded on Chicago's futures exchanges.

This chapter explains some of the economic, political, and market factors affecting the prices of a variety of agricultural commodities traded on U.S. and foreign futures exchanges. Of course, the information discussed is a general overview and should not be viewed as an all-inclusive study of agricultural commodities. For more information, consult the suggested reading list or the information sources given at the end of this chapter.

GRAINS

Many of the world's most important grains—particularly, corn, oats, rice, and wheat—are traded actively on domestic and international futures markets. Referred to as the *food and feed grains,* these commodities feed livestock and people alike around the world. Corn and oats are used primarily as feed grains and, to a lesser extent, in manufactured foods. Rice is almost exclusively a food grain. Wheat is generally grown and marketed for food uses, with strong secondary demand as a feed grain. (See Fig. 13.1.)

FIGURE 13.1

U.S. Harvested Acres by Crop, 2003

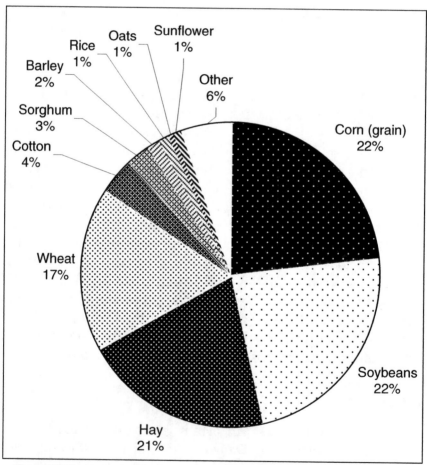

Source: USDA.

An emerging factor influencing the world supply and demand for grains and oilseeds has resulted from biotechnology. In the United States, biotechnology has been actively employed to produce new seed strains that are designed to protect crops from disease, weeds, and insects. In other parts of the world, however, there has been reluctance to use such engineered crops, commonly called *genetically modified organisms* (GMOs). As a result, distinct markets have emerged for both GMO and non-GMO commodities.

Corn

Corn (also called *maize*, chiefly outside the United States) is unique among the grasses cultivated as grain cereals. Used both for feed and as food, it is the only grain that originated in the Western Hemisphere. In fact, corn was unknown to the rest of the world until Christopher Columbus returned to Europe with samples.

Within a generation, the cultivation of corn spread to most of the farming areas of Europe. By the mid-sixteenth century, Chinese farmers were raising the crop. Today, there are 100 to 150 corn varieties. Most corn is used for animal feed, though it's a major part of the diet of the people of Mexico and Central America, who raise the crop mainly for food.

Farmers and commercial users have developed a grading system based on kernel tests. Dent, or field, corn is the most common variety, accounting for about 99 percent of U.S. corn production. Dent corn is named for the crease or trough that is formed in the top of the kernel by unequal shrinking of the starch components. Grain standards established for dent corn distinguish among yellow, white, and mixed. Yellow dominates all markets for livestock feed and for wet milling into flour and other products for human consumption and industrial uses. White corn goes to dry corn millers for flour production, for manufacturing hominy and grits, and for many industrial uses. Mixed corn—white and yellow corn accidentally combined during storage—is seldom traded commercially and is generally used in livestock feed.

The other major American corn is sweet corn. Its kernels are composed predominately of starch, making it easy to chew. The chemical structure of still another type, waxy corn, is well suited for certain wet milling processes. Squaw, or Indian, corn is used primarily for decorative purposes.

A number of factors affect corn production, with acreage and yields chief among them. Farmers' current practice of planting denser and narrower rows than in the past has lead to a higher plant population per acre. Pesticides and herbicides have helped minimize crop damage caused by insects and crop diseases. Fertilizers and new biotechnologies have increased yields as well. All together, these practices and others have increased corn yields to previously unheard-of levels. (See Fig. 13.2.)

Two of the primary, and less controllable, factors governing corn yields are moisture and temperature. To bring a large corn

FIGURE 13.2

U.S. Average Corn Yields, 1923–2003

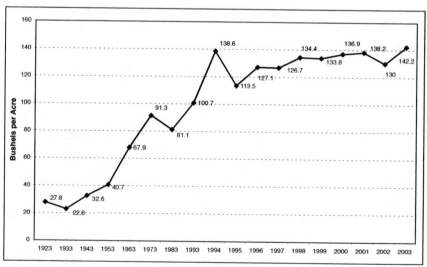

Source: USDA.

crop to successful harvest, the crop needs an even amount of moisture throughout the summer months. July and August, in particular, are the critical weather months for corn. Higher-than-normal rainfall favors high yields. Below-normal rainfall (especially during July) and higher-than-normal temperatures (particularly during August) tend to reduce yields.

The length of the growing season is another important production factor. During spring, late frosts or exceptionally wet weather can delay planting and thus reduce potential yields. And early fall frosts can critically stunt development of seedlings that are planted late in the season.

Most U.S. corn production is centered in the area known as the Corn Belt, namely Illinois, Indiana, Iowa, Minnesota, Missouri, Nebraska, Ohio, and South Dakota. (See Fig. 13.3.) Corn planting in most of these key production states begins in early May, while Minnesota and South Dakota tend to plant later. The corn plant reaches maturity in late August with one or two

FIGURE 13.3

Top 10 U.S. Corn Production States, 2003

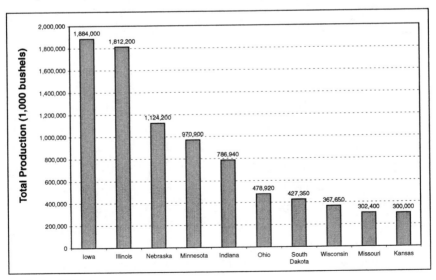

Source: USDA.

developed ears. Harvest usually begins around October 15, just
after the first hard frost. By mid-November, virtually all the corn
in the United States has been harvested. In recent years, however, corn has tended to be planted as early as March and April,
with harvests sometimes occurring prior to October 1. Because
of this trend, the U.S. Department of Agriculture (USDA) now
designates September 1 to August 31 as the official corn crop
year. Since October remains the principal harvest month, December is the first futures contract month for new-crop corn.

Approximately 55 to 60 percent of the cash corn crop is used
as livestock feed. In fact, in recent years, corn has accounted for
at least 25 percent of all livestock feed. Because feed is typically
the largest single cost item in raising livestock, the profitability
of feeding corn is determined by its cost relative to the price of
meat. When livestock-corn ratios are low, livestock feeders
reduce their use of corn by adjusting the number of animals fed
and the length of time livestock are kept on feed.

Two major factors account for the attractiveness of corn as
animal feed:

- Corn is generally good for fattening livestock and poultry
  because of its high starch content. In addition, it contains
  more oil than other cereal grains, so it is a high energy
  producer.

- An acre of corn yields more animal feed in both grain and
  forage than any other crop, although it costs no more in
  labor to produce and harvest. Because of the meat
  industry's traditional pattern of heavy corn consumption,
  any significant increase or decrease in animal production
  forces farmers to reevaluate their corn production.

Corn is used in various manufacturing industries; the
entire corn plant can be found in a variety of products. Paper and
wallboard are made from the stalks. Husks are used as fillers.
And cobs become fuel, charcoal, and industrial solvents.

Of course, the grain kernel remains the most valuable portion of the plant used commercially. In wet milling, corn kernels

are steeped or soaked in a solution of warm water and sulfur dioxide. Grinding and other operations then separate the hulls from the rest of the grain, which is further treated in various ways to produce corn oil, starches, dextrins, and syrups for human consumption as well as adhesives, glues, textile fibers, soaps, sizings, paints, ethanol fuel, varnishes, explosives, and a host of other useful industrial products. Dry milling, a process in which corn kernels are subjected to spray or steam softening and then ground, is used largely for the production of cereals, flour, hominy, grits, and feeds. (See Fig. 13.4.)

Of all the nonfood uses for corn, ethanol has emerged as the most successful by-product. As a fuel, ethanol contains a higher percentage of oxygen than gasoline, thus reducing emissions by

FIGURE 13.4

Corn Use by Product Segment, 2003

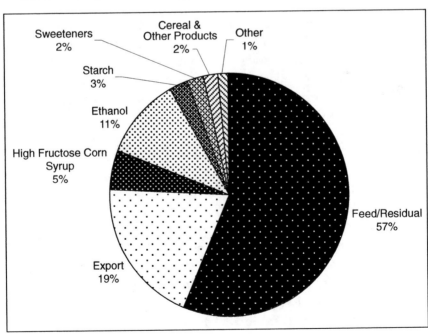

Source: USDA.

burning more completely. Ethanol-blended fuels account for 18 percent of all automotive fuels in the United States, with 11 percent of U.S. corn production going toward ethanol. It is Brazil, however, that leads the world in both ethanol production and consumption. More than 3.5 million Brazilian cars run on 100 percent ethanol fuel, with all automotive fuel containing at least a 24 percent ethanol blend.

Supply-and-demand factors in the principal corn exporting and importing nations have a significant impact on corn and its price. For instance, a bumper world corn crop might reduce foreign demand for U.S. corn or lead to increased competition between U.S. and foreign corn producers. On the other hand, a smaller world corn crop can cause increased demand for U.S. corn exports. Livestock price levels in other nations are another important factor affecting U.S. corn export demand. Low livestock prices abroad discourage feeding and lessen the demand for U.S. corn. Conversely, higher livestock prices tend to increase demand.

The USDA estimated total worldwide corn production for 2003–2004 at more than 23.9 billion bushels. The United States was the largest producer, with estimated production of more than 10 billion bushels—about 42 percent of the total world supply. Production in China, Brazil, the European Union, and Mexico followed the United States, although Europe and Mexico also import large amounts of corn. U.S. corn exports were 1.97 billion bushels, or 64 percent of all exports worldwide. The largest buyers of U.S. corn were Japan, Mexico, Taiwan, Canada, Egypt, and Colombia.

Corn futures and options trade at the Chicago Board of Trade. Outside the United States, corn futures also trade in Japan at the Tokyo Grain Exchange, the Fukuoka Futures Exchange, and the Kansai Commodities Exchange. Other non-U.S. exchanges trading in corn include the JSE Securities Exchange South Africa, the BM&F in Brazil, the Budapest Commodity Exchange, Euronext-Paris, and the Mercado a Termino de Buenos Aires. (See Table 13.1.)

TABLE 13.1

Major Corn Futures and Options Contracts

Contract	Futures Exchange	Annual Volume in 2004
Corn futures[1]	Chicago Board of Trade	24,038,233
Corn options[1]	Chicago Board of Trade	7,593,355
Corn futures[2]	Fukuoka Futures Exchange	2,406,808
Corn 75 Index futures[2]	Kansai Commodities Exchange	350,029
Corn futures[2]	Tokyo Grain Exchange	8,122,448
Corn options[2]	Tokyo Grain Exchange	16,072
White maize futures[2]	South African Futures Exchange	969,838
White maize options[2]	South African Futures Exchange	333,285
Yellow maize futures[2]	South African Futures Exchange	228,709
Yellow maize options[2]	South African Futures Exchange	33,385

[1]Data provided by CBOT.
[2]Data provided by Futures Industry Association, Inc.

Wheat

Wheat is one of the world's oldest and most widely used food crops. First cultivated in Asia Minor nearly 9,000 years ago, wheat gradually spread across much of Europe, Asia, and Africa. Early colonists introduced wheat to the United States in the seventeenth century, bringing seeds from Europe. Now grown on every continent except Antarctica, wheat is a huge part of worldwide food grain supplies. The USDA estimated world production for 2003–2004 at 2,160 million bushels.

Wheat has two distinct growing seasons: winter and spring. Winter wheat, which accounts for 70 to 80 percent of U.S. production, is planted in the fall, becomes dormant during the winter, resumes growth in the spring, and is harvested in the summer. Spring wheat is planted in the spring and harvested usually by early September.

The several hundred varieties of wheat grown in the United States all fall into one of five main classes: hard red winter, soft red winter, hard red spring, durum, and white. Each class is adapted to a particular set of growing conditions, is raised in a specific region, and has unique milling and baking properties. (See Table 13.2.)

The predominant class of wheat grown in the United States is hard red winter. During the 2003–2004 crop year, 856 million bushels of hard red winter wheat were produced. Hard red winter wheat is grown chiefly on the Great Plains, particularly in Kansas, Nebraska, Oklahoma, and the Texas Panhandle, where annual precipitation averages less than 25 inches, frequent dry periods occur, and winters produce subzero temperatures. Flour from hard red winter wheat is used primarily in bread.

The soft red winter wheat belt extends from central Texas northeastward to the Great Lakes and then east to the Atlantic coast. Soft red winter wheat is generally grown in a subhumid climate not conducive to the production of hard wheats. During the 2003–2004 crop year, 380 million bushels of soft red winter were harvested. Flour from soft red winter wheat is used in cakes, cookies, crackers, snack foods, and pastries.

TABLE 13.2

Top Five Wheat-Producing States in 2002

	Million Bushels	Percent of U.S. Total[1]
Kansas	267.3	17%
North Dakota	220.6	14%
Washington	129.7	8%
Montana	114.0	7%
Oklahoma	98.0	6%
Total Top Five	**829.6**	**51%**

[1]Numbers may not add because of rounding.

Source: National Association of Wheat Growers.

Hard red spring wheat is grown principally in northern states, such as Montana, North and South Dakota, and Minnesota, where the winters are too severe for winter wheat production. The principal hard red spring wheat districts have a fairly deep black soil and dry, hot summers, both important factors in the production of a high-grade wheat suitable for milling as bread flour. Hard red spring wheat accounted for 530 million bushels in 2003–2004 U.S. production.

Durum, a spring wheat, is produced primarily in North Dakota and Montana. Durum kernels are extremely hard and, along with hard red spring kernels, contain the highest percentage of protein of the wheat classes. Durum flour is used to make spaghetti, macaroni, and other pasta products and is not suitable for bread, cakes, or pastries. U.S. production of durum wheat totaled 90 million bushels in 2003–2004.

Various varieties of white wheat are grown mainly in southern Michigan, western New York, and the Pacific Northwest. It is primarily used for bakery products other than bread. However, the newer and sweeter hard white variety is used in breads and rolls. U.S. white wheat production for 2003–2004 was 306 million bushels.

The crop year in the United States for wheat is June 1 to May 31. Winter wheat is usually seeded in September or early October, whenever the soil has sufficient moisture to germinate the seed. At this time of the year, the danger of the seed being damaged from insects such as the Hessian fly is considerably less than in late summer.

At freezing temperatures, winter wheat enters a period of dormancy that lasts until warm weather returns. Ideally, a blanket of snow should cover the fields to insulate and protect the plants. Without adequate snow cover, wheat sometimes heaves—that is, the stem is severed from the root system—which results from alternate thawing and freezing of the soil.

In the spring, the head, which contains the kernels, develops on top of the stem. Later, after the kernels have fully developed and filled, the color of the plant begins to change from green to gold. Finally, when the heads are sufficiently dried, the fields are ready to be harvested. Harvest begins in late May and is usually completed in July.

In the northern United States, where winters are too severe for winter wheat, spring wheat is planted as early as possible in the spring. The dormancy period is thus eliminated. The crop matures and is harvested in July and August.

Wheat yields can vary substantially from one class to another and from one county or state to another. During the 2003–2004 crop year, for instance, durum wheat produced an average yield of slightly more than 33 bushels an acre, whereas white wheat yields were estimated at an average of nearly 60 bushels an acre. Overall U.S. wheat production yielded an average of 44.2 bushels an acre in 2003–2004.

Approximately 35 percent of the U.S. wheat crop is milled domestically for flour; as much as 50 percent is exported; and about 4 percent is set aside for subsequent crop plantings. The balance is used for animal feeds and in industrial products.

Since World War II, domestic flour consumption has declined at the retail level, while escalating standards of living have increased consumer demand for commercially prepared products using wheat flours. Average U.S. per capita flour consumption has grown from 110 pounds in 1972 to 139 pounds 30 years later in 2002. While U.S. flour consumption has increased, however, wheat acreage plantings have generally declined. This is partly the result of strong genetic improvements in corn and soybeans, allowing these crops to be planted farther west and north, and often replacing wheat acreage.

The USDA estimated U.S. wheat production for 2003–2004 at 2.34 billion bushels. Other major wheat producers include China, the European Union, India, Eastern Europe, Russia, and Australia. The largest importers of U.S. wheat are Japan, Mexico, Nigeria, the Philippines, Korea, the European Union, and Egypt.

Wheat futures and options trade at the Chicago Board of Trade (soft red winter wheat), the Minneapolis Grain Exchange

TABLE 13.3

Major Wheat Futures and Options Contracts

Contract	Futures Exchange	Annual Volume in 2004
Wheat (soft red winter) futures[1]	Chicago Board of Trade	7,955,155
Wheat options[1]	Chicago Board of Trade	1,465,760
Wheat futures[2]	Kansas City Board of Trade	2,833,370
Wheat options[2]	Kansas City Board of Trade	254,304
Spring wheat futures[2]	Minneapolis Grain Exchange	1,378,694
Spring wheat options[2]	Minneapolis Grain Exchange	34,260
Wheat futures[2]	South African Futures Exchange	200,663
Wheat options[2]	South African Futures Exchange	62,434

[1]Data provided by CBOT.
[2]Data provided by Futures Industry Association, Inc.

(hard red spring and a hard winter wheat index), and the Kansas City Board of Trade (hard red winter wheat). Outside the United States, various wheat contracts trade at the Budapest Commodity Exchange, Euronext LIFFE (London), Euronext-Paris, Mercado a Termino de Buenos Aires, the JSE Securities Exchange South Africa, and the Winnipeg Commodity Exchange. Though exchanges tend to designate a specific type and grade of wheat for delivery against futures contracts, most will allow substitutions at price differentials. (See Table 13.3.)

Oats

Oats, like other grains, belong to the grass family. Early records of oats indicate that they were first harvested as straw and used in mud bricks for Egyptian temples. The ancient Romans used oats as a forage crop for grazing livestock nearly 3,000 years ago. It was not until the Middle Ages that oats were grown for their grain. During much of the intervening period, they were considered little more than weeds that infested fields of barley and other small grains.

Over the centuries, though, oats were recognized as an excellent grain for feeding livestock and poultry. They were introduced in the United States around 1600 by English settlers, who raised oats throughout the northern colonies. As the nation was settled and animal numbers increased, U.S. oat production expanded as well.

Oats fall into five major classes: white, red, gray, black (including brown), and yellow. White oats comprise most of U.S. production. Oats of all sorts are less exacting in soil requirements than any other cereal grain except rye. To produce top yields, oats need at least medium levels of the essential nutrients—nitrogen, phosphate, and potash. Oats grow best in temperate climates that have plentiful moisture and cool weather at maturity time.

Most domestically grown oats are sown in the spring—early April to late May—and harvested between mid-July and late August. Top oat-producing states include South Dakota, Minnesota, North Dakota, and Wisconsin.

The official U.S. crop year for oats is July 1 through June 30. The USDA estimated U.S. oat production in 2003–2004 at 145 million bushels, with yields averaging 65 bushels per acre.

While yields have improved, the number of acres of oats planted has decreased steadily since about 1920. During the early 1900s, oat production declined rapidly when horses and mules, which eat oats as a primary feed, were replaced by automobiles, trucks, and tractors. In later years, oat production fell again as rising milk production per cow led to a steady reduction in the number of dairy cattle.

Most of the total oat crop is used as feed for livestock and poultry. A smaller share is used for rolled oats, meal, ready-to-eat breakfast cereals, and oat flour, as well as seed for upcoming crops. Exports account for less than 2 percent of the U.S. oat crop. In fact, in 2003–2004, the United States imported 90 million bushels of oats. Most regions of the world grow oats—major producers include Russia, the European Union, Eastern Europe, and Canada.

Oat futures and options trade at the Chicago Board of Trade, where annual volume for the futures contract was 416,448 in 2004.

Rice

Rice, an annual cereal grain, was probably first cultivated in China 5,000 years ago. Rice culture then gradually spread westward and was introduced to southern Europe during medieval times. Since then, rice has been the most important food staple for most of the world's population.

Rice is produced throughout the world in climates ranging from temperate to tropical. Cultivated on wetlands that provide the necessary uniform moisture, rice thrives under sunny, warm conditions and is highly vulnerable to either drought or unusually cool and overcast weather conditions. Cultivation practices vary widely among major rice-producing nations, reflecting differences in climate, other growing conditions, and levels of agricultural technology.

The harvested rice kernel, known as *paddy* or *rough rice,* is enclosed by the hull or husk. Three types of rice are grown in the United States—long, medium, and short grain. Arkansas, Louisiana, Texas, Mississippi, and Missouri produce nearly all the long-grain and some medium-grain rice, whereas California produces most of the medium- and short-grain rice. Arkansas is by far the largest rice producer, accounting for more than 57 percent of total U.S. output. The marketing year for rice in the United States is August 1 through July 31.

Rice use in the United States falls into three major categories: table rice (regular milled, parboiled, precooked, and brown rice), rice in processed foods (breakfast cereals, snacks, and other products), and brewers' rice.

Following harvest, rice is cleaned, sorted, and dried for further processing. Milling usually removes both the hull and bran layers of the kernel. Sometimes a coating of glucose and talc is applied to give the kernel a glossy finish. Rice that is processed to remove only the hulls is called *brown rice*. Rice that is milled to remove the bran as well is called *white rice* and is greatly diminished in nutrients. Parboiled white rice is processed before milling to retain most of the nutrients. Enriched rice has iron and B vitamins added.

The processing of precooked or quick-cooking rice is more complex and involves one of several methods, the most basic of which is known as the *freeze-thaw process*. Raw milled rice is steeped, immersed briefly in boiling water, drenched in chilled water, slowly frozen, and then thawed. This results in a porous kernel that readily absorbs water and reduces the required cooking time.

By-products of rice milling—including bran and rice polish, a finely powdered bran and starch resulting from polishing—are used in a variety of manufactured goods. For example, broken rice is used in brewing and distilling and in the manufacturing of starch and rice flour. Hulls are used for fuel, packing material, industrial grinding, and fertilizer manufacturing. Rice straw is used for feed, livestock bedding, roof thatching, mats, garments, packing material, and broom straws.

The International Rice Research Institute estimated world rough rice production for 2002 at 576.3 million metric tons. China, India, and Indonesia were the three largest rice producers, accounting for an estimated 31, 20, and 9 percent of total world production, respectively. Other major producers include Bangladesh, Vietnam, Thailand, Burma, Japan, the Philippines, Brazil, and the United States. U.S. rough rice production in 2002 was 9.57 million metric tons, accounting for less than 2 percent of world production.

Rough rice futures and options trade at the Chicago Board of Trade, where annual volume for the futures contract was 168,165 in 2004.

Barley

Other important grains such as barley are grown around the world. *Barley* is used chiefly as feed for hogs and cattle. The amount of barley planted and its price are thus related to the level of production and the price of other feed grains. Other barley finds use as a malt in beer, a minor source of flour, and in soups.

The Canadian Wheat Board estimated world barley production for 2003 at 143 million tons. Russia led world production with nearly 18 million tons in 2003. Other major barley producers are Germany, Canada, France, Spain, Australia, and Turkey.

Barley futures trade at Canada's Winnipeg Commodity Exchange, where annual volume for the futures contract was 204,635 in 2004.

OILSEEDS

Although they hold far less sway in the mainstream imagination than cereal grains such as corn and wheat, oilseeds such as soybeans are a huge part of U.S. agriculture. In 2003, the USDA estimated that the soybean crop comprised 28 percent of all U.S. crop acres planted. This places soybeans slightly behind corn at 30 percent, but ahead of wheat at 23 percent.

The Soybean Complex

It is nearly impossible to discuss soybeans without talking about soybean meal and soybean oil. The interrelationship between the soybean and its two principal by-products exists throughout the production, processing, and marketing phases. The term *soybean complex* refers to this interrelationship. This section presents the development of the soybean crop, its processing, and the intertwined supply-and-demand relationships of the soybean complex.

Soybeans, among the oldest of all cultivated crops, were first grown by the Chinese as early as 5,000 years ago. Through cooking, fermentation, germination, and other methods, the ancient Chinese developed a wide variety of soy foods. The development of these foods encouraged the spread of soybean production across much of the Pacific Basin. Historians believe Marco Polo may have introduced many of these soy foods to Europe upon returning from his travels through China in the thirteenth century. During the next few centuries, limited quantities of these foods were carried west over the trade routes between Asia and Europe.

Still, until the early twentieth century, little soybean production existed outside the Orient. Prior to then, U.S. farmers had grown limited quantities for soy sauce, as forage for cattle, even as "coffee berries" to brew "coffee" during the Civil War when real coffee was scarce. In 1904, however, George Washington Carver began studying the soybean at the Tuskegee Institute. His discoveries changed the way U.S. producers thought about soybeans. At that time, the Western world began to recognize the unique value of soybeans as a source of edible oil and high-protein meal, with secondary industrial and chemical applications.

Large-scale production of soybeans in the United States dates from the mid-1930s. The increase in production was largely the result of a trade embargo by China that cut off soybean supplies. Acreage restrictions on cotton, corn, and wheat to curb oversupply in those commodities also stimulated increased soybean plantings. The production of less cotton reduced the supply of cottonseed oil, once the preferred domestic edible oil, and soybean oil became a logical substitute.

Prior to World War II, the United States imported 40 percent of its edible fats and oils. But wartime trade restrictions necessitated the development of a domestic oilseed industry, further stimulating soybean production. Other factors increased demand as well. During the postwar recovery period, population growth and increased affluence in the United States, Western Europe, and Japan led to increased demand for meats and, therefore, for high-protein animal feeds such as soybean meal. These same factors were instrumental in increasing demand for both soybean oil and soybean meal from the 1950s to the present.

The USDA estimated 2004 U.S. soybean production at a new record of more than 3.1 billion bushels. In 2003, U.S. production accounted for 34 percent of the world total. Other major soybean producers include Brazil (28 percent), Argentina (18 percent), and China (9 percent). More than 37 percent of the 2003 U.S. crop went for exports, largely to China, the European Union, Mexico, Japan, and Taiwan. Note, too, that soybeans, by themselves, account for 58 percent of all world oilseed production. (See Fig. 13.5.)

FIGURE 13.5

World Oilseed Production, 2003

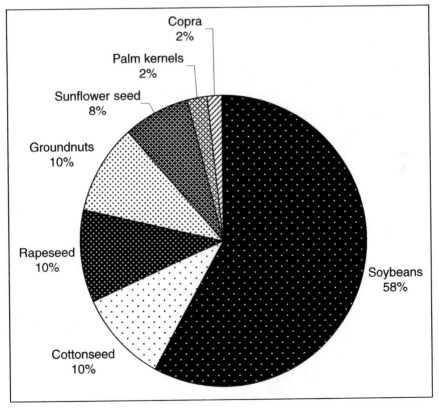

Source: USDA.

Producers grow more than 150 varieties of soybeans in the United States, from Arkansas to the Canadian border, according to soil and climate conditions. The dominant class of soybeans in commercial markets is the yellow soybean. Use of biotech-enhanced soybean seed stock has increased substantially in recent years, accounting for more than 80 percent of U.S. soybean acreage in 2003.

Illinois and Iowa are the two major soybean-producing states, followed by Minnesota, Indiana, Ohio, and Missouri. The important growing areas are more concentrated and roughly coincide with the central and southern sections of the Corn Belt. As a result, soybeans must compete for acreage with corn and cotton. (See Fig. 13.6.)

The soybean itself, a legume related to clover, peas, and alfalfa, is a bushlike plant that grows to heights ranging from 12 inches to 6 feet. An extensive root system gives the soybean

FIGURE 13.6

U.S. Soybean Production, 1978–2003

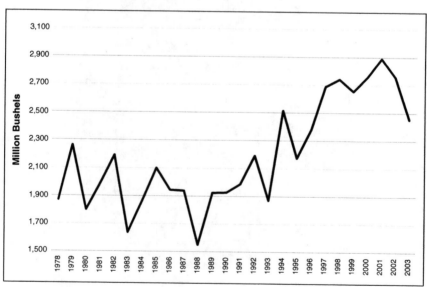

Source: USDA.

notable resistance to drought. After flowering, the plant develops several pods, each of which normally carries three seeds or beans. Soybeans grow best on fertile, sandy loam suitable for cotton or corn. Planting takes place in late May or June following corn planting. Harvest usually runs from early September through October.

The soybean plant is photoperiodic, which means that the flowering and opening of the pods are controlled by the length of daylight. Because of this photoperiodic growth, the soybean plant will mature within a few days of a given calendar date, regardless of planting time. Increased worldwide demand and higher overhead costs have thus prompted farmers in many cereal- and cotton-producing areas to double-crop using a short-term soybean hybrid as one of the two crops they plant.

Whole soybeans have limited uses. They are baked, puffed, roasted, or steamed to make feed for dairy animals, or they find use in certain soy-based food products. The greatest demand for soybeans is as meal and oil.

Approximately 98 percent of soybean meal is used as poultry and livestock feed to satisfy basic protein and amino acid requirements. Soybean meal demand is thus closely related to how much livestock and poultry are on feed. Any attempt to forecast consumption of soybean meal must focus on the demand for animal protein—meat and poultry products—which is influenced by such factors as consumer preferences.

Soybean meal faces competition from various animal and vegetable products. In the animal category, it competes with fish meal and tankage—the dried by-products of meat packing. Vegetable oilseed meals include those produced from rapeseed, cottonseed, flaxseed, and sunflower seeds, which livestock producers can substitute for soybean meal when they are priced more favorably.

Approximately 2 percent of the soybean meal consumed in the United States is used directly in food and industrial production. Food uses are the more significant of the two categories and include high-protein derivatives of soybean meal consumed in relatively small amounts in cake mixes, waffles, cereals, breads, snack foods, blended meat products, soups, and baby foods. Higher concentrations of soybean meal products are found in dietetic, health, and hypoallergenic foods and cosmetics as well as in antibiotics.

The greatest demand for soybean oil comes in the form of edible oil products such as shortening, margarines, salad oils, and cooking oils. To a lesser extent, soybean oil is used to manufacture chemicals, paints, varnishes, sealants, lubricants, and adhesives.

In food and industrial markets, soybean oil faces competition from a variety of animal and vegetable oils, competing with such animal oil products as butter, lard, and fish oils and vegetable oil products such as cottonseed oil, rapeseed oil, sunflower seed oil, flaxseed oil, olive oil, coconut oil, and palm oil. Because of the competition among these fat and oil products, soybean oil accounts for only about 31 percent of total world oil consumption.

Over the years, a radical change occurred in the technology of soybean processing methods—a shift from mechanical extraction to chemical extraction. Oil and meal were originally extracted from soybeans by hydraulic crushing, a method that left about 4 to 15 percent of the oil and solvent in the soybean flake or cake. (The cake is what remains after the extraction of the oil and solvent.) Today, nearly all U.S. and foreign processing plants use a chemical extraction method that leaves only 1 percent of the oil in the cake. In this hexane-solvent extraction method, the soybeans are first crushed and flaked. The oil is then extracted, and the solvent is removed from it by evaporation and is saved for reuse. In the refining process, crude oil can be degummed, refined, bleached, deodorized, or hydrogenated, depending on the end use.

After extraction, the soybean flake is toasted and ground into soybean meal, which contains 48 percent protein. For a lower protein meal, the hulls are mixed back in to lower protein content to 44 percent. Approximately half of all U.S. soybean meal is 48 percent protein, which is used primarily for high-performance feeds.

To make a profit, soybean processors must purchase soybeans at a lower cost than the combined sales income from the finished oil and meal. The difference, or margin, is called the gross processing margin (GPM). The GPM is key to a soybean processing plant's profitability.

The first step in calculating a processor's GPM is to determine the oil and meal dollar value in one bushel of soybeans. Each processor uses specific conversion factors to calculate these values. These factors vary slightly among processing facilities because of differences in plant efficiencies and the protein and oil content of the soybeans a processor typically purchases.

For example, assume standard conversion factors of 11 pounds of oil, 44 pounds of high-protein meal, 4 pounds of hulls, and 1 pound of foreign matter (dirt, stones, seeds) per soybean bushel. These are the same standards used by hedgers when calculating a futures "crush" margin, described below. (The average weight of a bushel of soybeans is 60 pounds. The example that follows does not include hulls and foreign matter factors.)

Processors using standard conversion factors convert oil prices to a bushel equivalent by multiplying the oil price by 11. For example, if soybean oil is selling at $18.24 per hundredweight, or $0.1824 per pound, the value of oil in a bushel of soybeans would be $0.1824 × 11, or $2.0064. Similarly, processors can convert the value of soybean meal per ton to its bushel equivalent by multiplying the price per ton by 0.022 (44 pounds divided by 2,000 pounds). With meal selling at $182.70 per ton, the value of soybean meal per bushel of soybeans would be $182.70 × 0.022, or $4.0194.

Given the above values for soybean oil and soybean meal and $5.27 per bushel of soybeans, processors would compute the GPM as follows:

Oil value	$2.0064/bu
Meal value	+$4.0194
Combined sales value	$6.0258
Soybean cost	−$5.2700
Gross processing margin	$0.7558/bu

Frequently, processing margins follow a seasonal pattern, with a favorable GPM after the fall harvest when soybeans are in abundance and priced low. During this period, there tends to be increased demand for feed as well, in anticipation of colder weather, lack of grazing, and feeding requirements for heavier livestock. The combination of lower soybean prices and strengthening soybean meal demand tends to increase the processing margin. Processing margins tend to decline later in the crop year for similar reasons. First, as demand for feed declines, soybean meal prices drop. Second, soybean prices tend to rise as the crop year progresses, because of lower supplies and the accumulation of carrying costs.

Applying the GPM to the soybean, soybean oil, and soybean meal futures markets makes it possible for processors to buy soybean futures to hedge later purchases of cash soybeans and, at the same time, sell soybean oil and meal futures to hedge later sales of meal and oil. This market position—long soybean futures and short soybean oil and meal futures—is known as a *crush spread* or *board crush*. Processors hold the long soybean portion of the hedge until they buy the required cash soybeans and the short portion of the hedge until they sell soybean oil and meal.

The opposite of a crush hedge is a *reverse crush*. This spreading opportunity results from distortions in normal price patterns. It may occur when the cost of soybeans is higher than the combined sales value of soybean oil and meal. The resulting unfavorable gross processing margin makes it unprofitable for soybean processors to manufacture meal and oil. Thus, when the GPM drops below a profitable level, processors may slow down or even stop crushing soybeans and at the same time possibly initiate a reverse crush spread—selling soybean futures and buying oil and meal futures. A decline in soybean processing eases the demand for tight soybean supplies and tends to curb rising soybean prices. At the same time, it tends to lead to tighter supplies of oil and meal, increasing their price levels. With downward pressure on soybean prices and upward pressure on meal and oil, the cost/price relationship may revert to a favorable GPM.

Soybean, soybean oil, and soybean meal futures and options trade at the Chicago Board of Trade. Soybean futures also trade at the BM&F (Brazil), the Dalian Commodity Exchange (China), the Tokyo Grain Exchange, the Fukuoka Futures Exchange, the Kansai Agricultural Exchange, and the Central Japan Commodity Exchange. (See Table 13.4.)

TABLE 13.4

Major Soybean and Related Futures and Options Contracts

Contract	Futures Exchange	Annual Volume in 2004
Soybean futures[1]	Chicago Board of Trade	18,846,021
Soybean options[1]	Chicago Board of Trade	6,045,952
Soybean oil futures[1]	Chicago Board of Trade	7,593,314
Soybean oil options[1]	Chicago Board of Trade	947,383
Soybean meal futures[1]	Chicago Board of Trade	8,569,243
Soybean meal options[1]	Chicago Board of Trade	971,335
No. 1 soybean futures[2]	Dalian Commodity Exchange	57,340,803
Soybean meal futures[2]	Dalian Commodity Exchange	24,750,958
U.S. soybean futures[2]	Tokyo Grain Exchange	2,125,458
U.S. soybean options[2]	Tokyo Grain Exchange	17,758
Non-GMO soybean futures[2]	Tokyo Grain Exchange	9,971,499
Non-GMO soybean futures[2]	Fukuoka Futures Exchange	308,943
Soybean meal futures[2]	Fukuoka Futures Exchange	187,926
Non-GMO soybean futures[2]	Kansai Agricultural Exchange	276,396

[1]Data provided by CBOT.
[2]Data provided by Futures Industry Association, Inc.

Palm Oil and Rapeseed/Canola

Like soybeans, other plants are cultivated to produce meal and oil. Palm oil is derived from the fruit of the oil palm, or *Elaeis Guinnesis* tree, which originated in West Guinea. The tree was first introduced into other parts of Africa, Southeast Asia and Latin America in the fifteenth century. In the mid-1990s, large commercial planting and cultivation began in Malaysia, which now produces nearly half the world's palm oil. According to the Malaysian Palm Oil Board, total world production reached 27.4 million tons in 2003. Indonesia is the second largest producer at 9.75 million tons. Palm oil is used as a cooking oil and shortening and margarine; it is also blended with other fats in a wide variety of food products.

Rapeseed production—including canola, a high-quality rapeseed—has escalated in recent years because of its growing use as an edible oil. Rapeseed meal is used as a feed supplement. In 2003, world rapeseed production reached 39 million metric tons. Major producers include the European Union, China, India, and Canada. The United States is a relatively small producer, generally importing twice as much as it produces.

Palm oil futures trade at the Bursa Malaysia. Canola futures and options trade at the Winnipeg Commodity Exchange. Rapeseed futures and options trade at Euronext (Paris). (See Table 13.5.)

TABLE 13.5

Other Major Oilseed Futures and Options Contracts

Contract	Futures Exchange	Annual Volume in 2004
Canola futures	Winnipeg Commodity Exchange	1,737,972
Canola options	Winnipeg Commodity Exchange	20,568
Crude palm oil futures	Malaysia Derivatives Exchange Berhad	1,378,334
Rapeseed futures	Euronext (Paris)	191,664
Rapeseed options	Euronext (Paris)	8,075

Source: Data provided by Futures Industry Association, Inc.

LIVESTOCK

Meat is the major source of protein in the diet of Americans and people of other developed nations. It is also a growing source of protein in the diet of those living in developing nations. By the turn of the twenty-first century, each American, on average, ate more than 197 pounds of meat, poultry, and fish—65 pounds of beef, 0.5 pounds of veal, 48.5 pounds of pork, 0.9 pounds of lamb, 53.9 pounds of chicken, 14.3 pounds of turkey, and 14.5 pounds of fish annually. (See Fig. 13.7.)

Pork Commodities

The public's attitude toward pork and its consumption has changed greatly over the years. Pork was once regarded as part of the rich man's diet. Now increased production efficiency has made pork readily available. In addition, a shift away from the fat-type hog, reflecting a widespread decline in the use of lard, and a corresponding emphasis on production of a lean, meat-type hog has boosted pork demand.

FIGURE 13.7

Cattle, Broilers, Hogs, and Turkeys; Pounds Produced, 1953–2003

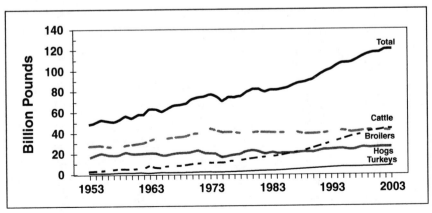

Source: USDA-NASS, April 2004.

U.S. pork production is concentrated in the Corn Belt, with the exception of North Carolina, which through notable recent growth has become the nation's second largest producer. Iowa still claims the largest share, however, with more than one-quarter of all U.S. pork production.

Total U.S. production was 98 million head slaughtered in 2001, making the United States the third largest producer of pork. China solidly holds the number one position, with 554 million head, followed by the European Union at 202 million head slaughtered.

Historic price patterns and current price trends are among the most important influences on the level of pork production. Hog producers, as do producers of most other commodities, tend to cut back on production when the price outlook is bearish. Yet cutbacks in periods of weakening prices are not as pronounced as they once were. Hog-feeding operations tend to be much larger than they were in the past, and operators attempt to feed at or near capacity to offset the higher fixed costs of automated feeding facilities. As operations have grown substantially in size, their total numbers have declined dramatically, creating a very concentrated market among fewer and larger players. (See Fig. 13.8.)

Feed is the primary cost in livestock production operations. Feed cost, in relation to the sales value of finished market-weight hogs, is thus the primary determinant of how much pork will be produced. In addition, feed prices may influence the producer's decision of when and at what weight to market hogs. Generally, when feed costs are high relative to the sales value of finished hogs, producers tend to breed, feed, and market fewer hogs, at lighter weights, than they would in periods of lower feed costs. When the cost-to-sales-price ratio is more favorable, breeding, feeding, marketing, and average market weights increase.

The hog/corn ratio, measured by dividing the price of hogs ($/hundredweight) by the price of corn ($/bushel), expresses the relationship of feeding costs to the dollar value of hogs. For instance, if the price of hogs in Omaha is $49.50 per hundredweight and the Omaha price of No. 2 yellow corn is $3.20¼ per

FIGURE 13.8

Number of U.S. Hog Operations, 1980–2003

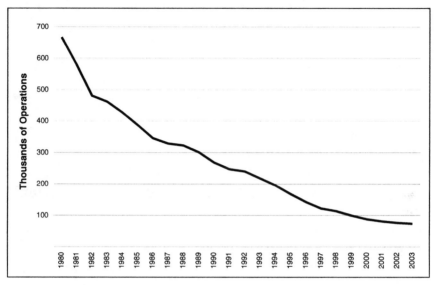

Source: USDA.

bushel, the hog/corn ratio is 15.5 ($49.50 divided by $3.2025). In other words, 15.5 bushels of corn have the same dollar value as 100 pounds of live pork.

When corn prices are high relative to pork prices, it takes fewer units of corn to equal the dollar value of 100 pounds of pork. Conversely, when corn prices are low relative to pork prices, it takes more units of corn to equal the value of 100 pounds of pork. A hog/corn ratio of 13.3 indicates higher corn costs and perhaps weaker hog prices than does a ratio of 22.5. The higher the ratio, the more profitable it is to feed hogs.

By closely controlling breeding and feeding operations, hog producers can be relatively certain about the number and weight of hogs they will have ready for market at a given date. A producer's first decision is how many sows to breed. In making this decision, producers take into account the gestation period of nearly four months and the average yield of 7.3 pigs per litter.

By knowing the number of sows bred and then multiplying that number by the average litter size, producers can accurately project feeding requirements and develop a marketing plan. Depending on their feed plan and seasonal factors that can affect weight gain, producers normally can bring newly born pigs to market weight in five to seven months.

Note that producers make this kind of calculation not only in terms of their own production but, based on reports from the USDA, apply it as well to total U.S. hog production in an attempt to get a reasonably sound picture of total production, available market supply, and probable price outlook.

Hog production usually follows a seasonal pattern, though these seasonal production trends are now of less importance than they once were. The largest number of *farrowings* (pig births) occurs during March, April, and May. Ordinarily, the smallest number occurs during December, January, and February. Since it takes five to six months to bring newly born pigs to market, spring pigs farrowed in March, April, and May come to market from August through December. During this period, pork commodities are traditionally at their lowest price level of the year, reflecting the increased hog supply.

In the past, most sows were bred only twice a year. Now they are commonly bred three times a year, which tends to even out the number of hogs coming to market throughout the year. Better management, improved feeding programs, and higher fixed costs (such as heated production facilities) make it desirable to consistently maintain production at near-capacity levels. (See Fig. 13.9.)

Along with the historic seasonal trends in production, there are long-term cycles in hog prices, which may last up to five or six years. They occur chiefly because of producers' reactions to price levels. Relatively high prices stimulate hog production for several years thereafter. This increased production leads to depressed prices, which, in turn, influences producers to cut production. Volatile feed prices have affected these patterns as well. As in the beef industry, hog price cycles now tend to be shorter in

FIGURE 13.9

U.S. Quarterly Hogs and Pigs Inventory, December 1, 1993–2004

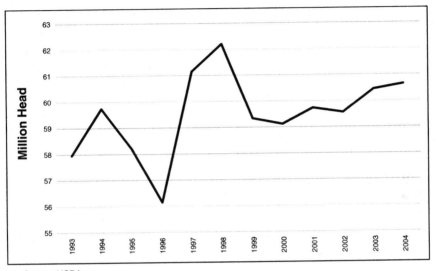

Source: USDA.

duration than in the past as a result of better price forecasting, greater production planning, and the trend toward more even production levels.

Various long- and short-term factors affect the supply situation for both pork bellies and other pork products—hams, loins, and butts. Some factors have greater impact on the supply and price level of pork bellies than they do on other cuts of pork. The most important long-term factors affecting supplies include the current livestock situation—feed costs and profitability considerations—general consumer income levels, the number of hogs and pigs on farms, and the birth of new pigs. In the short run, the current rate of weekly hog marketings at major markets tends to be the strongest influence on both the supply and price of pork products. Weekly bacon slicings and cold storage figures also figure prominently in forecasting pork belly supplies and price levels.

TABLE 13.6

Major Pork Futures and Options Contracts

Contract	Futures Exchange	Annual Volume in 2004
Lean hog futures	Chicago Mercantile Exchange	3,204,186
Lean hog options	Chicago Mercantile Exchange	179,093
Pork bellies, frozen futures	Chicago Mercantile Exchange	151,949

Source: Data provided by Futures Industry Association, Inc.

The demand for pork—such as chops, hams, bacon, and pre-pared meat products—is most strongly affected by the price relative to general income of the public and to the price of competitive meat products. The consumer trend toward greater weight consciousness has increased the demand for leaner pork products, particularly those made from hams and loins. Hams and loins account for 24 percent and 18 percent of carcass weight, respectively.

Pork bellies, the end product of which is cured sliced bacon, account for 14 percent of the carcass weight of hogs. The demand for bacon has risen because of increasing demand for pork in general and increases in population and per capita consumption. Bacon is unique among meat products in that it has relatively few substitutes. Consumption tends to remain stable from one year to the next, except in situations of major price changes.

Futures and options on lean hogs and frozen pork bellies trade at the Chicago Mercantile Exchange. (See Table 13.6.)

Beef Commodities

The U.S. cattle/calf inventory peaked in the mid-1970s. On January 1, 1975, for instance, the cattle/calf inventory was 132 million head. By 1980, it had decreased to about 111 million head. It then held somewhat steady for a few years, but liquidation resumed because of volatile financing costs and shifts in consumer tastes. By January 1, 1991, the U.S. cattle/calf inventory had dropped to 98.9 million head, one of the lowest inventories in 30 years. By 2004, inventories had declined further to 94.9 million head. (See Fig. 13.10.)

The U.S. cattle industry has three sectors: cow-calf operations, feedlots, and meat packers. Cow-calf operations produce calves, which soon become what are called feeder cattle. Feedlots in the surplus feed grain production areas of the Corn Belt and the Great Plains buy calves and feeder cattle from Western ranchers and commercial breeders and then feed them until they reach a desired market weight. Meat packers slaughter cattle for beef.

The three largest beef-producing states are Texas, Nebraska, and Kansas. The level of beef production is affected by many interrelated factors, the most influential of which are current and recent-past price levels. When prices are high, commercial

FIGURE 13.10

U.S. Cattle Inventory, January 1, 1968–2004

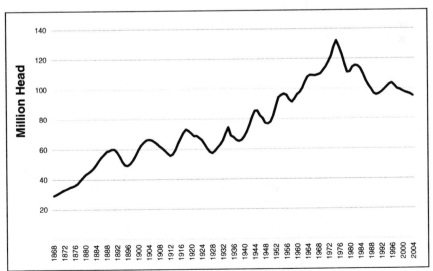

Source: USDA.

breeders increase their breeding programs in anticipation of increased demand for feeder cattle. When prices are low, feeders (feedlots) cut back their production, and breeders reduce the number of feeder cattle produced. In periods of extremely low prices, breeders may even liquidate some of their breeding stock.

In addition, drought and crop failure in the Corn Belt may reduce feed grain production and cut back on cattle feeding. Sustained periods of excessively hot, cold, or rainy weather slow the rate of cattle weight gain and subsequently increase feeding costs. Conversely, less extreme weather generally results in better feed grain yields, creating cheaper feed supplies and improved profits for the cattle feeder.

The steer/corn ratio, an important influence on the level of production, measures the cost of feed in relation to the market price of beef. This ratio, released monthly by the USDA, divides the price of cattle ($/hundredweight) by the price of corn ($/bushel). For instance, if the price of choice steers in Omaha is $66.69 per hundredweight and the Omaha price of No. 2 yellow corn is $3.20¼ per bushel, the steer/corn ratio is 20.8 ($66.690 divided by $3.2025). In other words, 20.8 bushels of corn are equal in dollar value to 100 pounds of choice steer beef.

When the value of corn is high relative to the sales value of beef, fewer units of corn equal the dollar value of 100 pounds of beef. Conversely, when corn prices are low relative to beef prices, it takes more units of corn to equal the value of 100 pounds of beef. A steer/corn ratio of 17.6 thus indicates higher corn costs and weaker beef prices than a ratio of 22.5. The higher the ratio, the more profitable it is to feed the cattle.

Beef production requires a lengthy start-up time. A heifer, a female that has not yet produced a calf, is normally not bred until it is 14 to 18 months old, and gestation requires another 9 months. At six to eight months of age, calves are weaned from their mothers and either sent directly to a feedlot or to an intermediate stage lasting from six to ten months where they are fed roughage. Both steers and heifers are placed in feedlots, although fewer heifers are placed because their retention is necessary to maintain cow herds. To bring feeder cattle to a desired market weight requires another five to nine months. Because of the time required from breeding to finished market weight, adjustments in beef breeding and feeding to meet demand and price changes are difficult to make.

The *cattle cycle,* a cyclical change in the size of the cattle herd, arises from several factors, including this lengthy start-up time, changes in demand for beef, and the availability and cost of feed. Cattle cycles generally last 10 to 12 years.

The expansion phase of a typical cattle cycle begins when producers decide to expand their breeding stock in response to rising prices or expectations that prices will rise. When breeding stock is held back to expand herds, prices rise. Rising prices also keep calves, yearlings, and steers out of the market and on feed until they are older and at a heavier weight. Eventually, however, the large number of new calves from the expanded herds mature, and slaughter begins to increase. That starts the down cycle. Prices start to drop because of the cattle oversupply. Since herd expansion is no longer profitable, the slaughter of cows and calves increases, further depressing prices. Eventually, herds become so small that prices go up, and a new cycle begins.

Still, despite these seasonal breeding and feeding patterns, beef production has only a small seasonal trend, tending to rise slightly from the second to the fourth quarter after declining slightly from the first to the second quarter. Similarly, there is a fairly weak seasonal trend in prices, tending to reach a low in February and to peak in August. (See Fig. 13.11.)

Various government regulations, programs, and information, particularly from the USDA, affect the production and marketing of beef. In the past, annual farm programs sometimes used acreage controls or crop production incentives to influence the amount of feed grain raised during a given crop production marketing year. The dairy program also affects beef supply. For instance, if the government initiates a program to reduce milk production, farmers participating in the program may be required to reduce dairy cattle numbers. More dairy cattle will be

FIGURE 13.11

U.S. Monthly Commercial Slaughter, Cattle, 2002–2004

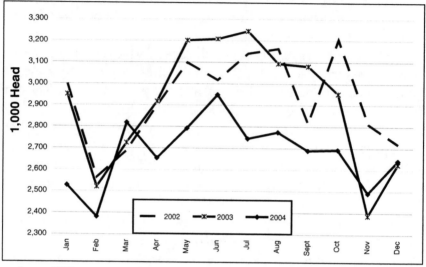

Source: USDA.

slaughtered, increasing beef supplies and ultimately forcing beef prices down.

Other government actions are aimed directly at beef production. In periods of depressed meat prices, for example, the government may attempt to stimulate demand through subsidized school lunches and other donation programs. At other times, the government may use export or import quotas on beef products to influence domestic beef production and price levels.

The USDA also provides information on cattle and livestock inventories, the number of heads of cattle and calves on feed, and production and stocks data on competitive meat and poultry. The cattle-breeding, feedlot, and meat-packing segments of the industry watch this information closely to anticipate future beef demand and price trends.

The amount of U.S. beef produced depends on domestic demand factors. Meat consumption tends to increase as a result of population growth and rising affluence. Production has barely kept pace with the demand for choice beef and has never exceeded demand for any significant period. In inflationary periods and in times of steeper feed costs, however, consumers tend to avoid the more expensive beef varieties in favor of cheaper cuts. At such times, a change in diet—substituting poultry or pasta products—is not uncommon.

Since 1975, for instance, the annual per capita consumption of beef declined from 88 pounds (retail weight) to about 68 pounds in 2001, while the annual per capita demand for chicken increased from about 37 pounds to nearly 77 pounds over the same time period. Pork consumption, on the other hand, has remained fairly steady through the years at an annual rate of around 49 pounds. Consumers increasingly prefer white meat products—fish and poultry—and more and more convenience foods include chicken.

Although beef has historically commanded higher prices than either pork or poultry, price movements for the three commodities are somewhat parallel, because they are all affected by the general availability and cost of feeds, chiefly corn. When beef supplies are scarce, however, higher beef prices tend to lead to greater consumption of lower-priced meat products—pork, poultry, and fish.

In recent years, disease outbreaks and related trade restrictions have hampered world trade in beef and other animal products. For cattle, the chief concern has been bovine spongiform

TABLE 13.7

Major Beef Futures and Options Contracts

Contract	Futures Exchange	Annual Volume in 2004
Live cattle futures	Chicago Mercantile Exchange	4,510,128
Live cattle options	Chicago Mercantile Exchange	500,927
Feeder cattle futures	Chicago Mercantile Exchange	741,265
Feeder cattle options	Chicago Mercantile Exchange	142,638
Live cattle futures	BM&F (Brazil)	225,200

Source: Data provided by Futures Industry Association, Inc.

encephalopathy (BSE), or "mad cow disease," which devastated the British beef industry during the late 1990s.

Live cattle and feeder cattle futures and options trade at the Chicago Mercantile Exchange, in addition to contracts on various classes of milk from dairy cattle. Cattle futures also trade at the BM&F (Brazil). (See Table 13.7.)

FURTHER READING

Atkin, Michael, *International Grain Trade*. Cambridge, England: Woodhead Publishing, 1995.

Ball, C. E., *Building the Beef Industry: A Century of Commitment 1898–1998*. Saratoga, Wyoming: The Saratoga Publishing Group, 1998.

Broehl, Wayne G., Jr., *Cargill: Trading the World's Grain*. Hanover, NH: University Press of New England, 1992.

Chambers, William, *Forecasting Feed Grain Prices in a Changing Environment*. Outlook Report No. FDS-04F-01. Washington, DC: United States Department of Agriculture, Economic Research Service, July 2004.

Ferris, William G., *The Grain Traders: The Story of the Chicago Board of Trade*. East Lansing, MI: Michigan State University Press, 1988.

Fussell, Betty, *The Story of Corn*. Albuquerque, NM: University of New Mexico Press, 2004.

Grandmill, William, *Investing in Wheat, Soybeans, Corn*. New York: Windsor Books, 1990.

Hoeft, Robert G., *Modern Corn and Soybean Production*. Savoy, IL: MCSP Publications, 2000.

Lesser, William H., *Marketing Livestock and Meat*. New York: Food Products Press, 1993.

Mathews, Kenneth H., Jr., William F. Hahn, Kenneth E. Nelson, Lawrence A. Duewer, and Ronald A. Gustafson, *U.S. Beef Indus-*

try: Cattle Cycles, Price Spreads, and Packer Concentration. Technical Bulletin No. 1874. Washington, DC: United States Department of Agriculture, Market and Trade Economics Division, Economic Research Service, April 1999.

McBride, William D., and Nigel Kay, *Economic and Structural Relationships in U.S. Hog Production.* Agricultural Economic Report No. AER818. Washington, DC: United States Department of Agriculture, Economic Research Service, February 2003.

Morgan, Daniel, *Merchants of Grain.* New York: Viking Press, 1979.

Thu, Kendall M., and E. Paul Durrenberger, *Pigs, Profits, and Rural Communities.* New York: State University of New York Press, 1998.

Warnken, Philip, F., *The Development and Growth of the Soybean Industry in Brazil.* Ames, Iowa: Iowa State Press, 1999.

INFORMATION SOURCES

American Soybean Association	www.soygrowers.com
National Association of Wheat Growers	www.wheatworld.org
National Cattlemen's Beef Association	www.beef.org
National Corn Growers Association	www.ncga.com
National Pork Producers Council	www.nppc.org

CHAPTER 14

Financial Markets: Debt Instruments, Stock Indexes, Currencies

Financial futures make up more than 80 percent of the world's futures trading volume. Since they first appeared on the financial scene in the 1970s, increasing numbers of financial managers have found them to be important risk management tools during periods of market volatility. Financial futures and options provide financial managers with efficient vehicles for protecting investments from adverse price changes in debt, equity, or currency markets. To understand how financial futures perform these vital functions, it is first necessary to understand how the underlying cash markets work. Accordingly, this chapter provides an overview of several important cash markets underlying U.S. futures markets.

FINANCIAL MARKETS OVERVIEW

The role of the financial markets in a market economy is to match up savings and investment. This can be illustrated by examining the major market participants and the flow of goods, services, and funds among them. A competitive market economy can be divided into households, businesses, and governments, each of which performs different economic functions. For example, in the *goods and services market,* households purchase food, clothing, entertainment, and other goods or services from businesses. In the *resources market,* businesses employ factor inputs such as labor to produce these goods and services. *Governments* provide public goods and services, such as defense, which are financed by taxes.

Beyond providing for immediate needs, households, businesses, and governments plan for the future. Households save a portion of their income for retirement, home purchases, education, and other needs. Businesses borrow money to invest in future productive capacity, for instance, with office buildings, power plants, research and development, and so on. Governments borrow money to finance the difference when spending exceeds tax revenues.

Financial markets provide the means for households, businesses, and governments to combine savings with investment. With their savings, households can purchase securities such as stocks or bonds. Businesses and governments use these funds to finance upcoming projects. A flowchart depicting these capital flows is shown in Figure 14.1.

Like all models, this economic picture is oversimplified. Households are not the sole source of funds, and businesses and governments are not the only sources of securities. In general, though, U.S. households are net providers of funds, and businesses and governments are net users of funds. Also absent from the picture is the international flow of funds. But the central point remains: competitive financial markets are an integral component of a well-functioning market economy.

Within the financial markets, there are many different types of instruments. Some are debt securities, some are equities, and some are hybrids. The quality of the instruments can also vary, as can the maturity of the debt instruments. Furthermore, the instruments can be issued many different ways.

Debt versus Equity

There are two basic types of financial instruments: debt and equity. *Debt instruments* are loans with an agreement to pay

FIGURE 14.1

Circular Flow: A Market Economy Overview

The combined activities of households, businesses, and governments produce the flows of a market economy. The outer circle, running counterclockwise, illustrates businesses channeling goods and
services to households through the goods and services market. In
turn, households offer their labor skills to businesses through the
resources market. The inner circle, running clockwise, depicts
money payments—income dollars to households, households
spending dollars to pay for goods and services, businesses taking
sales revenues back to their firms, and businesses paying employees. The very center shows the financial markets' role—providing the
means by which households with surplus dollars transfer savings to
corporations, governments, and other spending units.

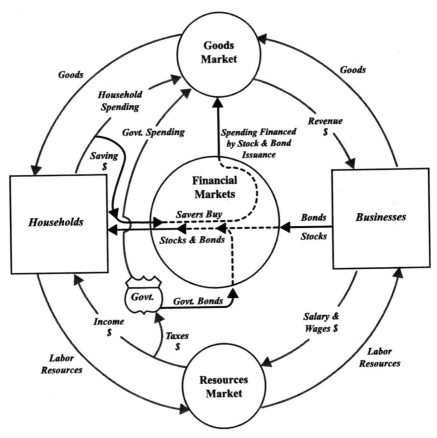

back the funds with interest. Depending on the terms of the debt instrument, the interest payment can be either fixed or variable. Examples of debt securities include bonds, notes, and mortgages.

Equity securities are shares of stock representing ownership in a company. Those who purchase equity securities thus become company owners. As owners, they may be entitled to a share of the company's profits, typically in the form of quarterly dividends. If for some reason a company goes out of business, the stockholders are last in line to receive a portion of the company's assets. In contrast, those who purchase debt securities are lenders, and their claim to principal and interest has a higher priority. In general, equity securities are riskier than debt securities, and so equity holders expect higher returns.

Financial Intermediaries

Banks, credit unions, insurance companies, savings and loans, pension funds, mutual funds, and other "middlemen" act as financial intermediaries, facilitating the flow of funds between savers and users of funds. Having pooled the funds of many savers, they buy debt and equity securities from governments and corporations and resell them to savers in more manageable increments. Because they provide economies of scale, financial intermediaries reduce transaction costs and make it easier for small investors to participate in financial markets. Considered in the aggregate, various types of financial intermediaries transfer billions of dollars each year. (See Table 14.1.)

Maturity

Debt securities have maturities ranging from overnight to 30 years or more. Some securities, such as Treasury bills, mature in 90 days, whereas others mature only after decades, like the 50-year bonds issued by the Tennessee Valley Authority. In the past companies issued so-called *century bonds,* as well as perpetual bonds. Equities have no stated maturity; they remain outstanding in perpetuity unless some event (like a takeover or

TABLE 14.1

Financial Intermediaries
Total Financial Assets, 2004

	Total Financial Assets ($ billions)
Commercial banking	$8,487.0
Mutual funds	5,435.3
Private pension funds	4,444.4
Life insurance companies	4,159.9
Agency- and GSE-backed mortgage pools	3,542.6
Government-sponsored enterprises (GSEs)	2,895.0
Issuers of asset-backed securities (ABSs)	2,817.2
State and local government employee retirement funds	2,072.4
Money market mutual funds	1,879.9
Security brokers and dealers	1,836.0
Savings institutions	1,691.2
Finance companies	1,458.0
Funding corporations	1,275.5
Other insurance companies	1,182.9
Federal government retirement funds	1,024.0
Bank personal trusts and estates	924.6
Credit unions	654.7
Closed-end and exchange-traded funds	246.1
Real estate investment trusts (REITs)	222.8
Mortgage companies	32.1
Total	**$46,281.6**

Source: Flow of Funds Accounts of the United States, March 10, 2005, Board of Governors of the Federal Reserve System.

bankruptcy) prompts a change in their status or existence. (See Table 14.2.)

The information in Table 14.2 only scratches the surface. For instance, besides the debt and equity securities noted, there are other interest-bearing instruments, such as Eurodollar deposits, with a stated maturity, and checking accounts, which are payable on demand.

TABLE 14.2

Securities: Time to Maturity

Security	Maturity
U.S. Treasury bills	Less than one year
Notes (corporations; municipal, state, and federal government agencies)	One year to ten years
Bonds (corporations; municipal, state, and federal government agencies)	More than ten years
Corporate stock	Perpetual

Primary versus Secondary Market

When a company or government first sells a stock or bond in the marketplace, it is issuing a security in the *primary market.* Typically, companies issue new securities through investment banking firms that provide underwriting services. The investment bank buys the new issue and reoffers it to the public. Alternately, an issuer of a new security can hold an auction in which bids are accepted, and the winning bidders receive the securities. Typically the U.S. Treasury raises money through auctions. In either case, the company or government issuing the securities receives the proceeds of the sale, less the underwriting fees.

Once securities make their debut in the primary market, they are traded from that point on in the resale or *secondary market* through an interdealer network or on an organized exchange, such as the New York Stock Exchange. Note, however, that while any security may be traded through these organized channels, there is no guarantee that a security will have an active, liquid secondary market.

DEBT INSTRUMENTS

Since debt instruments are loans, they must state the terms agreed upon by the lender and borrower. Debt instruments identify the borrower, the amount loaned, when repayment is due, the rate of interest, and how the interest is to be paid. This section gives an overview of the cash markets for many of the debt instruments that have futures contracts associated with them. Today's menu of interest rate futures contracts spans the entire yield curve giving banks, insurance companies, savings and loans, and other institutions the ability to hedge debt instruments with virtually any maturity.

Short-term debt instruments, such as Eurodollars, fed funds, and Treasury bills, comprise what financial market participants call the *money market*. Longer-term debt securities, such as notes and bonds issued by the U.S. Treasury, municipalities, and corporations, join equities as capital market instruments, because they are generally issued to finance long-term objectives.

Eurodollar Deposits

Eurodollar deposits are nonnegotiable, fixed-rate, U.S. dollar–denominated deposits held in banks outside the United States. Because they are held offshore, Eurodollar deposits are generally more lightly regulated than are conventional deposits.

Originally, most of these dollar-deposits were held in Europe, hence the name. Now, however, the term *Eurodollar* is applied to any dollar deposits in banks outside the United States. The interest rate that banks pay on Eurodollar deposits is the London interbank offer rate (LIBOR), which is paid using a simple add-on method. With this method, if $100 is deposited for one year at 5 percent, the bank adds $5 to the account balance at the end of 360 days (a year for money market calculations), and the depositor can withdraw $105.

The origin of Eurodollars is just one example of financial market innovation in response to changing economic conditions and government regulations. During the Cold War, the Soviet Union, its Eastern European satellites, and the People's Republic of China feared that the United States would someday freeze their bank accounts and confiscate dollar balances held in New

York banks. Anticipating this possibility, the Soviets transferred their dollar balances from New York to London and other European financial centers. This transfer of funds was achieved via the Soviet bank in Paris, Banque Commerciale pour l'Europe du Nord, also known as Eurobank. The term *Eurodollar* emerged as a result.

Regulatory controls in the United States, including the Fed's Regulation Q—which limited the interest banks could pay on deposits—and the Fed's requirement that its member banks hold cash reserves against deposits, accelerated the creation of the Eurodollar market. These controls imposed costs and restrictions that made it attractive for banks to enter the Eurodollar market to compete for funds and, at the same time, to provide depositors with higher interest rates than were possible on domestic deposits. (See Table 14.3.)

Today's Eurocurrency market is so large that financial intermediaries hold not only Eurodollars, but also other currencies from outside their borders as well, such as the Japanese yen (Euroyen).

Fed Funds

The fed funds market is the heart of the U.S. money market. The Federal Reserve requires banks and other depository institutions in the United States to hold reserves with Federal Reserve Banks based on their customers' deposits and loans. Yet bank customers change their balances almost constantly. As a result, each day some banks end up with excess reserves, while others come up short.

Since these reserves do not earn interest, banks with excess reserves have an incentive to lend any excess funds to banks that need funds in order to meet reserve requirements. Funds in excess of reserve requirements lent to other banks needing reserves are referred to as *fed funds,* and such interbank transactions are collectively known as the *fed funds market.* The vast majority of transactions in the fed funds market

TABLE 14.3

Eurodollar Liabilities of Banks in BIS Reporting Categories
Q4 1977 to Q4 2003

Q4 Period	Outstanding Amount ($ billions)
1977	$444.9
1978	$552.7
1979	$704.1
1980	$877.3
1981	$1,055.4
1982	$1,137.9
1983	$1,282.2
1984	$1,429.2
1985	$1,481.8
1986	$1,877.9
1987	$2,224.4
1988	$2,399.1
1989	$2,777.9
1990	$3,018.1
1991	$2,852.5
1992	$2,848.3
1993	$2,851.4
1994	$3,170.9
1995	$3,253.3
1996	$3,314.9
1997	$3,791.4
1998	$3,950.9
1999	$4,001.5
2000	$4,530.2
2001	$4,933.8
2002	$5,100.8
2003	$6,226.7

Notes:
U.S. dollar-denominated liabilities of banks in all BIS reporting countries vis-à-vis the United States are excluded.

U.S. dollar-denominated liabilities of banks in the United States vis-à-vis nonresident of the United States are included.

Source: Bank of International Settlements, Monetary and Economic Department, International Financial Statistics.

are overnight borrowings. The remaining transactions are longer-maturity borrowings known as *term fed funds*. These term loans typically have maturities of anywhere from one week to six months.

Larger money center banks are usually net borrowers of fed funds, whereas smaller banks are typically net lenders. Interest is paid from bank to bank using the add-on method, as with Eurodollars. The fed funds market trades continuously during the day, although the bulk of trading occurs before 11:00 a.m. (U.S. Eastern time zone).

The fed funds rate at any given moment is such a significant indicator of the cost of credit that the Federal Reserve Bank of New York reports the dollar-weighted average of fed funds rates daily. This average rate is based on the previous day's activity and is referred to as the *fed effective rate*. The Fed uses the fed effective rate as an important measure of the effectiveness of its policies.

The fed funds rate is the primary tool of Federal Reserve monetary policy. Accordingly, most short-term U.S. interest rates are keyed to the fed effective rate. Anticipated changes in Fed policy, expectations about government reports and economic indicators, and intermarket concerns about the strength of the U.S. dollar—reflected in the fed effective rate—can all affect general money market expectations. Uncertainty about monetary policy may lead to increased fed funds volatility.

U.S. Treasury Bills

T-bills have become increasingly popular with individuals and corporations worldwide for several reasons. First, T-bills are extremely liquid instruments. Second, like all securities issued by the U.S. Treasury, T-bills are virtually free of credit risk. In addition, interest received on Treasury securities is free from taxation by state and local governments.

Treasury bills pay interest using the discount method, which is different from the add-on method used by Eurodollars, fed funds, and personal savings accounts. Rather than adding interest onto the principal, Treasury bills subtract the interest from the face amount of the bill at the time of issue and then pay the face amount at maturity. The difference between the purchase price and the redemption value is the interest. For example, in one auction the U.S. Treasury sold $11.043 billion face value of 13-week bills. The average price of the 13-week bills was 99.272 percent of par, or $9,927.20 for a $10,000 face value T-bill. Thirteen weeks later, at T-bill maturity, the investor who bought this T-bill received $10,000—$9,927.20 plus $72.80 in interest.

The interest rate, or discount yield, in this example equals 2.88 percent and is calculated using the following formula. (Note that the T-bill in this example matures in 91 days.)

$$\text{Discount yield} = \frac{par - price}{100} \times \frac{360 \text{ days}}{\text{no. of days}}$$

$$= \frac{100 - 99.272}{100} \times \frac{360 \text{ days}}{91 \text{ days}}$$

$$= 0.00728 \times 3.956$$

$$= 0.0288 \text{ or } 2.88\%$$

As this example shows, discount yield is calculated as a percent of face value using the 360-day year, which is customary for securities with an original maturity of one year or less. Treasury instruments with original maturities greater than one year compute yield based on the price paid, rather than the face value, using the actual number of days in the year. To adjust for these differences, investors can calculate the bond equivalent yield of a T-bill. This way they can compare the discount yield of a T-bill with the yield of a bond.

$$\text{Bond equivalent yield} = \frac{par - price}{price} \times \frac{365 \text{ days}}{\text{no. of days}}$$

$$= \frac{100 - 99.272}{99.272} \times \frac{365 \text{ days}}{91 \text{ days}}$$

$$= 0.007333 \times 4.010989$$

$$= 0.0294 \text{ or } 2.94\%$$

U.S. Treasury Notes and Bonds

Governments around the world issue longer-term debt instruments to finance their borrowing needs. In Germany, the securities are referred to as bunds, bobls, and schatz; in England, as gilts, and in the United States, as Treasuries.

The U.S. Treasury market has grown dramatically over the years as the U.S. Treasury has issued increasing numbers of debt instruments to finance increasing U.S. government budget deficits. In 1973, for instance, there were $263 billion in outstanding Treasury securities. By 1996, marketable U.S. Treasury debt had exploded to more than $3.4 trillion. And by 2004, it reached nearly $4 trillion. (See Fig. 14.2.)

Unlike Treasury bills, Treasury notes and bonds are considered capital market instruments because they represent the medium- to long-term segment of the maturity spectrum. Notes are issued at maturities between of 1 and 10 years, but most often with maturities of 2, 3, 5, and 10 years. For all Treasury securities, the minimum purchase amount is $1,000.

Treasury bonds may be issued at any maturity greater than 10 years. Although U.S. long bond issuance was suspended for nearly five years, the U.S. Treasury resumed issuing 30-year bonds in February 2006. Because of the long-term nature of these instruments and the size of outstanding issuance, the secondary market in T-bonds has traditionally been very active.

The coupon rate on a bond is quoted as an annualized percentage rate, but is typically paid in semiannual installments. An 8 percent bond, for example, would pay two 4 percent coupons per year. The actual interest amount is determined by multiplying the coupon rate by the face amount of the bond. Since neither the coupon rate nor the face amount of the instrument changes, interest payments do not change during the life of the note or bond, hence the name *fixed-income security* is often used for intermediate- and long-term debt instruments.

The term *coupon* is a holdover from earlier times when bond holders received certificates with interest coupons attached.

FIGURE 14.2

Marketable U.S. Treasury Debt

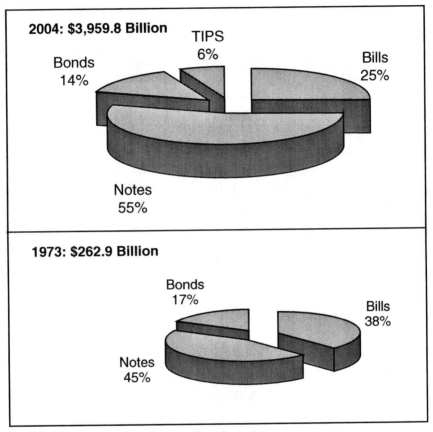

Note: TIPS represents Treasury inflation-protected securities.
Source: Economic Report of the President 2005; U.S. Department of the Treasury.

Bond holders clipped these coupons and presented them to the issuer to receive their interest. Because of the rising cost of printing and distributing debt certificates and the growing use of computers, standard practice has now changed to book entry. Debt issuers now simply ask a transfer agent, typically a commercial bank or trust company, to electronically transfer interest payments to a creditor's bank account. In the Treasury market, this process began with U.S. Treasury bills issued in 1979. By

1986, all marketable Treasury debt was issued by electronic book entry.

T-note and T-bond prices are quoted as a percent of the face value of the instrument, or par, and 32nds of a percent. For example, a $1,000 face value note priced at 105-16 ($105^{16}\!/_{32}$ percent of par) is a note whose current market price is $1,055 (105.5 percent × $1,000). This quoted price excludes any interest due. Since holders of T-notes and T-bonds receive interest payments at six-month intervals, purchases and sales must account for interest that has been earned but not yet paid to the holder, commonly called *accrued interest.* If a bond or note is sold in the secondary market between interest payments, the buyer pays the quoted price plus accrued interest. (See Fig. 14.3.)

In 1997, the United States began issuing a new category of marketable debt called Treasury inflation-protected securities, or TIPS. Issued in terms of 5, 10, and 20 years, the principal value of these securities is tied to inflation (utilizing the Con-

FIGURE 14.3

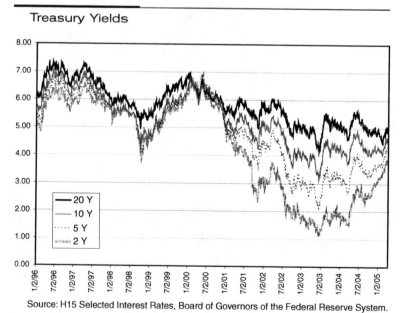

Treasury Yields

Source: H15 Selected Interest Rates, Board of Governors of the Federal Reserve System.

sumer Price Index). Interest payments and the final payment at maturity are based on this inflation-adjusted principal. Because TIPS are designed to appeal to buy-and-hold investors, they are less actively traded in the secondary market.

U.S. Treasury Security Market Structure

There are three major participants in the U.S. Treasury debt markets: the Federal Reserve, the U.S. Treasury Department, and primary dealers. Their roles in the marketplace govern and shape the flow of funds from savers to borrowers through U.S. government debt.

The *Federal Reserve System,* frequently called the Fed, is the central bank of the United States. The Fed was created by the Federal Reserve Act, passed by Congress in 1913 to provide a safer and more flexible banking and monetary system than the one that existed at the time. The Federal Reserve helps attain the nation's economic and financial goals through its ability to set monetary policy and influence money supply and credit in the economy. As the nation's central bank, it attempts to maximize long-term sustainable growth along with reasonable price stability. In the short run, the Federal Reserve seeks to adopt policies that combat deflationary or inflationary pressures as they may arise—in other words, the Fed "leans against the wind." Finally, as a lender of last resort, it has the responsibility to use the policy instruments available to it to prevent national liquidity crises and financial panics.

The Federal Reserve also has been entrusted with many supervisory and regulatory functions to promote stable financial markets in the United States. Its responsibilities include regulating the foreign activities of all U.S. banks and the activities of foreign banks in the United States as well as administering the laws that regulate bank holding companies.

The U.S. central bank is a complex organization composed of the Board of Governors of the Federal Reserve System, the Federal Open Market Committee (FOMC), and 12 regional Federal Reserve Banks. The 12 regional Federal Reserve Banks operate a check-clearing process, distribute coin and currency, conduct bank examinations, and assist the Treasury at auction time. On a larger scale, the Board of Governors oversees the system, but its primary responsibility is to formulate monetary policy. (See Fig. 14.4.) The Fed has three primary tools at its disposal for executing its monetary policy—open market operations, reserve requirements, and discounting.

Open market operations are the Federal Reserve's purchase or sale of U.S. government securities in the secondary market. They are the most powerful and flexible monetary policy tool the Federal Reserve has to influence money supply and hence inflation, interest rates, and the overall U.S. Treasury market. These operations are the Fed's preferred method for injecting or draining reserves from the banking system. When the Fed buys securities, it adds to member-bank reserves, thereby increasing the lending capacity of the banking system. As bank lending increases, the supply of money grows. When the Fed sells securities, it collects money from member banks, thus reducing the banking system's lending capacity. This cutback in lending decreases money supply. As the supply of money changes, so do interest rates. The greater the supply of money (assuming inflationary expectations remain the same), the lower the rates, and vice versa. The FOMC directs the Federal Reserve's open market operations and, consequently, is the most important monetary policy-making body of the Federal Reserve System.

In addition to open market operations, the Federal Reserve can change its *reserve requirements* to influence monetary policy. By law, depository institutions in the United States are required to have a certain amount of "spare cash," or reserves, on hand either in their vaults or on deposit at the Federal Reserve Bank. The higher the reserve requirement, the less lending capacity banks have and the slower the growth in money supply. The lower the reserve requirement, the more lending capacity and the faster the growth in money supply.

FIGURE 14.4

The Fed's Structure

The Federal Reserve System

- The nation's central bank
- A regional structure with 12 districts
- Subject to general Congressional authority and oversight
- Operates on its own earnings

Board of Governors	Federal Open Market Committee	Federal Reserve Banks
• 7 members serving staggered 14-year terms	• The system's key monetary policy-making body	• 12 regional banks with 25 branches
• Appointed by the U.S. President and confirmed by the Senate	• Decisions seek to foster economic growth with price stability by influencing the flow of money and credit	• Each independently incorporated with a 9-member board of directors from the private sector
• Oversees System operations, makes regulatory decisions, and sets reserve requirements	• Composed of the 7 members of the Board of Governors and the Reserve Bank presidents, 5 of whom serve as voting members on a rotating basis	• Set discount rate, subject to approval by Board of Governors
		• Monitor economy and financial institutions in their districts and provide financial services to the U.S. government and depository institutions

Source: *The Fed: Our Central Bank* (The Federal Reserve Bank of Chicago).

Since reserves are non-interest-bearing deposits, banks try to minimize the amount of reserves in excess of the Fed's requirements. Overnight bank lending of excess reserves (fed funds) to banks with insufficient reserves arose as a market solution to provide interest for bank reserve lenders and a source of funds for bank reserve borrowers.

The third monetary tool the Federal Reserve uses is *discounting*. The Fed uses this tool either by adjusting the amount it will lend to member banks or by changing the *discount rate*— the interest rate the Fed charges member banks for loans. By cutting the discount rate, the Fed confirms its intention to stimulate bank lending, a clear signal to the marketplace of the Fed's easing monetary policy stance. If the Fed is trying to rein in the economy, it raises the discount rate.

Distinct from the Federal Reserve, the U.S. Treasury is part of the executive branch of the government and is responsible for administering to the financial needs of the federal government. Its responsibilities include raising funds to finance the federal deficit (government expenditures in excess of federal tax revenues) through Treasury auctions and handling the repayment of the nation's maturing federal debt. The Treasury funds the deficit and the repayment of debt by issuing Treasury bills and notes.

The following lists distinguish the U.S. Treasury from the Federal Reserve:

U.S. Treasury

- Part of the executive branch of the federal government
- Monitors U.S. government budget, including receipts and disbursements
- Determines size and maturity of government securities
- Issues interest-paying Treasury notes and bills in the primary market
- Mints coins and authorizes the issuance of new currency

Federal Reserve

- Created by and responsible for semiannual reports to Congress
- Uses three tools to influence the availability of money and credit: open market operations, reserve requirements, and changes in the discount rate
- Acts as fiscal agent of the Treasury in auctions of government securities and services and redeems securities on the Treasury's behalf
- Net demander of Treasury debt in the secondary market
- Applies net earnings to the reduction of the federal debt
- Issues Federal Reserve notes, which pay no interest

Throughout the 1980s and into the 1990s, deficits ran into the hundreds of billions of dollars, increasing the federal debt as a percent of gross domestic product (GDP) and necessitating the issuance of more and more government securities. In the late 1990s, however, federal budget cutbacks and strong economic growth shrank the annual deficit considerably as a percent of GDP, leading to lower gross debt as a percent of GDP. With a lower deficit to fund, the Treasury issued far fewer securities, which significantly affected the Treasury market. Since 2000, however, the combined impacts of an economic downturn, federal tax cuts, and increased spending have prompted the gross federal debt, as a percent of GDP, to rise again. (See Fig. 14.5.)

Primary dealers are the third major participant in the Treasury securities market. Representing the core of the cash market for Treasury securities, primary government securities dealers—currently 22 banks or bank subsidiaries and brokerage firms—act as underwriters of new Treasury debt, purchasing the bulk of the securities at Treasury auctions.

Once Treasury securities are issued, the dealers maintain a secondary market for existing issues. Almost all the secondary market activity occurs in an over-the-counter dealer market that

FIGURE 14.5

Gross Federal Debt as a Percentage of GDP

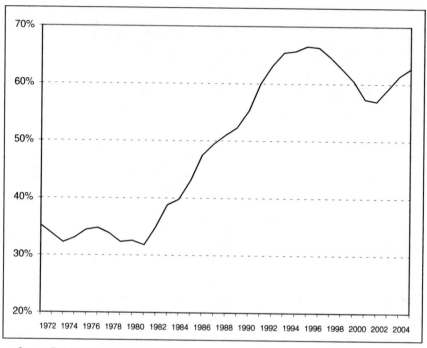

Source: Federal Reserve Bank of St. Louis.

trades more than $100 billion in Treasuries each day. Ready sup-
ply and active demand make the most recent issues extremely
liquid at each maturity. Older issues are traded less, yet the
dealers remain willing to quote continuous firm bids and offers,
providing the Treasury cash market with unparalleled liquidity.

In addition to primary dealers, as many as 500 secondary
dealers participate to varying degrees in the secondary market.
Both primary and secondary dealers generally hold an inventory
of U.S. Treasury securities and seek to profit from favorable security price changes, proprietary trading, and commissions. Because
the secondary market is so competitive, commissions are slight
and bid-ask spreads are narrow, reflecting a liquid market.

Carrying Treasury securities in inventory can be profitable when the yield curve has a positive slope—that is, when long-term interest rates are higher than short-term rates. A positive yield curve environment implies *positive carry*—named positive because the coupon income is greater than the short-term cost of financing inventory. Because the majority of the dealers' inventories are financed with short-term loans called *repurchase agreements,* these costs are pivotal to their profit margins.

Using government securities as collateral, a dealer initiates a repurchase agreement, also referred to as a *repo* or *RP,* by selling specific securities to receive cash now and simultaneously arranging to buy back the securities—repurchase them—at a certain price on a specific day in the future, usually the next day. With this repo transaction, the dealer obtains funds via a short-term collateralized loan. The repurchase price is higher than the selling price, reflecting interest expense. There are also *term repos* that cover a longer period of time, though rarely more than 30 days.

A *reverse repo,* also called a *matched sale-purchase agreement,* is the opposite side of a repo transaction. With a reverse repo, a dealer buys specific securities and simultaneously agrees to sell them back at a certain price on a specified future date.

The Fed's open market operations typically rely on repos and reverse repos to supplement outright purchases and sales of government securities. Repos initiated by the Federal Reserve have the opposite meaning of repos initiated by dealers. With Fed-initiated repos, the Federal Reserve buys securities for cash and simultaneously agrees to resell the securities at a certain price by a specific date in the future.

Municipal and Corporate Bonds

Like the U.S. government, city and state governments also issue longer-term debt instruments. Local governments sell municipal notes and bonds to generate funds to finance new developments and local improvements. Many investors find these municipal securities, often simply called *munis,* particularly attractive because the interest earned is exempt from federal taxes and, in some cases, state and local taxes as well.

Corporations also issue notes and bonds to finance their operations. Corporate issues have features similar to those of municipal and Treasury securities, although the interest received on *corporates* is not exempt from federal, state, or local income taxes.

Corporate bonds and notes typically pay higher interest rates than do benchmark Treasuries with the same maturity because of the increased credit risk. Investors often refer to the yield of the most recently issued, or on-the-run, Treasury of a certain maturity as representing the risk-free rate of return at that maturity. Since U.S. Treasury securities are backed by the full faith and credit of the U.S. government, market participants consider such issues to have zero credit, or default, risk. (Note that "risk free" in this context refers only to credit risk and does not mean freedom from market or other kinds of risk.)

Credit risk, and credit rating, becomes crucial, however, in the very large corporate and municipal securities markets. If the current 10-year Treasury yields 5.90 percent, a given corporate issue with the same maturity might yield 6.80 percent, while another corporation might have to accept 6.95 percent for otherwise similar paper. The 90 basis point spread (a basis point is $\frac{1}{100}$ of a percent) between the 5.90 Treasury yield and the 6.80 corporate yield represents in part the market's estimate of the probability of default, the credit risk, of the corporate issue. And the 15 basis point difference between the yields of the two corporate issues represents the difference between the market's estimates of the creditworthiness of the two firms relative to each other.

To help the market make these determinations, private agencies research and rate municipal, corporate, and sovereign debt (debt secured or guaranteed by a government) instruments according to the issuer's ability to pay back the loan. Three of the most prominent debt-rating agencies—Moody's Investors Service, Standard and Poor's (S&P), and Fitch Ratings—give debt instruments a rating ranging from Aaa or AAA, the best, to C or D, the worst. These agencies determine ratings for thousands of debt instruments by analyzing the history, previous borrowing and repayment records, and other economic factors of the issuers. Ratings are not fixed. If a debt issuer's economic condition changes in the estimation of a rating agency, it adjusts the issuer's credit rating. (See Table 14.4.)

Ratings are important to both borrowers and lenders. Lenders get a snapshot view of the overall financial condition of the firm or municipality they are lending to. Borrowers are rewarded for their financial stability and receive independent verification of their financial condition. Borrowers with high

TABLE 14.4

Debt Ratings

	Moody s	Standard & Poor's	Fitch Ratings
Investment Grade			
Highest quality	Aaa	AAA	AAA
High quality	Aa1, Aa2, Aa3	AA+, AA, AA–	AA+, AA, AA–
Upper medium grade	A1, A2, A3	A+, A, A–	A+, A, A–
Medium grade	Baa1, Baa2, Baa3	BBB+, BBB, BBB–	BBB+, BBB, BBB–
High Yield or "Junk" Debt			
Predominately speculative	Ba1, Ba2, Ba3	BB+, BB, BB–	BB+, BB, BB–
Low grade	B1, B2, B3	B+, B, B–	B+, B, B–
Default likely	Caa1, Caa2, Caa3	CCC+, CCC, CCC–	CCC+, CCC, CCC–
Very speculative	Ca	CC	CC
Lowest quality or in default	C	C D	C DDD, DD, D

credit ratings can sell their debt at lower interest rates than can borrowers with low credit ratings.

Debt Instruments' Price/Yield Relationship

For all conventional debt securities with fixed interest payments, the security's price and its yield are inversely related. That is, when the yield of a fixed-income security rises, the price falls. When the yield falls, the price rises.

This inverse relationship holds because a note's worth is the present value of expected future cash flows. As the discount rate rises, the expected value of future cash flows declines. For example, if current market yields are around 5 percent when a debt security is issued, borrowers issuing a $10,000 face value note would set the coupon rate at 5 percent in order to be competitive in the market. Suppose, however, that as time passes and financial conditions change, market yields rise to 8 percent. If newly issued notes with an 8 percent coupon are paying $800 of interest a year, what happens to the existing 5 percent coupon notes paying $500 a year? To remain competitive in the market, the price of the 5 percent coupon note must fall. (See Fig. 14.6.)

To see why the price of the 5 percent note falls, consider the choice buyers have when purchasing a $10,000 face value note. They can either earn $800 of interest per year by purchasing a newly issued 8 percent coupon note or $500 a year in interest by buying the older 5 percent coupon note. If the two notes were sold at the same price, everyone would buy the newer 8 percent coupon note to get the higher interest payment. Competitive market pressures thus force sellers of the older note to reduce its price to attract buyers.

Several formulas can be used to determine the price of a fixed-rate note when yields change. The simplest (and least precise) of these is current yield—the amount of annual interest receipts divided by the current price of the security. While market participants do not use current yield to value debt instruments, current yield does provide a convenient way to illustrate the inverse relationship between price and yield.

FIGURE 14.6

Price/Yield Inverse Relationship

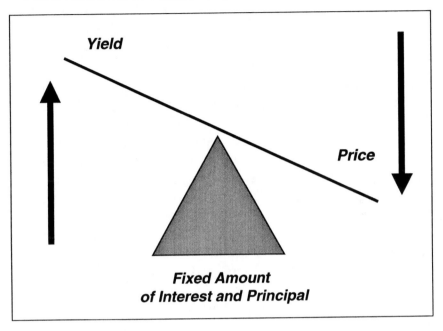

$$\text{Current yield } (Y) = \frac{\text{annual coupon income } (C)}{\text{current price } (P)}$$

Suppose an investor holds a $10,000 note with a 5 percent coupon, and current yield rises to 7.5 percent. The price of the note must fall below $10,000. Using the current yield formula, the note's price falls to $6,666.66.

$$7.5\% = \frac{\$500 \text{ (coupon income on 5\% note)}}{\text{current price } (P)}$$

$$= \frac{\$500}{\$6,666.66}$$

Table 14.5 illustrates the inverse relationship for the 5 percent note at three different yield levels using current yield calculations. Note that the table also shows that increasing and decreasing yield by the same amount results in different changes in price. A 2.5 percent yield increase (from 5 percent to 7.5 percent) causes the price to decrease by $3,333.34 (from $10,000 to $6,666.66), whereas a 2.5 percent yield decrease (from 5 percent to 2.5 percent) causes the price to increase by $10,000 (from $10,000 to $20,000).

This differing price response for the same change in yield suggests the complexity of the inverse relationship. What's more, the magnitude of the differing results also reveals a drawback in the current yield formula—namely, that the formula does not account for key factors such as an instrument's maturity and the timing of coupon payments. Because of this, the market uses a more sophisticated formula called *yield to maturity*.

Yield to maturity (YTM) measures the rate of return an investor receives when holding a fixed-income security to maturity. To measure this effectively, YTM must account for several variables, including time remaining to maturity, the amount and timing of coupon payments and principal repayment, and two other income sources not accounted for in current yield: (1) capital gains or losses (the difference between the price paid for the debt instrument and the amount received at maturity) and (2) the interest earned on reinvested coupons. Yield to maturity assumes that the coupons received are reinvested at the YTM rate.

Yield to maturity is the rate that satisfies the following formula, which appears imposing but is easily calculated with financial calculators. For simplicity, the yield to maturity formula used here accounts for annual coupon payments even

TABLE 14.5

Price/Yield Inverse Relationship at Three Different Levels

Current Yield	Annual Interest Payment of 5 Percent Note	Market Price
2.5%	$500	$20,000.00
5.0% (par)	$500	$10,000.00
7.5%	$500	$6,666.66

though Treasury notes (and bonds) have semiannual coupon payments. The formula becomes more complicated when semiannual payments are used, yet one can calculate YTM either way.

$$P = \frac{C_1}{(1 + \text{YTM})^1} + \frac{C_2}{(1 + \text{YTM})^2} + \ldots + \frac{C_n}{(1 + \text{YTM})^n} + \frac{F}{(1 + \text{YTM})^n}$$

where:

P = price of instrument

C = annual coupon payments

n = number of years to maturity

YTM = yield to maturity

F = face value of instrument

To see how the formula works, consider a $10,000 face value bond with a 10 percent coupon, paying $1,000 annually, and with three years left to maturity. If the bond's yield to maturity is currently 15 percent, an investor would find the price by using the formula:

$$P = \frac{\$1,000}{(1 + .15)^1} + \frac{\$1,000}{(1 + .15)^2} + \frac{\$1,000}{(1 + .15)^3} + \frac{\$10,000}{(1 + .15)^3}$$

In this equation, price equals $8,858.39. (Alternatively, given a target price, investors can use the formula to compute a security's yield to maturity.) The inverse relationship between price and yield thus exists in YTM calculations as well as in current yield calculations. As yields rose from 10 to 15 percent, the price of the bond fell from $10,000 (par value) to $8,858.39.

This inverse relationship depends most heavily on two factors: the instrument's maturity and its coupon. The longer the time to maturity, the greater the effect a yield change has on the price of a security. (See Table 14.6.) For example, given a 30-year T-bond and a 5-year T-note with the same 8 percent coupon, the T-bond will experience a greater price change for a given change in yield. The price of the 5-year T-note would fall by $^{14}\!/_{32}$ if yield increased by 0.1 percent, or 10 basis points, whereas the price of

TABLE 14.6

Yield Change Impact on Price

Maturity	Coupon	Yield	Price	Price Impact of 0.10 Yield Change
5-year T-note	8%	8.00	100-00	
5-year T-note	8%	8.10	99-18	$-^{14}\!/_{32}$
30-year T-bond	8%	8.00	100-00	
30-year T-bond	8%	8.10	98-28	$-^{36}\!/_{32}$

a 30-year T-bond with the same coupon rate would fall by $^{36}\!/_{32}$.* The differing price sensitivity of T-bonds versus T-notes is an important consideration to many traders of yield curve spreads in the cash and futures markets. Traders of 10-year NOBs (notes over bonds), for example, who have positions in both 10-year notes and 30-year bonds frequently weight their positions in each futures contract to adjust for this difference in price sensitivity.

The differing price sensitivity of debt instruments is also evident when comparing coupon rates. (See Table 14.7.) With all else being equal, low-coupon instruments are more sensitive to a given change in yield than are high-coupon instruments. For example, as yields rise 10 basis points, the price of a 10-year T-note with a 2 percent coupon priced at par would fall by $^{29}\!/_{32}$, whereas a 10-year T-note issued when yields were 14 percent would fall by only $^{17}\!/_{32}$.

Yield Curves

Fixed-income analysts study the relationship between yield to maturity and the time to maturity of debt instruments of the same quality using a yield curve graph. By plotting yields

---

* One percent of yield is divided into smaller parts called basis points; 100 basis points equal 1 percent. Note: *basis* used in this context does not refer to the basis between cash and futures prices.

TABLE 14.7

Yield Change Impact on Coupons

Maturity	Coupon	Yield	Price	Price Impact of 0.10 Yield Change
10-year T-note	2%	2.00	100-00	
10-year T-note	2%	2.10	99-03	$-{}^{29}/_{32}$
10-year T-note	14%	14.00	100-00	
10-year T-note	14%	14.10	99-15	$-{}^{17}/_{32}$

against maturities, a yield curve provides a snapshot view of the current interest rate environment. Because the most recently issued Treasury instrument at each maturity provides the benchmark for the pricing of other debt, most yield curve analysis refers to the U.S. Treasury yield curve. Further, the Treasury yield curve serves as a foundation from which other yield curves can be built.

Figure 14.7 illustrates three different yield curve environments. In July 2003, the yield curve was positively sloped, with long-term yields higher than short-term yields. While still exhibiting a positive slope, the yield curve in April 2005 was less steep. Because a positive yield curve is most common, it is often called a *normal yield curve*. But yield curves can also take on other shapes. In April 2000, the yield curve was relatively flat. When a yield curve is flattish, it means that yields held within a narrow range across all maturities. Yield curves can also be negatively sloped, with short-term yields sloped higher than long-term yields. A negatively sloped yield curve is referred to as an *inverted yield curve.*

Financial economists offer several explanations for the shape of a yield curve. Many believe its shape is influenced by the market's expectation of future interest rates. That is, by analyzing a yield curve, one can get an idea of what the market currently expects interest rates to be in the future. Rates extracted from a yield curve and expected to prevail in the future are known as *forward rates*. Forward rates are important for the Eurodol-

FIGURE 14.7

Treasury Yield Curves

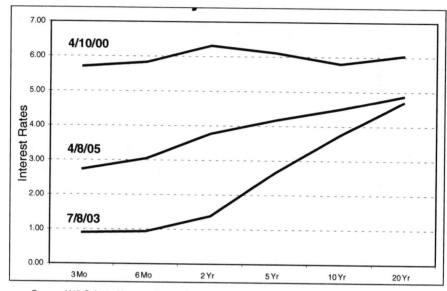

Source: H15 Selected Interest Rates, Board of Governors of the Federal Reserve System.

lar, Treasury bill, and fed funds futures markets because these futures markets price according to the forward rates embedded in the yield curve.

Yield curves shift all the time. Because market yield reflects the current price of credit, yield fluctuates with changes in (1) the behavior of demanders and suppliers of credit, (2) expected inflation/deflation during the life of the loan, and (3) the creditworthiness of the borrower (generally not a factor in Treasury securities). Complicating matters, each of these factors can move in opposing directions with differing intensities, such that the net impact on yield may be difficult to discern.

The competition between those who supply funds and those who demand funds determines the basic "rent" on borrowed money. Changes in the behavior of suppliers and demanders affect the demand and supply of credit and, ultimately, yields. Major suppliers and demanders of funds are households, businesses, governments, and financial intermediaries. In the United

States, businesses and governments are net demanders of funds. Households and financial intermediaries are net suppliers.

For example, businesses may increase spending to upgrade plants and equipment. Or a local park district may face a cut in tax revenues, while its spending remains unchanged. In either case, there would be an increased demand for funds. This demand for additional funds leads to higher yields, provided other economic forces remain constant.

On the supply side, household demographics have an impact on yield. For example, household members may spend most of their income during the early career years, when they are purchasing first homes and starting families. Once careers are established and children raised, spending could be reduced and saving increased. This increase in household saving, other forces remaining constant, increases the supply of funds and leads to lower yields.

The premium paid by borrowers to cover inflationary expectations can also affect yields. That is, increases in expected inflation lead to higher market yields. Decreases in expected inflation lead to reduced market yields.

Because lenders want to be rewarded for lending funds, they build an anticipated inflation premium into lending rates. This premium is in addition to the basic "rent" for lending. If the inflation premium were absent, lenders would see their purchasing power erode. Suppose, for instance, that a lender agrees to a $1,000 one-year loan at 3 percent interest. If inflation rises from an anticipated level of 0 percent to, say, 5 percent, the lender's $1,000 would not have the same purchasing power that it did a year earlier. In fact, the lender needs to receive $1,050 just to get back the same purchasing power.

Futures Markets

The preceding is just an overview of today's debt markets. Yet even an overview reveals the risk exposures faced by debt market participants—exposures that futures and options on futures can help manage. For example, consider the primary dealers who buy Treasury securities in bulk at auction and hold inventories until they can sell the portion they want. Perhaps a dealer's bid is more aggressive than intended, and the dealer acquires more securities than planned in the auction. Suppose, too, that for various business reasons, the primary dealer's usual customers temporarily defer their purchase of securities. The primary dealer thus remains stuck with more securities than it wants and remains dangerously exposed to a decline in Treasury prices. Short hedging with Treasury futures or options can help the dealer manage this exposure and minimize the risk.

Alternatively, consider a municipality planning to issue a note. Perhaps there's a time lag between the time the decision is made to issue the securities and the time the issue is brought to market. Like the primary dealer above, the municipality is exposed to rising rates and falling note prices, an exposure that skillful short hedging with futures or options could help manage until the municipality successfully markets the issue. Selling futures acts as a temporary substitute sale of the note and locks in an issuing price.

The Chicago Board of Trade offers a full spectrum of futures and options on U.S. government debt instruments, including Treasury bond futures and options, 10-, 5-, and 2-year T-note futures and options, and 30-day fed funds futures. The CBOT also offers 5- and 10-year interest rate swap futures and options. The Chicago Mercantile Exchange trades 3-month Eurodollar, Euroyen, and 1-month LIBOR futures and options. Outside the United States, various government debt and other interest rate futures contracts trade actively at Euronext LIFFE, Eurex, Singapore International Monetary Exchange (SIMEX), Tokyo International Financial Futures Exchange, BM&F (Brazil), Sydney Futures Exchange, and other exchanges.

To illustrate the size and diversity of exchange-traded debt futures, Table 14.8 lists a sampling of the most actively traded contracts. Most of these futures contracts also have active options markets.

TABLE 14.8

Major Interest Rate Futures Contracts

Contract	Futures Exchange	Annual Volume in 2004
U.S. Treasury bonds[1]	Chicago Board of Trade	72,949,053
10-year Treasury notes[1]	Chicago Board of Trade	196,119,150
5-year Treasury notes[1]	Chicago Board of Trade	105,469,410
2-year Treasury notes[1]	Chicago Board of Trade	9,454,774
30-day fed funds[1]	Chicago Board of Trade	11,940,120
3-month Eurodollars[2]	Chicago Mercantile Exchange	297,584,038
Interest rate[2]	BM&F (Brazil)	100,290,263
Interest rate – exchange rate swap[2]	BM&F (Brazil)	1,189,805
Euro-Bund[2]	Eurex	239,787,517
Euro-Bobl[2]	Eurex	159,166,394
Euro-Schatz[2]	Eurex	122,928,076
3-month sterling[2]	Euronext LIFFE	51,324,125
3-month Euroswiss[2]	Euronext LIFFE	7,296,932
3-month Euribor[2]	Euronext LIFFE	157,746,684
Long gilt[2]	Euronext LIFFE	14,045,404
Eurodollar[2]	SIMEX	8,241,545
90-day bank bills[2]	Sydney Futures Exchange	14,213,188
3-year Treasury bonds[2]	Sydney Futures Exchange	22,805,279
10-year Treasury bonds[2]	Sydney Futures Exchange	8,557,437
3-month Euroyen[2]	Tokyo International Financial Futures Exchange	7,259,779

[1]Data provided by CBOT.
[2]Data provided by Futures Industry Association, Inc.

EQUITY SECURITIES

Bonds, notes, bills, commercial paper, and other debt instruments provide one way for companies and governments to finance their spending plans. Another major source of funding comes from equity securities.

While some companies are privately held, others are held publicly, meaning that they sell ownership rights—shares of stock—in their firm to the general public. Since stockholders are owners of a company, they can take an active role in the firm's management and prosperity. They elect a board of directors and vote on various company resolutions proposed at the annual shareholders' meeting. By contrast, owners of debt instruments are not entitled to any voting rights.

Along with having a voice in the company, shareholders either reap the benefits of a company's success or experience losses if the company falters. Consequently, unlike debt holders who earn a fixed interest rate on their investment, the rewards of owning stock are limited only by the company's profits. Profitability typically translates into larger stock dividends and increased stock prices, which owners can realize by selling shares. On the other hand, if the company fails and is liquidated, stockholders are paid after all other creditors, including debt holders.

Companies that elect to go public and sell shares of stock do so by conducting an initial public offering (IPO). Through this process, companies sell shares to an initial group of primary shareholders. After the IPO, shares are publicly traded on the various stock exchanges or markets, which are often referred to collectively as the secondary market. These markets are discussed in the following sections.

Exchange versus OTC Trading

Shares of stock trade on "the stock market," which is actually composed of both stock exchanges and organized over-the-counter (OTC) markets such as NASDAQ and electronic communications networks (ECNs). All U.S. equity trading, whether on an exchange or over the counter, is supervised by the Securities and Exchange Commission (SEC).

Stock Exchanges   Stock exchanges have traditionally provided centralized locations where orders to buy and sell shares of stock are executed for individuals and businesses. In the United

States, the oldest and largest stock exchange is the New York Stock Exchange (NYSE), also known as the "Big Board." The NYSE lists more than 2,700 companies with a combined market value in 2004 in excess of $17 trillion. In fact, NYSE companies represent over 80 percent of the U.S. public equity market's total capitalization. Other U.S. stock exchanges include the American Stock Exchange (Amex) in New York and other regional exchanges in Boston, Philadelphia, Cincinnati, and Chicago. In addition to these U.S. stock exchanges, stock exchanges exist in financial market centers throughout the world, including Hong Kong, Tokyo, London, Frankfurt, Paris, Amsterdam, Madrid, Sydney, Taipei, and Sao Paulo, just to name a few.

In the United States, the NYSE and Amex use a specialist trading system that differs from the open auction method of trading used in the futures pit. The specialist, a designated individual or firm, must maintain a fair and orderly market in a specific stock. In maintaining fair and orderly markets, specialists are required to buy stock from sellers if there are no other buyers available or to sell stock to buyers if there are no other sellers. They are not expected to prevent a stock from rising or falling in value. Specialists are also required to disseminate bid and ask prices on a continuous basis.

OTC Markets In addition to stock exchanges, stocks are bought and sold in the OTC markets. Instead of one central location, OTC markets link buyers and sellers through computerized trading systems that match buy and sell orders. These systems are also extensively used for the after-hours trading of equities. OTC markets have traditionally listed small companies. However, in recent years, a number of leading, larger companies have elected to list their companies for trading in the OTC markets instead of on an exchange.

NASDAQ (originally shorthand for the National Association of Securities Dealers Automated Quotation system) is currently the largest U.S. electronic stock market in terms of listings with approximately 3,300 companies. The National Association of Securities Dealers (NASD) owns and operates the NASDAQ system. This screen-based system connects market participants over a telecommunications network. Market makers trade out of their own inventory of stock and have stated responsibilities to continuously post two-sided markets (bids and offers) and buy and sell NASDAQ stocks.

The trading of NASDAQ securities has evolved over the past decade. A key development was the SEC's 1997 implementation of new order handling rules that allowed ECNs to compete directly on the NASDAQ National Market System. ECNs were originally structured to facilitate trading for institutional investors and broker/dealers. Over time, however, ECNs have widened access of their systems to allow for participation by a larger number of institutions as well as individual investors. The key aspect of these networks involves the fact that they allow for direct electronic interaction of buy and sell orders. ECNs feature electronic order books and computerized algorithms to execute trades instead of specialists or floor traders.

Stock trading on the ECNs is primarily geared toward NASDAQ-listed securities. However, a number of the ECNs have been making inroads and have increased their market share in NYSE- and Amex-listed stocks. The leading ECNs currently include Arca, Bloomberg's Tradebook, BRUT, and INET.

Advances in technology and automation have been important drivers in increasing market efficiency, and they have allowed for the growth and expansion of all the major equity markets. Systems that have played key roles include the NYSE's Direct+ and Super Designated Order Turnaround (DOT) system, the Common Message Switch (CMS) at the Amex, and the NASDAQ's Super Montage system.

In recent years, the equity markets have displayed significant growth both in trading volume and in the dollar value of equities traded. In 1985, for example, average daily volume at the NYSE totaled 109.2 million shares with a dollar value of about $3.9 billion. By 1992, average daily volume was 202 million shares, amounting to a dollar value of $6.9 billion. And by 2004, average volume reached almost 1.46 billion shares a day, with a dollar value exceeding $46 billion. On the NASDAQ, trading volume has also displayed tremendous growth as average daily volume has increased from roughly 82 million shares in 1985 to over 1.8 billion shares per day in 2004. (See Table 14.9.)

TABLE 14.9

NYSE and NASDAQ Volume

Year	Stock Market Volume (daily average, millions of shares)		Value Traded (daily average, $ billions)	
	NYSE	NASDAQ	NYSE	NASDAQ
1985	109.2	82.1	$3.9	$0.9
1986	141.0	113.6	$5.4	$1.5
1987	188.9	149.8	$7.4	$2.0
1988	161.5	122.8	$5.4	$1.4
1989	165.5	133.1	$6.1	$1.7
1990	156.8	131.9	$5.2	$1.8
1991	178.9	163.3	$6.0	$2.7
1992	202.3	190.8	$6.9	$3.5
1993	264.5	263.0	$9.0	$5.3
1994	291.4	295.1	$9.7	$5.8
1995	346.1	401.4	$12.2	$9.5
1996	412.0	543.7	$16.0	$13.0
1997	526.9	647.8	$22.8	$17.7
1998	673.6	801.7	$29.0	$22.9
1999	808.9	1,081.8	$35.5	$43.7
2000	1,041.6	1,757.0	$43.9	$80.9
2001	1,240.0	1,900.1	$42.3	$44.1
2002	1,441.0	1,752.8	$40.9	$28.8
2003	1,398.4	1,685.5	$38.5	$28.0
2004	1,456.7	1,801.3	$46.1	$34.6

Source: Investment Company Institute.

Shareholder demographics have changed too. In 1950, according to the Federal Reserve, households, personal trusts, and nonprofit corporations accounted for more than 91 percent of common stock purchases. By 1991, that percentage had declined to 54 percent and went down even further to 40 percent in 1998. Institutions such as public and private pension funds, insurance companies, banks, and mutual funds now invest in equities in ever-increasing numbers. U.S. pension funds and institutions increased their share of stock holdings from 8 percent in 1950 to about 48 percent in 2001.

Quite simply, more and more individual investors now invest in stocks indirectly through mutual funds and other institutional intermediaries rather than directly through a broker. The reason is the growing acceptance of modern portfolio theory—the idea, as it applies to equities, is that asset diversification, or not putting all your eggs in one basket, can reduce the unsystematic risk faced by holders of relatively undiversified portfolios.

Systematic and Unsystematic Risk

There are any number of reasons why a company, once profitable, could face a downtrend. Perhaps the company's visionary dies, the production process the firm uses becomes obsolete, or consumers change their buying patterns. That is why investors typically do not want to invest all their savings in the stock of just one firm. Putting all your eggs in just that basket exposes you to that firm's specific risk.

To avoid firm-specific risk, called *unsystematic risk,* equity owners often hold diversified portfolios. Modern portfolio theory suggests that diversification achieved by holding as few as 20 different company stocks eliminates most firm-specific risk.

In recent years, individual investors have achieved diversification through mutual funds. Mutual funds, first created in the 1920s, pool the funds of individuals or businesses and invest them in a variety of securities to achieve a defined investment objective. Common stock mutual funds offer opportunities to invest in a diversified and professionally managed portfolio of equities with initial investments of as little as $100 and subsequent contributions of $50 to $100. Common stock funds may be international funds that invest in equities of non-U.S. companies, global funds that invest in securities issued in the United States and other countries, or sector funds that invest in a particular group of stocks, such as technology, health care, or financial services.

According to the Investment Company Institute, the group that monitors the mutual fund industry, there were a total of 1,528 mutual funds with $495.4 billion in assets and more than 34 million shareholder accounts in 1985. By 1996, there were 6,293 mutual funds with $3.53 trillion in assets distributed among 151 million shareholder accounts. In 2004, the number of mutual funds totaled 8,046 with $8.1 trillion in assets. These 2004 totals include not only 4,551 stock funds but also 3,495 funds specializing in debt securities, including bond and money market funds. Money market mutual funds invest in short-term debt securities that offer stability of principal and current market yields. Bond funds invest in fixed-income securities that typically pay higher interest rates than do short-term money market instruments. (See Table 14.10.)

Stock Indexes

Holding a diversified portfolio helps people manage firm-specific risk, but even the diversified portfolio holder remains exposed to the general, overall volatility of the market, referred to as *systematic risk*. In many instances, the value of a portfolio is based on how the stock market or a particular group of stocks moves. To track general market direction, a number of market averages or indexes have emerged to allow continuous monitoring of the stock market's overall movement. To hedge against systematic

TABLE 14.10

U.S. Mutual Fund Industry Total Net Assets ($ Billions)

| End of Year | Total | Long-Term Funds | | | Money Market Funds |
		Equity Funds	Hybrid Funds	Bond Funds	
1984	$370.68	$79.73	$11.15	$46.24	$233.55
1985	$495.39	$111.33	$17.61	$122.65	$243.80
1986	$715.67	$154.45	$25.76	$243.31	$292.15
1987	$769.17	$175.45	$29.25	$248.37	$316.10
1988	$809.37	$189.38	$26.35	$255.69	$337.95
1989	$980.67	$245.04	$35.64	$271.90	$428.09
1990	$1,065.19	$239.48	$36.12	$291.25	$498.34
1991	$1,393.19	$404.73	$52.23	$393.78	$542.44
1992	$1,642.54	$514.09	$78.04	$504.21	$546.19
1993	$2,069.96	$740.67	$144.50	$619.48	$565.32
1994	$2,155.32	$852.76	$164.40	$527.15	$611.00
1995	$2,811.29	$1,249.08	$210.33	$598.87	$753.02
1996	$3,525.80	$1,726.01	$252.58	$645.41	$901.81
1997	$4,468.20	$2,368.02	$317.11	$724.18	$1,058.89
1998	$5,525.21	$2,977.94	$365.00	$830.59	$1,351.68
1999	$6,846.34	$4,041.89	$378.81	$812.49	$1,613.15
2000	$6,964.67	$3,961.92	$346.28	$811.19	$1,845.28
2001	$6,974.95	$3,418.16	$346.32	$925.12	$2,285.35
2002	$6,390.36	$2,662.46	$325.49	$1,130.45	$2,271.96
2003	$7,414.40	$3,684.16	$430.47	$1,247.77	$2,052.00
2004	$8,106.87	$4,384.08	$519.29	$1,290.32	$1,913.19

Data for funds that invest in other mutual funds were excluded from the series.
Components may not add to the total because of rounding.

Source: Investment Company Institute.

market risk, portfolio managers have turned to futures and options contracts based on these different stock indexes.

The most familiar stock indexes are the Dow Jones Industrial Average (DJIA) (see Table 14.11) and the Standard & Poor's 500 (S&P 500). Others include the New York Stock Exchange Composite, the NASDAQ Composite, the Russell 2000, and the

TABLE 14.11

Components of the Dow Jones Industrial Average

Company Name	Primary Exchange	Ticker	Subsector
3M Co.	New York	MMM	Diversified Industrials
Alcoa Inc.	New York	AA	Aluminum
Altria Group Inc.	New York	MO	Tobacco
American Express Co.	New York	AXP	Consumer Finance
American International Group Inc.	New York	AIG	Full Line Insurance
AT&T, Inc.	New York	T	Fixed Line Telecommunications
Boeing Co.	New York	BA	Aerospace
Caterpillar Inc.	New York	CAT	Commercial Vehicles & Trucks
Citigroup Inc.	New York	C	Banks
Coca-Cola Co.	New York	KO	Soft Drinks
E.I. DuPont de Nemours & Co.	New York	DD	Commodity Chemicals
Exxon Mobil Corp.	New York	XOM	Integrated Oil & Gas
General Electric Co.	New York	GE	Diversified Industrials
General Motors Corp.	New York	GM	Automobiles
Hewlett-Packard Co.	New York	HPQ	Computer Hardware
Home Depot Inc.	New York	HD	Home Improvement Retailers
Honeywell International Inc.	New York	HON	Diversified Industrials
Intel Corp.	NASDAQ	INTC	Semiconductors
International Business Machines Corp.	New York	IBM	Computer Services
Johnson & Johnson	New York	JNJ	Pharmaceuticals
JPMorgan Chase & Co.	New York	JPM	Banks
McDonald's Corp.	New York	MCD	Restaurants & Bars
Merck & Co. Inc.	New York	MRK	Pharmaceuticals
Microsoft Corp.	NASDAQ	MSFT	Software
Pfizer Inc.	New York	PFE	Pharmaceuticals
Procter & Gamble Co.	New York	PG	Nondurable Household Products
United Technologies Corp.	New York	UTX	Aerospace
Verizon Communications Inc.	New York	VZ	Fixed Line Telecommunications
Wal-Mart Stores Inc.	New York	WMT	Broadline Retailers
Walt Disney Co.	New York	DIS	Broadcasting & Entertainment

Wilshire 5000. Outside the United States, the most familiar indexes include the Nikkei 225 Stock Average, the Financial Times Stock Index 100 (FT-SE, pronounced "footsie"), the Deutsche Antienindex (DAX), and the EuroStoxx 50. All of these are quoted daily in the financial press.

How a particular index tracks the market depends on the index's composition, that is, the sample of stocks chosen from the universe of stocks, the weighting of the individual stocks, and the method of averaging. When selecting a sample of stocks for an index, the aim is to choose stocks whose aggregate price movement reflects, as closely as possible, the overall movement of the market or some specific market segment. After selecting these stocks, the index constructor must then decide how to appropriately weight each stock's influence on the index.

Some indexes, such as the Dow Jones Industrial Average (DJIA), are price-weighted. That is, the prices of all component stocks are added and divided by a divisor. The divisor is used to maintain the comparability of the average over time. By adjusting the divisor, the effects of stock splits, divestitures, mergers, stock dividends, and changes in the component stocks are offset so that the index reflects only the effects of price changes. With price-weighted indexes, a 1 percent change in the price of a lower-priced stock causes a smaller movement in the average than does a 1 percent change in the price of a higher-priced stock.

With capitalization-weighted indexes, such as the S&P 500, the impact of a single stock's price change is proportional to its market capitalization as compared with the total market capitalization of all stocks in the index. A stock's market capitalization is the share price multiplied by the number of outstanding shares. So, a 1 percent price change in larger capitalization issues, called *large caps,* has more impact on the index than a 1 percent price change in smaller capitalization issues, or *small caps.* In fact, the top 10 stocks in the S&P 500 alone account for about 24 percent of the overall index. (See Table 14.12.)

TABLE 14.12

Major U.S. Stock Indexes

Name of Index	Weighting Method	Futures/Options on the Index
Dow Jones Industrial Average (DJIA)	Price-weighted average of 30 blue-chip securities	DJIA futures, DJIA futures options, mini-sized Dow futures, mini-sized Dow futures options
Standard & Poor's 500 (S&P 500)	Capitalization-weighted index of 500 common stocks	S&P 500 futures, S&P 500 futures options, E-Mini S&P 500 futures, and E-Mini S&P 500 futures options
NASDAQ 100	Capitalization-weighted index of 100 of the largest nonfinancial stocks traded on NASDAQ	NASDAQ 100 futures, NASDAQ 100 futures options, E-Mini NASDAQ 100 futures, and E-Mini NASDAQ 100 futures options
Russell 2000	Capitalization-weighted index of 2,000 of the smallest U.S. stocks based on market capitalization.	Russell 2000 futures, Russell 2000 futures options, E-Mini Russell 2000 futures, and E-Mini Russell 2000 futures options

Futures Markets

A diversified portfolio helps equity owners manage unsystematic risk. But even a diversified portfolio holder remains exposed to the general volatility of the market. If, for example, the overall market—as measured by the DJIA or the S&P 500—falls, then even individuals and institutions holding diversified portfolios would see the value of their holdings decline.

Those with a bearish outlook could sell stocks to avoid the anticipated decline. But this entails disassembling a portfolio built through careful evaluation and the timely purchase of hundreds of individual securities, as well as incurring brokerage costs and the costs associated with the bid-ask spread. Selling large blocks of stock, as an institutional investor might, can even move the market lower as the sale occurs.

Alternately, many portfolio managers have learned from experience that specific equities have price movements that go counter to the market's trend. Thus, a market bear could reorient the allocation of new funds (reinvestment of dividends or pension fund contributions or inflow of insurance premiums) toward the purchase of those equities that rise in price when the market trends downward and actually benefit from a market decline. Yet such a portfolio would be adversely affected by a market rise. Exposure to market volatility still remains.

Portfolio managers need a tool to manage their exposure to the general trend of the market—the systematic risk. Stock index futures provide this by giving equity owners a useful way to manage their exposure to the systematic risk inherent in their cash market positions. By selling stock index futures to protect against a market decline, portfolio owners can keep their portfolios intact while managing their market exposure. Any decline in the value of the portfolios would be more or less offset by the corresponding gain on the short stock index futures position.

Stock index futures also provide portfolio managers with a flexible tool for when the market is expected to rise. Consider an insurance company that thinks the equity market will rise before it receives its premium inflow for the month. Lacking the cash, it cannot acquire the stocks that it believes are "good values" now. Yet the company can buy stock index futures now, thus giving it "synthetic" exposure to the market that allows it to participate in the expected market rise. When the premiums flow in, the company can then purchase the actual stocks it wants and unwind its futures position.

Or suppose that a mutual fund company has a large amount of cash now and is very bullish. But it believes that the size of its purchases in the cash market would have too large an impact and move prices higher, eroding some of the gain it anticipates from buying the securities. The company could instead buy futures. Positioned for the anticipated major market move up through its long futures position, the company can acquire cash securities slowly, thus minimizing its impact on the cash price.

Stock and bond index futures can be combined as well to manage the exposure of a combined portfolio. Suppose a portfolio manager has a portfolio allocated 65 percent to bonds and 35 percent to equities but believes that stocks will outperform bonds in the coming year. The manager could sell bonds and buy stocks in their respective cash markets. Or, using futures, the manager could modify the portfolio's exposure to a 50-50 debt-equity allocation—even while keeping the cash portfolio intact—by selling bond futures and buying stock index futures.

TABLE 14.13

Major Equity Index Futures Contracts

Contract	Futures Exchange	Annual Volume in 2004
Mini-Dow[1]	Chicago Board of Trade	20,695,848
S&P 500 Index[2]	Chicago Mercantile Exchange	16,175,584
E-Mini S&P 500[2]	Chicago Mercantile Exchange	167,202,962
NASDAQ 100[2]	Chicago Mercantile Exchange	4,011,983
E-Mini NASDAQ 100[2]	Chicago Mercantile Exchange	77,168,513
E-Mini Russell 2000[2]	Chicago Mercantile Exchange	17,121,233
DJ Euro STOXX 50[2]	Eurex	121,661,944
CAC 40 10 Euro[2]	Euronext (Paris)	24,058,528
KOSPI 200[2]	Korea Futures Exchange[3]	55,608,856
Nikkei 225[2]	SIMEX	7,769,675
TAIEX Futures[2]	Taiwan Futures Exchange	8,861,278
Hang Seng Index[2]	Hong Kong Exchange & Clearing[4]	8,601,559
Nikkei 225[2]	Osaka Securities Exchange	14,415,884
TOPIX Stock Index[2]	Tokyo Stock Exchange	10,305,318

[1]Data provided by CBOT.

[2]Data provided by Futures Industry Association, Inc.

[3]These contracts were transferred from the Korea Stock Exchange as of January 2, 2004, and now trade on KFE.

[4]Hong Kong Exchange & Clearing Derivatives Unit (HKFE & HKSE).

The Chicago Board of Trade offers futures and options on futures on the Dow Jones Industrial Average as well as on mini-sized Dow futures and options. The Chicago Mercantile Exchange lists large-sized and mini-sized futures and option contracts on a number of indexes including the S&P 500, Nikkei 225 Stock Average, NASDAQ 100, and the Russell 2000. Stock index futures and options trade actively around the world as well, at such exchanges as the BM&F (Brazil), Korea Futures Exchange, Singapore International Monetary Exchange (SIMEX), Osaka Securities Exchange, Tokyo Stock Exchange, Eurex, and others.

Table 14.13 contains a sampling of several of the largest equity index futures contracts traded throughout the world. In most cases, options are also actively traded on these futures contracts.

FOREIGN EXCHANGE

The foreign exchange market, also called the forex or FX market, is the world's largest financial market. Operating virtually around the clock, the forex market trades enormous amounts of money. In 2004, daily transaction volume, worldwide, amounted to roughly $1.9 trillion in U.S.-dollar equivalents.

Unlike a futures exchange with a central location bringing buyers and sellers together, the forex market is an over-the-counter market where buyers and sellers conduct business linked by telephones, computers, and other means of communication. Participants include corporations, commercial banks (money center and regional), pension funds, and investment banking firms.

Quite simply, foreign exchange is the exchange of one country's currency for another's. When individuals or companies from one country trade across borders, they need foreign currency. For example, when a U.S. importer buys French wine, either the importer must buy euros to pay the French merchant or the French merchant must accept U.S. dollars and convert them to euros.

Exchange Rates

International trade directly affects the rate of exchange between currencies—the price of one currency in terms of another. In the cash market, exchange rates between the U.S. dollar and foreign currencies are generally quoted in European terms. This method measures the amount of foreign currency needed to buy one U.S. dollar, that is, foreign currency units per dollar. The other method used to quote exchange rates is the reciprocal of European terms, which measures the U.S.-dollar value of one foreign currency unit, that is, dollars per foreign currency unit.

For example, if the European-terms quote is 0.7705 euros (or €) per $1, or €0.7705:$1, then the reciprocal of European terms quote is $1.2979 per euro ($1.2979:€1). The reciprocal of European quote is the method used by the U.S. futures exchanges where most foreign currency futures trade. Also, the British pound is usually quoted in reciprocal of European terms.

Knowing whether the rate of exchange is quoted in reciprocal of European terms or European terms is crucial in determining whether the value of one currency has risen or fallen in relation to another. Suppose it takes $1.8678 to buy one British pound (£), but a week later it takes $2.0000 to buy one British pound. Has the value of the dollar risen or fallen? The dollar has fallen in value, either because it takes more dollars to buy one British pound (the dollar/pound ratio rose from $1.8678:£1 to $2.0000:£1) or because it takes fewer pounds to buy $1 (the pound/dollar ratio fell from £0.5354 to £0.5000). While both statements are correct, the first one quotes the exchange rate in reciprocal of European terms, whereas the second quotes the exchange rate in European terms.

Analyzing exchange rates as the price of a currency suggests that competitive market forces—supply and demand—determine exchange rates. This type of free market environment in foreign exchange is often referred to as a floating exchange rate environment. In a *floating exchange rate environment,* the exchange rate responds to many factors, such as imports and exports, capital flows, and relative inflation rates. At times, however, government policies limit these exchange rate fluctuations.

One factor affecting the exchange rate between the U.S. dollar and other currencies is the merchandise trade balance. By definition, the *merchandise trade balance* is the net difference between the value of a country's merchandise imports and its exports. For example, consider the market for Japanese yen and the yen's rate of exchange. The United States imports products from Japan. To pay for them, Americans need Japanese yen. On the other hand, the Japanese want American-made goods and supply Japanese yen to the foreign exchange market to acquire U.S. dollars.

The U.S. demand for Japanese goods and services thus contributes to the demand for Japanese yen, while Japanese purchases of American goods and services contribute to the supply of Japanese yen. In this case, the net difference between U.S. purchases of Japanese goods and services and Japanese purchases of American goods and services is the merchandise trade balance between the two countries. Table 14.14 provides trade data for leading trading partners with the United States in 2004.

The flow of funds between countries to pay for stock and bond purchases also contributes to the foreign exchange rate. In the near term, these capital flows are greatly influenced by yield differentials. For example, all else being equal, the higher the yield on German securities compared to U.S. securities, the more attractive German securities are relative to U.S. securities and the less attractive U.S. securities are relative to German securities. An increase in German yields would tend to raise the flow of U.S. funds into German securities as well as decrease the outflow of German funds to U.S. securities. Combined, this increased flow of funds into Germany increases demand for the euro and would raise the value of the euro and, therefore, the dollar:euro ratio.

The rate of inflation is another factor influencing exchange rates. People try to avoid the eroding effect inflation has on their

TABLE 14.14

Total Trade with the United States, 2004 ($ Billion)

Rank	Country	Exports	Imports	Total, All Trade	Percent of Total Trade
—	Total, All Countries	$819.0	$1,471.0	$2,289.6	100.0%
—	Total, Top 15 Countries	$614.2	$1,107.1	$1,721.3	75.2%
1	Canada	$190.2	$255.9	$446.1	19.5%
2	Mexico	$110.8	$155.8	$266.6	11.6%
3	China	$34.7	$196.7	$231.4	10.1%
4	Japan	$54.4	$129.6	$184.0	8.0%
5	Federal Republic of Germany	$31.4	$77.2	$108.6	4.7%
6	United Kingdom	$36.0	$46.4	$82.4	3.6%
7	Korea, South	$26.3	$46.2	$72.5	3.2%
8	Taiwan	$21.7	$34.6	$56.3	2.5%
9	France	$21.2	$31.8	$53.1	2.3%
10	Malaysia	$10.9	$28.2	$39.1	1.7%
11	Italy	$10.7	$28.1	$38.8	1.7%
12	Netherlands	$24.3	$12.6	$36.9	1.6%
13	Ireland	$8.2	$27.4	$35.6	1.6%
14	Brazil	$13.9	$21.2	$35.0	1.5%
15	Singapore	$19.6	$15.3	$34.9	1.5%

Source: Foreign Trade Division, U.S. Census Bureau, Washington, D.C.

purchasing power. Consequently, investments in countries with lower inflation become more attractive than investments in countries with higher inflation. In turn, currency from the lower inflation country rises in value, while the currency from the higher inflation country falls in value. If the United States is experiencing lower inflation than its trading partner Japan, for instance, the dollar:yen ratio falls to reflect the growing price level in Japan relative to the United States. This fact is rooted in the concept of purchasing power parity, which holds that, over the long run, an exchange rate adjusts to reflect the difference in price levels between countries.

Exchange Rate Risk

All these examples illustrate how exchange rates can float in the foreign exchange market. They also hint that free-floating exchange rates create risk. For example, when a U.S. wine merchant contracts to buy 1,000 cases of French wine, the merchant may agree to pay in euros, say €50 per case, when the vintage is ready for shipment in two years. Over the next two years, the value of the dollar could drop from $1.2980:€1 to $1.3500:€1, thereby raising the price of each case from $64.90 to $67.50. Pricing the wine in euros exposes the U.S. wine merchant to exchange rate risk.

Of course, the wine could be priced in dollars at $64.90 per case. This relieves the U.S. merchant from foreign exchange rate risk, but now the French wine producer would be hurt if the value of the dollar fell from $1.2980:€1 to $1.3500:€1. Instead of receiving €50 per case, the producer would only receive €48.0741 per case.

Because of these risks, governments throughout history have intervened to fix exchange rates. In 1944, Western world leaders met in Bretton Woods, New Hampshire, to create the International Monetary Fund to cope with world economic and financial problems that arose following the Great Depression and World War II. As part of the agreement, the value of the U.S. dollar, the world's leading currency at the time, was set at $\frac{1}{35}$ of an ounce of gold. And world central banks were called upon to keep the exchange rates of their currencies pegged to the dollar's gold content, with variations limited to plus or minus 1 percent. (See Fig. 14.8.)

Since 1944, world leaders have made various attempts to exert at least some control over exchange rates. Following the demise of the Bretton Woods Agreement in the early 1970s, exchange rates floated more or less freely until the early 1980s, when central bankers and treasury officials meeting at the Plaza Hotel in New York crafted the Plaza Accord. But that, too, proved ineffective and has long since disappeared from the scene. Volatility in the currency market continues.

FIGURE 14.8

U.S. Dollar versus Euro, Pound, and Yen (divided by 100)

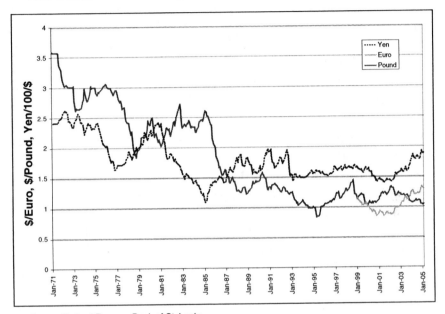

Source: Federal Reserve Bank of St. Louis.

European Union

More recently, the European Union has tried to regulate exchange rates within that community of nations as a prelude to the European Monetary Union (EMU) and the introduction of a common currency—the euro.

The European monetary system (EMS) was established in 1978 to create "a zone of monetary stability" to help member nations limit exchange rate volatility, control inflation, and coordinate exchange rate policy relative to non-EMS currencies like the U.S. dollar. Essentially, each EMS member currency had to trade within bands (a predetermined standard range) plus or minus 15 percent of defined parity. The reference currency had been the deutsche mark. Should a currency drift beyond those limits, the countries involved had to intervene to return the errant member to its proper course.

But, as with earlier attempts to fix exchange rates, the EMS encountered difficulties. The summer of 1992, for example, saw remarkable volatility in the deutsche mark. Britain, Italy, and Spain all violated the EMS discipline. Several countries experienced devastating currency devaluation and interest rate shocks. Ultimately, Britain dropped out.

After a period of recovery from that trauma, the EMU renewed its focus and pushed toward the widespread adoption of the euro as its official currency. History was made on January 1, 1999, when 11 of the countries established conversion rates between the euro and their respective currencies and created a monetary union with a single currency—the euro. The original 11 member states included Belgium, Germany, Spain, France, Ireland, Italy, Luxembourg, the Netherlands, Austria, Portugal, and Finland. Greece became the twelfth member to officially add the euro on January 1, 2001.

On January 1, 2002, 144 billion of euro currency notes and coins were put into general circulation by the central banks of the 12 participating countries. Concurrent with this, each member country started to withdraw its respective currency notes and coins from circulation and established a transition period of dual circulation. During this period, the public could exchange their national currency for euros or spend it on goods and services.

Futures Markets

Firms exposed to foreign exchange rate risk have turned both to the forex market and to currency futures markets to manage exchange rate risks. In customized forex market transactions, both parties negotiate and agree on the rate of exchange and other terms in what is essentially a forward contract. Market participation is limited to very large customers. On the other hand, currency futures contracts are, like all futures contracts, standardized and remain open to anyone who needs a vehicle to hedge currency risk. Futures also provide a formal clearing process in which accounts are settled daily.

TABLE 14.15

Major Currency Futures Contracts

Contract	Futures Exchange	Annual Volume in 2004
British pound	Chicago Mercantile Exchange	4,676,512
Canadian dollar	Chicago Mercantile Exchange	5,611,328
Euro FX	Chicago Mercantile Exchange	20,456,672
Japanese yen	Chicago Mercantile Exchange	7,395,322
U.S. dollar	BM&F (Brazil)	23,943,757

Source: Data provided by Futures Industry Association, Inc.

The Chicago Mercantile Exchange trades a number of currency futures and options contracts including the euro, Australian dollar, Brazilian real, British pound, Canadian dollar, Russian ruble, Japanese yen, Mexican peso, and Swiss franc. The FINEX, a division of the New York Board of Trade, trades a variety of cross-rate and U.S. dollar–based currency futures and options contracts as well as U.S. Dollar Index futures and options. Outside the United States, U.S.-dollar contracts are traded at the BM&F (Brazil) and the Mercado a Termino de Buenos Aires (MATBA). (See Table 14.15.)

FURTHER READING

Burghardt, Galen, *The Eurodollar Futures and Options Handbook*. New York: McGraw-Hill, 2003.

Choudhry, Moorad, *Analysing and Interpreting the Yield Curve*. New York: John Wiley & Sons, 2004.

Choudhry, Moorad, *Bond and Money Markets: Strategy, Trading, Analysis*. Boston: Butterworth-Heinemann, 2001.

Dailger, Robert, *Financial Futures and Options Markets: Concepts and Strategies*. New York: HarperCollins, 1994.

Fabozzi, Frank J., *The Handbook of Financial Instruments*. New York: John Wiley & Sons, 2002.

Fabozzi, Frank J., *The Handbook of Fixed Income Securities,* 7th ed. New York: McGraw-Hill, 2005.

Powers, Mark, and Mark Castelino, *Inside the Financial Futures Market,* 3d ed. New York: Wiley & Sons, 1991.

Ray, Christina I., *The Bond Market: Trading and Risk Management.* New York: McGraw Hill, 1992.

Riehl, Heinz, *Managing Risk in the Foreign Exchange, Money and Derivative Markets.* New York: McGraw-Hill, 1998.

Stigum, Marcia, *The Money Market,* 3d ed. New York: McGraw-Hill, 1989.

INFORMATION SOURCES

Dow Jones & Company	www.djindexes.com
Economic Report of the President	www.access.gpo.gov/eop
Federal Reserve Bank of St. Louis	www.stls.frb.org
Federal Reserve System Board of Governors	www.federalreserve.gov
Fedstats	www.fedstats.gov
Investment Company Institute	www.ici.org
Oanda: The Currency Site	www.oanda.com
U.S. Census Bureau	www.census.gov
U.S. Department of the Treasury	www.ustreas.gov

CHAPTER 15

Metals Markets: Gold, Silver, Copper, Platinum

Futures contracts in gold, silver, copper, and the platinum group of metals trade on various commodity exchanges throughout the United States and the world. This chapter covers the supply, demand, current production, known reserves, and U.S. government policies for each of these metals.

GOLD

Gold is used primarily for jewelry and monetary investment purposes, with jewelry accounting for roughly 80 percent of demand worldwide in 2003. Because of its predominant usage, gold is regarded as a precious metal rather than an industrial metal.

Gold does, however, have industrial qualities—malleability, ductility, reflectivity, resistance to corrosion, and unparalleled ability as a thermal and electrical conductor. Because of these qualities, gold is used to a small extent (about 400 metric tons annually) in electronic and industrial applications, such as plating salts for electronic contacts; fine gold wire or strips to connect transistors and integrated circuits; printed circuit boards to link electronic components; dental fillings; and decorative plating for costume jewelry, watch cases, pens and pencils, eyeglass frames, bathroom fittings, china, and glass.

The Gold Exchange Standard

Gold has been used for domestic and international exchange for centuries. But it was not until the mid-nineteenth century that gold became the formal exchange standard for modern governments. In modern history, the first formal monetary role for gold was established in 1816 when England made the gold sovereign its primary monetary unit. Soon the economies of many nations were based on the gold standard, including the United States, as provided for by the U.S. Coinage Act of 1873.

The gold standard system, in its pure form, specified that payments between nations be made in gold, either bullion or coins. The system worked until World War I when Britain suspended payments in gold. The United States sought to continue the gold standard, but the economic strains of war prevailed and eventually caused the United States to abandon gold as its means of international settlement.

In 1922, the United States modified the pure gold standard by creating the gold exchange standard, which allowed international payments to be made in both gold and U.S. dollars. The system worked because the United States continued to honor its commitment to redeem the dollar in gold on demand.

By 1931, however, in the midst of worldwide economic depression, Britain came off the gold standard entirely. Two years later, to lend stability to U.S. banks, President Franklin Roosevelt broke the link between the dollar and gold by banning gold ownership for monetary purposes and the public exporting of gold bullion. Two years later, in 1933, the United States changed its official price of gold from $20 an ounce—a level at which it had been since 1869—to $35 an ounce, the level at which it remained until 1971.

Economic depression gave way to World War II and, by the war's close, a completely new system of international exchange.

During the war, the world's major trading nations, anticipating the severe economic and financial problems that would follow the conflict, met at Bretton Woods, New Hampshire, to deal with separate proposals by the United States, Great Britain, Canada, and France for a new international system of payments. There, in July 1944 the International Monetary Fund (IMF) was created as a compromise between U.S. and British plans. Central to this system, which functioned until the early 1970s, was the concept that each IMF member nation's currency would have a par value related to the gold value of the U.S. dollar.

Throughout most of the 1950s, the Bretton Woods system worked comparatively well, despite the economic disruption of the Korean War and the Suez crisis. Less-developed nations, however, often faced a chronic shortage of money, because they tended to spend more for imports than they generated from their exports.

Yet, in the 1960s, the economies of the less-developed nations strengthened. At the same time, the United States began to experience a slight balance-of-payments deficit rather than a surplus, as U.S. foreign expenditures outdistanced export income. (A trade deficit occurs when a nation's foreign purchases exceed its foreign sales.)

In 1968, a two-tier gold market started. Gold had both an official price of $35 an ounce, to be used in all international settlements, and a free market price, to be used in all other transactions. At the same time, the Special Drawing Right (SDR) was created as a new international medium of exchange. SDRs were issued by the IMF to its member nations. Initially, SDRs were priced at 35 SDRs per ounce of gold, reflecting the price of gold at the time. After 1973, the link to gold was severed, and SDRs were based on a weighted value of member-nation currencies.

Yet U.S. inflation and balance-of-payments deficits continued to worsen. As a result, in the spring of 1971, the United States suspended converting dollars to gold bullion and formally devalued the dollar to $\frac{1}{38}$ of an ounce of gold, thus raising the official price of gold to $38 an ounce.

With the balance-of-payments deficit approaching $6 billion in 1973, the United States again devalued the dollar to $\frac{1}{42}$ of an ounce of gold and applied the resulting official value of gold to international payments between central banks. The old order could not hold. On December 31, 1974, the United States lifted its ban on the ownership of gold bullion by private citizens, and the first gold futures contract began trading.

From 1975 through 1979, the IMF and U.S. Treasury continued efforts to eliminate the use of gold as a monetary standard. Both, for example, increased gold sales significantly during this period. In 1978, official gold sales accounted for 20 percent of total world gold supplies, compared to 1971 when official gold sales accounted for only 7 percent of total supplies.

In 1982, the question of gold's role in the international monetary system received attention once more with the formation of the Gold Commission by President Reagan. This panel voted against any move to return to the gold standard.

Official gold sales picked up again in 1997, as governments shifted even further away from the traditional notion of gold as the medium of international exchange and store of value (held in defense of inflation). Faced with strict eligibility requirements for European Monetary Union membership, for instance, European governments either sold or weighed plans to sell their large gold reserves to pay down their debt. And the Australian central bank announced in July 1997 that it had sold two-thirds of its gold reserves, 167 metric tons, to buy higher-yielding U.S., German, and Japanese government securities. Despite these sales, governments continue to hold about one-quarter of all gold in existence. (See Fig. 15.1.)

World Supply and Demand

Gold derives at least part of its value from its scarcity. In the last 6,000 years, only a little over 150,000 metric tons of gold have been mined, and more than 60 percent of that since 1950.

Total gold production averages about only 2,600 metric tons annually. South Africa is the world's largest producer of gold,

FIGURE   15.1

World Official Gold Holdings, October 2004

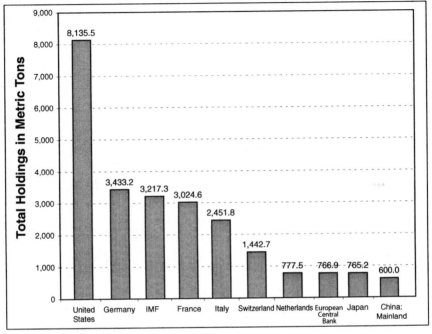

Source: World Gold Council.

mining 363 metric tons in 2003, which was a decline of more than 25 percent since 1996. In fact, gold accounts for 14 percent of South Africa's exports. The United States is the second largest producer, mining 285 metric tons, mostly from Nevada. Australia, the third largest producer, mined 284 tons in 2003. China, Peru, Russia, and Indonesia are also large gold producers.

In 2003, the total gold supply came to an estimated 3,865 metric tons—2,302 from mine production, 617 from net official sales, and 945 from gold scrap. Net official sales and gold scrap account for an increasing share of the supply, while mine production has declined because of a variety of factors, including the increasing difficulty in attracting financing for marginal properties and the depletion, scaling back, or closing of older mines, which offsets gains in new capacity elsewhere.

Gold prices, having fallen significantly in real terms since the early 1970s, have also affected gold producers. In South Africa, for instance, gold output continues to decline, in part because of low gold prices. One expert noted that with gold at $320 an ounce, fully 60 percent of South Africa's mines could be classified as either economically marginal or loss-making. Although many mines have adapted to lower prices through production cost reductions, the savings gained have often been accompanied by lower production.

Demand for gold has declined somewhat since peaking in the mid-1990s. In 2002, total demand hit 3,415 metric tons, down from 1997's record 4,190 tons. Gold jewelry fabrication accounted for 80 percent of the total demand. Electronic and industrial applications accounted for about 10 percent of the

FIGURE 15.2

CBOT Nearby Mini Gold Futures Price, October 1, 2001– June 16, 2005

*2001 high and low settlement prices are based on October 1–December 31.
**2005 high and low settlement prices are based on January 3–June 16.
Source: CBOT Market Data.

TABLE 15.1

Major Gold Futures and Options Contracts

Contract	Futures Exchange	Annual Volume in 2004
Gold futures	COMEX (New York)	14,959,617
Gold options	COMEX (New York)	4,667,523
Gold futures	Tokyo Commodity Exchange	17,385,766
Gold options	Tokyo Commodity Exchange	64,308

Source: Data provided by Futures Industry Association, Inc.

total. Investment demand represented 10 percent, rebounding from 4 percent in 2000, as world political tensions rose. (See Fig. 15.2.)

The United States is the world's second largest market for gold, behind India. U.S. gold consumption in 2002 was 431 metric tons, up by 16 percent from 1997. Jewelry manufacturers were by far the largest gold consumers, accounting for 90 percent of all U.S. gold consumption in 2003. In fact, demand from the U.S. gold jewelry industry has grown steadily from 1997 to 2002.

Futures Markets

Futures and options markets in gold are conducted at the New York Mercantile Exchange's COMEX division and the BM&F (Brazil). Additionally, the Chicago Board of Trade and the Tokyo Commodity Exchange trade gold futures. (See Table 15.1.)

SILVER

Silver has been used in coins, ornaments, and jewelry for centuries. Times have changed, though. Now these uses account for considerably less than half of total world silver consumption. Today, the electronics and photography industries consume most of the world's silver, taking commercial advantage of its light sensitivity, malleability, ductility, high electrical and thermal conductivity, and resistance to corrosion.

World Supply and Demand

Mine production is the primary source of silver, with most of the silver recovered as a by-product of mining other metals such as copper, gold, lead, nickel, and zinc. As a result, the demand and price of these other metals directly influences the amount of silver produced and, in turn, silver's price. An important but smaller percentage of silver is produced by mines in which silver is the main product.

Estimated total world production of silver reached 596 million ounces in 2003. Mexico, the world's leading silver producer, produced about 16 percent of the world total. Peru produced more than 15 percent, while the United States produced about 7 percent, mostly from Nevada, Idaho, and Arizona. Australia, China, Poland, Chile, Russia, and Canada are major producers as well. (See Fig. 15.3.)

World consumption of silver in 2003, at 859 million ounces, exceeded total production. Inventories covered the production deficit. Of total consumption, 351 million ounces went for industrial fabrication, 196 million ounces for photographic uses, 277 million ounces for jewelry and silverware, and 35 million ounces for coinage. The United States, despite its significant silver production, imported about 106 million ounces of silver in 2003.

Uses

Historically, silver has been used for monetary purposes. In the United States, for instance, silver, like gold, has been used in coins, and its price has been supported by the government as a result. Yet silver's uses and value for monetary purposes have decreased significantly since 1968.

In 1965, the U.S. Coinage Act stopped the use of silver in quarters and dimes and cut back on the amount of silver in half

FIGURE   15.3

Top 10 Silver Producing Countries, 2003

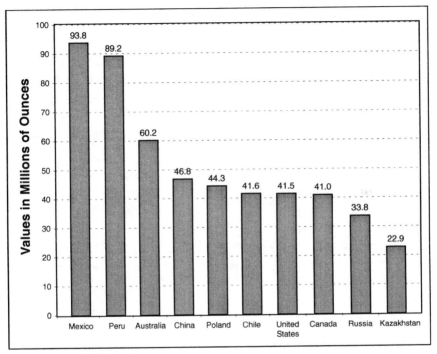

Source: World Gold Council.

dollars from 90 to 40 percent. Two years later, the U.S. Treasury stopped selling silver at $1.2929 per fine, or *troy,* ounce (the description of a troy ounce of silver that is assumed to be 995 pure, unless otherwise specified), and the price of silver immediately increased to $1.87 per ounce. Silver coins were thus worth more than their face value, and the government issued a ban on melting down coins. In the middle of 1967, Congress authorized the Secretary of the Treasury to rule that outstanding silver certificates worth about $150 million were either lost, destroyed, or privately held and would not be redeemed. By 1968, then, holders of U.S. silver certificates could no longer redeem them for silver.

The international demand for silver coin has declined as well; Great Britain, Canada, and Australia no longer use silver coinage. The use of silver in coinage fabrication worldwide reached 35 million ounces in 2003, reaching a nine-year high that was driven primarily by sharply higher minting in Germany.

In today's markets, the price of silver is determined mainly by its industrial applications and to a lesser extent by its use in jewelry. Its value is not based on monetary purposes. In 2002, industrial purposes, including the manufacture of photographic, electrical, and electronic products, accounted for about 75 percent of U.S. silver consumption. About 10 percent went for electroplated ware, sterling ware, and jewelry. (See Fig. 15.4.)

The photographic film, plate, sensitized paper, and photocopying machine industries comprise the largest single market

FIGURE   15.4

CBOT Nearby Mini Silver Futures Price, October 1, 2001–June 16, 2005

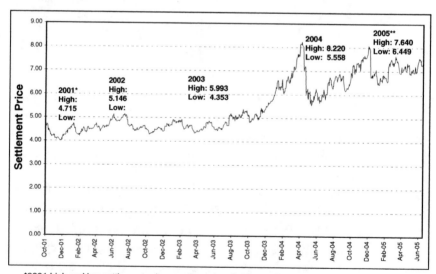

*2001 high and low settlement prices are based on October 1–December 31.

**2005 high and low settlement prices are based on January 3–June 16.

Source: CBOT Market Data.

for silver in the United States today. The photographic industry, in particular, is also the leader in the reclamation and recycling of silver, primarily from waste solutions from film development. Digital photography has made inroads into traditional photography recently, and the extent of its impact on demand for silver has not yet been determined.

The electrical and electronic industries are major silver consumers as well, taking commercial advantage of silver's thermal and electrical conductivity and high heat resistance. In fact, silver electrical contacts are used in practically every on-off switch and electrical appliance. Silver is also used in computer, telephone, and aviation systems.

Substitutes for silver in the electrical and electronic fields are available, but at the moment they are both costly and somewhat inferior. Stainless steel, pewter, and aluminum are popular substitutes for silver tableware. Aluminum and rhodium substitute for silver in mirrors and other reflecting surfaces, while tantalum substitutes for silver in surgical sutures, plates, and pins.

Futures Markets

Silver futures and options trade at the New York Mercantile Exchange's COMEX division. Silver futures also trade at the Chicago Board of Trade and the Tokyo Commodity Exchange. (See Table 15.2.)

TABLE 15.2

Major Silver Futures and Options Contracts

Contract	Futures Exchange	Annual Volume in 2004
Silver futures	COMEX (New York)	5,006,125
Silver options	COMEX (New York)	1,022,348
Silver futures	Tokyo Commodity Exchange	1,473,370

Source: Data provided by Futures Industry Association, Inc.

COPPER

The open-pit mining of copper and the use of copper in weapons, tools, and utensils dates back to prehistoric times. A nonferrous metal, copper is a highly versatile substance valued for its excellent conductivity, noncorrosiveness, and heat resistance. It has applications in automotive, electrical and electronic, communications, and construction products, as well as lesser uses in jewelry, decorative arts, and housewares.

Mining, Processing, Refining, and Manufacturing

Copper is obtained both from mining and from secondary recovery of scrap. Approximately 80 to 90 percent of copper is mined in open pits. The remainder is mined by various underground methods.

Most mined copper comes from base-metal sulfide ores that contain varying amounts of other metals, including gold, silver, nickel, lead, zinc, platinum, and palladium. As a result, a rather complex processing, using milling, smelting, and refining, is necessary to obtain pure, refined copper. The milling process involves crushing the ore and using water, chemicals, and air to concentrate the copper and isolate it from other metals and waste. In the smelting process, the copper concentrate is roasted, melted, and treated with air. Prior to smelting, the concentrate is only 20 to 30 percent copper. By the end of the three-part smelting operation, however, the resulting product, called *blister copper,* is 98.5 percent pure.

Copper can be refined by two different methods—electrolysis and firing. Electrolytic refining is used to produce nearly 90 percent of all refined copper. In this process, the blister copper is melted in a furnace and cast into anodes (positive terminals of an electrolytic cell). The anodes are then placed in tanks of electrolytic solution with thin sheets of copper called *cathodes.* When an electrical charge is run through the electrolyte solution, pure copper is deposited onto the cathodes, leaving impurities behind in the tank and solution. The pure copper cathodes can then be melted and cast into ingots.

Finally, to manufacture finished copper products, ingots of various kinds and sizes are normally rolled to produce sheets, melted and extruded to make wire products, or melted and recast to make parts of many shapes and sizes. Throughout the world, only a few large companies mine, refine, and manufacture copper, and they vary greatly in the type of functions they perform. Some firms are involved in all stages of copper production, from mining through the manufacturing process, while others specialize in refining or manufacturing.

World Supply and Demand

World mined copper production in 2003 was estimated to be 15.2 million metric tons. Leading copper producing countries include Chile, the United States, Indonesia, Australia, and Peru. In 2003, Chile and the United States accounted for 35 percent and 8 percent, respectively, of world mined copper production. Most copper mined in the United States comes from Arizona, with other mines in New Mexico and Utah.

Note, however, that newly refined copper is not the only source of supply. Secondary recovery—the reclamation of old copper scrap—can account for as much as 30 percent of the total U.S. consumption of copper.

The United States, once the world's largest copper consumer, has been overtaken in the last decade by Asian countries, which in 2003 accounted for 43 percent of world consumption. China is the leading copper consumer in Asia. The United States and Europe accounted for 16 and 24 percent, respectively, in 2003. Strong growth of demand is expected to continue in Asia, while demand is expected to recover somewhat in the United States and experience modest growth in Europe.

Copper is used in a wide range of products. Because copper is resistant to corrosion and can conduct heat, the construction, electrical, industrial machinery, and transportation industries are major consumers of copper in the U.S. market.

The construction industry is the primary user of copper, applying it in roofs, plumbing fixtures and pipes, hardware, and decorative products. In 2003, the construction industry accounted for about 46 percent of U.S. demand. Copper does, however, face some competition from aluminum in roof construction and from plastic in pipes.

Electrical and electronic products are the second largest end-use market for copper in the United States, accounting for 23 percent of demand in 2003. Copper is used in a variety of communications equipment, such as telephones, telegraphic equipment, televisions, radio receivers, and communications satellites. Copper also is used in motors, power generators, batteries, fans, and heating and refrigeration equipment.

The transportation industry consumes about 10 percent of all U.S. copper to manufacture motors and turbines in automotive, rail, and aircraft applications and for use in steering, air conditioning, switching, and signal devices. Another 11 percent is used in consumer and general products, and 10 percent in industrial machinery. Because copper is used in a variety of products, its price is highly sensitive to fluctuations in supply and demand.

TABLE 15.3

Major Copper Futures and Options Contracts

Contract	Futures Exchange	Annual Volume in 2004
High-grade copper futures	COMEX (New York)	3,190,625
High-grade copper options	COMEX (New York)	216,350
Copper—grade A futures	London Metal Exchange	18,171,204
Copper—grade A options	London Metal Exchange	1,721,914
Copper futures	Shanghai Futures Exchange	21,248,370

Source: Data provided by Futures Industry Association, Inc.

Futures Markets

Copper futures and options trade on the New York Mercantile Exchange's COMEX division and on the London Metal Exchange. Copper futures also trade on the Shanghai Futures Exchange. (See Table 15.3.)

THE PLATINUM GROUP

Six metals comprise the platinum group: platinum, palladium, iridium, osmium, rhodium, and ruthenium. Of these, platinum and palladium are the most important, accounting for about 90 percent of the total metal refined in the United States from this group of platinum ores.

Platinum and palladium have many similarities and common metallurgical characteristics. Often they are used in combination with each other. Both have excellent electrical conductivity and are noncorrosive. Platinum, particularly, is used in settings for fine jewelry.

World Supply and Demand

World reserves of platinum-group ores were estimated at 71,000 metric tons in 2003. Platinum-group ores are found in placers (glacial deposits that contain particles of valuable minerals), in loose rock formations shifted by glacial movements, or in deposits in rock fissures. Both South Africa and Russia's Ural Mountain region are rich in platinum-group ores, with reserves estimated at 63,000 metric tons and 6,200 metric tons, respectively. There are smaller, but significant, reserves of platinum-group ores in Canada and the United States, holding 310 and 900 metric tons, respectively.

Platinum-group production is thus unique in that two countries—South Africa and Russia—account for most of the world's supply. Together, South Africa and Russia produce 90 percent of the world's platinum, with South Africa alone producing more than 70 percent. Russia and South Africa produce 43 and 38 percent of the world's palladium, respectively. Total world production of platinum and palladium was estimated at 6.01 million ounces and 5.50 million ounces, respectively, for 2003.

Platinum-group metals are used primarily by the automotive industry to manufacture catalytic converters. The automotive industry accounted for 39 percent of platinum consumption and 58 percent of palladium consumption in 2003. Properties of platinum-group metals, used in the catalytic converter, help break down poisonous carbon monoxide and hydrocarbon emissions into harmless oxygen and hydrogen. The use of platinum metals by the auto industry has grown in recent years because of strict government exhaust-emission standards.

Platinum and palladium can also be used in combination or singly as catalysts in the production of nitric acid, an important element used to make fertilizers and explosives. In addition, both platinum and palladium are used as catalysts in the production of pharmaceuticals, high-octane gasoline, and other petroleum products.

Platinum, in particular, is used as well in the manufacturing of blown glass, pressed glass, and glass and synthetic fibers, accounting in 2003 for 23 percent of the U.S. end-use market. It also finds significant use as a precious metal in jewelry and other decorative pieces, accounting for about 37 percent of demand, and some use as an investment, about 1 percent of platinum demand.

Finally, because of their excellent electrical conductivity, both platinum and palladium are important products used in the manufacture of telephones, other telecommunications equipment, and industrial controls. The use of palladium in low-voltage electrical contacts is far greater than the use of platinum in these products, accounting for about 17 percent of palladium demand. The dental industry also represented 17 percent of demand for palladium in 2003.

Note that as a major consumer of platinum and palladium but with only light domestic mine production, the United States

TABLE 15.4

Major Platinum and Palladium Futures Contracts

Contract	Futures Exchange	Annual Volume in 2004
Palladium futures	Tokyo Commodity Exchange	438,934
Platinum futures	Tokyo Commodity Exchange	13,890,300
Palladium futures	NYMEX (New York)	267,552
Platinum futures	NYMEX (New York)	295,695

Source: Data provided by Futures Industry Association, Inc.

relies heavily on secondary refining and imports, as does any large platinum-group consumer outside of South Africa and Russia.

Because of the use of platinum, palladium, and rhodium in the manufacture of catalytic converters, demand for these metals is expected to grow. Worldwide, regulation of automotive emissions has increased, and in Europe, sale of diesel engines has grown. Prices for this metal group hit all time highs in 2004.

Futures Markets

Platinum and palladium futures trade at the New York Mercantile Exchange's NYMEX division and the Tokyo Commodity Exchange. (See Table 15.4.)

FURTHER READING

Bernstein, Jake, *Jake Bernstein's New Guide to Investing in Metals*. New York: Wiley & Sons, 1991.

Green, Timothy, *The New World of Gold: The Inside Story of the Mines, the Markets, the Politics, the Investors*. New York: Walker & Company, 1984.

Rapson, W. S., and T. Groenewald, *Gold Usage*. New York: Academic Press, 1978.

INFORMATION SOURCES

U.S. Geological Survey	minerals.usgs.gov/minerals/
Minerals Information	
World Gold Council	www.gold.org
The Silver Institute	www.silverinstitute.org
Copper Development Association	www.copper.org
Johnson Matthey's LCC	www.platinum.matthey.com
World Bureau of Metal Statistics	www.world-bureau.com

Forest, Fiber, and Food Markets: Lumber, Cotton, Orange Juice, Sugar, Cocoa, Coffee

This chapter covers the basic economic and political factors that affect the price of lumber, cotton, orange juice, sugar, cocoa, and coffee. All these commodities are traded on U.S. futures exchanges. Note that the information presented here is a general overview and is not meant to cover all the factors affecting prices for these products. To learn more about them, see the suggested reading list or information sources given at the end of the chapter.

LUMBER

Forests are among this country's most valuable natural resources. Their timber provides a wide variety of wood products used in housing, nonresidential construction, furniture, packaging, transportation, and paper products. This section discusses two-by-four lumber, a commonly used timber product.

Ownership of commercial forestland is divided among private individuals, lumber firms, local and state governments, and the federal government. Three major forest areas exist in the United States: the Pacific Northwest, the Rocky Mountains, and the South. The Pacific Northwest and Rocky Mountain regions are sometimes referred to as the coastal and inland regions, respectively. The Pacific Northwest yields mainly Douglas fir and hemlock pine, while Rocky Mountain forests produce white fir, Douglas fir, larch pine, Engelmann spruce, and lodgepole pine. Nearly all timber produced in the Southern region is southern yellow pine.

Timber, a renewable resource, is typically regarded as an agricultural commodity. So the U.S. Department of Agriculture (USDA) monitors timber production. But timber differs greatly from crops that have annual growing seasons, because timber must grow for years before it is ready to harvest and mill into wood and paper products. (See Table 16.1.)

The production of lumber is generally not affected by seasonal considerations. Instead, levels are determined primarily by the rate of demand and price. Most lumber mills operate five days a week, two shifts a day, as long as prices are sufficient to produce a profit. This puts a continuous supply of lumber into the distribution pipeline.

To produce two-by-four lumber, sawlogs are fed through automated sawmills onto planing machinery. From there, the lumber is transferred to train boxcars and flatcars and transported to where it is sold. Sawmills that make two-by-fours also produce other lumber products. When prices for two-by-four lumber production are weak, sawmill equipment can be realigned to produce lumber products of other dimensions with better profit potential.

TABLE 16.1

U.S. Timberland Ownership, 2003

Farms and private	56%
Under federal government management	24%
Forest industry	13%
State, county, and municipal governments	7%

Source: USDA.

Approximately 40 percent of all dimensional lumber produced in the United States is used in residential construction—framing applications, including external and internal walls, rafters, roofing, and floor joists. About 30 percent of dimensional lumber goes for repairs and remodeling, while nonresidential construction applications consume about 15 percent. The remainder is used in material handling, furniture manufacturing, and other wood products.

Because lumber is used primarily in residential construction, the monthly housing starts report, compiled by the U.S. Department of Commerce, is the most critically watched indicator of lumber demand. In 2003, new housing starts were at 1,848,000, up from 1,705,000 in 2002.

In addition to housing starts, a variety of other economic factors dictate lumber demand. In particular, higher mortgage interest rates can cause construction of single-family housing to decrease with a corresponding decrease in the demand for lumber. Lower mortgage rates can have the opposite effect.

Substitute materials also influence lumber demand. Steel and aluminum, for instance, are increasingly used in place of lumber for residential construction.

In recent years, the export level of U.S. lumber products has been a major factor in the overall demand and price for two-by-four lumber. This was particularly true in the mid-1970s, when Japan imported large quantities of U.S. lumber. U.S. exports have declined somewhat since then, but significant foreign demand for plywood, lumber, and sawlogs still exists.

Random-length lumber futures and options trade at the Chicago Mercantile Exchange, where the futures contract annual volume was 242,873 in 2004.

COTTON

Cotton, one of the oldest fibers known, is the world's leading natural textile fiber. It is produced in more than 75 countries and on every continent of the world except Antarctica. Furthermore, the

demand for cotton continues to grow, driven by worldwide population growth and the desire for quality fabrics. In 1960–1961,
worldwide cotton production was an estimated 45.1 million
bales. By 2003–2004, experts were forecasting a crop of more
than double that size—94.3 million bales. (One bale of cotton
weighs 480 pounds.) Increased yields account for almost all the
growth as the harvested area worldwide has remained primarily
the same.

Despite worldwide supply-and-demand expansion, synthet-
ics such as rayon and polyester have affected U.S. cotton demand.
In 1981–1982, in fact, U.S. cotton consumption was at its lowest
point since 1911. In the 1990s, however, U.S. consumers began
once again to value the superior quality of cotton as a textile,
and U.S. demand rebounded strongly. U.S. mill use peaked in
1997 at roughly 11 million bales. Since then, demand by U.S.
mills has declined as U.S. exports of cotton have grown robustly.
U.S. exports of cotton reached an all-time high of 13.8 million
bales in 2004, more than double the 6.5 million bales consumed
by U.S. mills that year. (See Table 16.2.)

China, the world's leading cotton producer, is expected to
break previous records with an estimated 30 million bales in the

TABLE 16.2

U.S. Cotton Balance Sheet (millions of 480 lb bales)

	1999/2000	2000/2001	2001/2002	2002/2003	2003/2004
Beginning stocks	3.9	3.9	6.0	7.4	5.4
Production	17.0	17.2	20.3	17.2	18.3
Imports	0.1	0.0	0.0	0.1	0.0
Total supply	**21.0**	**21.1**	**26.3**	**24.7**	**23.7**
U.S. mill use	10.2	8.9	7.7	7.3	6.5
Exports	6.7	6.7	11.0	11.9	13.8
Total demand	**16.9**	**15.6**	**18.7**	**19.2**	**20.2**
Ending stocks	**3.9**	**6.0**	**7.4**	**5.4**	**3.5**

Source: USDA.

2004–2005 marketing year, after producing 22.3 million bales in 2003–2004. In 2003–2004, the United States and India followed China in production, with 18.3 and 13.8 million bales, respectively. Pakistan and Brazil are also major cotton producers.

At 32.4 million bales in 2003–2004 marketing year, China is also the world's largest cotton consumer and a major export market for U.S. cotton. Following China were India, consuming 13.5 million bales, Pakistan at 9.6 million bales, and the United States, with 6.5 million bales.

The U.S. cotton crop year begins on August 1 and ends on July 31. Planting begins in March and continues through mid-June, depending on the area of the country where cotton is grown. Major cotton-producing states include Texas, California, Georgia, Mississippi, Arkansas, and Louisiana.

The price of cotton and the number of acres planted relative to other crops each year have a major effect on cotton production. When cotton is priced low and other crops are priced high, fewer acres of cotton are planted. When cotton is priced high and other crops are priced low, producers plant more.

Cotton production is also sensitive to weather and insects. Extremes in temperature and rainfall during planting, growing, and harvesting can affect the quantity and quality of the cotton crop.

Government policies likewise play an important role in the supply and price level of cotton. U.S. government production and price programs for cotton began in 1929, when the Agricultural Marketing Act established a cotton loan rate. During the 1940s, 1950s, and 1960s, U.S. cotton carryover grew under government programs. Basically, farmers were producing cotton for the government, and artificially high price levels made U.S. cotton unattractive on the world market.

In the 1970s and 1980s, the government moved toward a free market system, but nonetheless retained government support programs, including acreage reduction, payment-in-kind, and export programs. One government cotton program, established under the 1985 Farm Bill, was designed to make U.S. cotton competitive in world markets and to lower stockpiles. Under the program's rules, cotton farmers were allowed to borrow money using their crop as collateral, just as they did under past government programs. But when it came time to pay back the loan, they needed to repay only an amount equal to the prevailing world price for cotton, as calculated by the USDA.

This marketing program made U.S. cotton prices more competitive in foreign markets. As a result, U.S. cotton carry-over fell drastically. The USDA reported that cotton carryover stocks dropped from more than 9 million bales in 1985 to 5 million bales in 1987 and to a little more than 3.5 million bales in 2004.

The 1996 Federal Agriculture Improvement and Reform Act (FAIR) effectively eliminated government acreage reduction and price support programs. Moving toward a more market-oriented farm program, FAIR gives U.S. producers total planting flexibility while calling for more market-oriented risk management to wean producers from government price supports.

After harvest, the marketing route for cotton starts with the producer. Cotton producers can sell their crop to the local gin, use it to redeem a preexisting government loan, or sell it to cotton merchants or large textile mills, where it is eventually processed into fiber and oilseed.

At a gin, the cotton is cleaned and fiber, called *lint,* is removed from the seed and pressed into 480-pound gross weight bales. The cottonseed is usually sold to oil mills, where it is processed into both a variety of edible and industrial oil products and cottonseed meal, an animal feed ingredient.

Quality and grade are determined after the cotton is processed. Quality is established by the grade, staple length, and fiber fineness. Merchants then classify the cotton and price it according to similar types. Cotton is graded on the basis of color, brightness, and foreign matter, as well as on the ginning preparation that determines the smoothness of cotton. Actual grading and classifying are done by trained classers who are licensed and supervised by the USDA. Both the grade and class tell a buyer how a specific lot of cotton will perform under additional manufacturing.

Cotton represented 61.5 percent of the U.S. fiber market in 2004. The greatest use of cotton is for apparel, followed by household items such as linen goods, upholstery, draperies, and carpeting.

U.S. cotton futures and options are traded on the New York Board of Trade, where the 2004 annual futures and options contracts traded were 3,156,018 and 1,725,982, respectively.

ORANGE JUICE

The popularity of frozen concentrated orange juice has skyrocketed since World War II, causing orange production to increase significantly. World production of oranges tripled between 1965 and 2000, reaching 63.7 million metric tons during the 2000 crop year. The United States, a major producer, grew roughly 20 percent of the world's oranges that year.

U.S. orange production since 1985–1986 has increased steadily, with the exception of 1999, and has held at between 11.5 and 13 million tons from 2000 to 2004. (See Fig. 16.1.) Florida produced the most oranges in 2004, at 242 million boxes, about 84 percent of all U.S. production. California followed with 52 million boxes. (See Table 16.3.) Note that the size of one box of oranges varies from state to state. In Florida, one box equals 90 pounds, whereas in Texas, one box equals 85 pounds. In Arizona and California, one box equals 75 pounds.

The U.S. crop year for oranges runs from December through November. Florida's production runs from January through mid-June or July, with a break in late February and early March. Frozen concentrated orange juice (FCOJ), also known as *pack,* is processed from mid-December through mid-July. FCOJ yield is measured in gallons of juice per box. In 2003–2004, one box yielded about 1.57 gallons of Florida FCOJ.

Orange juice production is directly related to the number of oranges each tree yields. Orange yield varies according to the

FIGURE 16.1

U.S. Oranges Utilized Production, 1994–2004

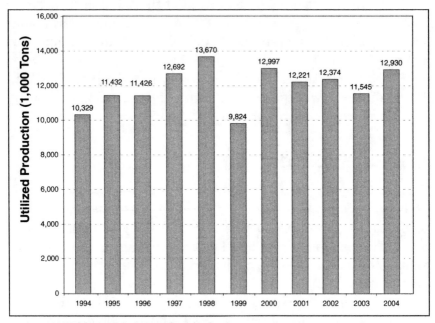

Source: USDA/National Agricultural Statistics Service.

age of the tree and weather conditions. An orange tree requires more than four years of intensive care before it begins to bear fruit. A 5-year-old tree, for example, can be expected to yield only one box of oranges per year, while a mature tree—20 to 45 years old—yields about six boxes each year. Weather affects yield as

TABLE 16.3

U.S. Citrus Production Areas, 2003–2004

State	Bearing Acreage
Florida	564,800
California	182,000
Texas	8,800
Arizona	5,800

Source: USDA/National Agricultural Statistics Service.

well. Cold spells, sudden heat, dryness, and strong winds can damage orange growth and production.

The sweetness of the oranges depends on the length of time the fruit remains on the tree. The longer an orange is on the tree, the sweeter it will be. Processors measure sweetness by the yield of pounds of solids. Solids, which are mostly sugar, are what remain when the water is evaporated from the orange juice.

Approximately 80 percent of the orange crop is processed into various food products. Of the oranges processed in Florida in the 2003–2004 season, 60 percent went into frozen concentrated orange juice. The best measure of demand is found in the movement of pack from Florida processors to wholesalers, supermarket chains and other distributors, and manufacturers of food products that use the concentrate as an ingredient. This figure is released every Thursday by the Florida Citrus Processors. The U.S. government is also a large consumer of frozen concentrated orange juice because of its purchases for school lunch and various food programs. U.S. exports represent significant demand as well, at about 10 percent of all FCOJ produced. Primary export markets include Canada, the European Union, and Japan.

Although it has become a staple breakfast item over the years, FCOJ has not escaped competition from market competitors such as artificial orange juice products, other pure fruit juices, and diluted fruit drinks.

FCOJ futures and options are traded on the New York Board of Trade, where the 2004 annual futures and options contracts traded were 970,437 and 554,432 respectively.

SUGAR

Historically, sugar has been an important item of international trade because it is considered a luxury item and because it is produced in many countries throughout the world. Over the past 20 years, sugar consumption has grown by about 2 percent per year. This fairly steady year-to-year expansion in sugar use on a global basis reflects population growth, the stability of the human diet, and sugar's role as a basic staple in most of the world.

There has been a dramatic shift in world sugar production since 1985. Countries in the Southern Hemisphere have significantly increased their production, whereas production from the Caribbean countries, the European Union, and the United States has remained fairly stable. (See Fig. 16.2.)

F I G U R E   16.2

World Sugar Production, 1983–1984 and 2002–2003

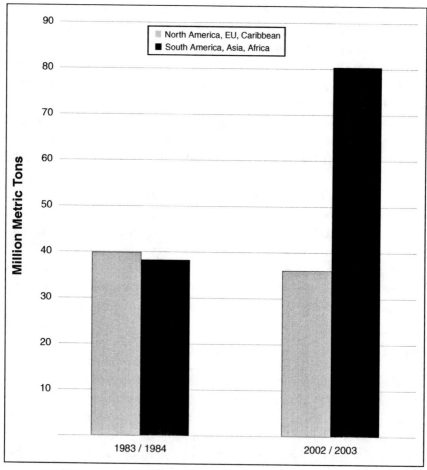

Source: USDA.

In 2003–2004, more than 142 million metric tons of sugar was produced worldwide. Brazil is now the largest producer of sugar, supplying 25.5 million metric tons in 2003–2004, an increase in production of approximately 150 percent since 1985. Production continued on a sustained basis in Australia and South Africa, while it increased in India, China, Pakistan, and Thailand, further contributing to the dominance of the Southern Hemisphere in sugar production.

Total world consumption of sugar reached a record 140.1 metric tons in 2003–2004. India was the leading consumer of sugar that year with 20.5 metric tons, followed by the European Union, China, Brazil, and the United States. Together they accounted for 49 percent of world consumption.

Sugar is produced from both sugarcane and sugar beets. Except for the United States and China, which raise both sugarcane and sugar beets, most areas of the world produce sugar from only one type of plant. The nature and location of production and the processing techniques for sugarcane and sugar beets are different, but the refined sugar from each is indistinguishable.

Sugarcane, a bamboolike grass that grows in tropical and semitropical climates, can be harvested approximately 18 months after planting and continues to produce for several years. Sugarcane is usually harvested from fall through spring. India, Brazil, China, the United States, and Thailand are large sugarcane producers. In the United States, sugarcane is grown predominantly in Florida, Louisiana, Hawaii, and Texas.

Sugar beets are white, tapering roots about 12 inches long and weighing about 2 pounds each. They are planted in early spring and harvested before the first winter freeze. Sugar beets are grown in Europe, the Ukraine, and the United States. Minnesota, Michigan, Idaho, California, and North Dakota are the major sugar beet-producing states.

Several economic and political factors affect the supply of and demand for sugar, which, in turn, affect price. On the demand side, per capita income and population are two important economic factors. Increases in the level of income and population growth in Third World countries, for example, have led to an increase in sugar demand. In recent years, however, sugar demand has slowed somewhat because of the use of corn sweeteners as a substitute for sugar.

Variables affecting production and, eventually, the supply of sugar include weather, the number of acres of sugar beets and sugarcane planted, and disease problems. Other variables affecting sugar prices include government stocks, protective agreements, and government policies. Reports of sugar stocks, which measure the balance between supply and demand, are an important indication of total supply and expected price levels.

Most of the world production remaining after domestic consumption is sold internationally under special protective agreements, such as the U.S. tariff rate quota or the European Union import quota. This trade accounts for most of the sugar sold to major importers, such as Russia, the United States, the European Union, Japan, and China. Just five places of origin—Australia, Brazil, Cuba, the European Union, and Thailand—account for about 70 percent of global exports.

Because of the trade agreements, approximately 20 percent or less of world sugar production is traded in the world market at the world price. The remainder is sold in the country in which it is produced, usually at a price higher than the world market price, or it is traded under the special agreements. The International Sugar Organization (ISO), a voluntary alliance of sugar exporting and importing countries, monitors the world sugar trade and attempts to maintain a stable, orderly, and free world sugar market.

U.S. sugar supplies, in particular, are governed by a quota system, established by the USDA, wherein domestic production is supplemented by imports. Each exporting nation is given a quota for which the United States will pay a certain price, usually above the world market price. The United States exports virtually no raw sugar, but is an exporter of refined sugar.

Sugar futures and options are traded in the United States on the New York Board of Trade. Outside the United States, var-

TABLE 16.4

Major Sugar Futures and Options Contracts

Contract	Futures Exchange	Annual Volume in 2004
Sugar No. 11 futures	New York Board of Trade	9,766,550
Sugar No. 11 options	New York Board of Trade	2,854,683
White sugar futures	Euronext LIFFE	1,251,233
Raw sugar futures	Tokyo Grain Exchange	355,659

Source: Data provided by Futures Industry Association, Inc.

ious sugar contracts are traded on the BM&F (Brazil), Euronext LIFFE (London), the Fukuoka Futures Exchange (Japan), and the Tokyo Grain Exchange. (See Table 16.4.)

COCOA

Cocoa is produced from the cocoa, or cacao, tree, a tropical plant that bears cantaloupe-sized pods. The pods contain cocoa beans that can be processed into cocoa, cocoa butter, and various sweetened and unsweetened chocolate products.

The cocoa plant was originally cultivated in Central and South America and introduced to the European explorers of the Western Hemisphere in the sixteenth century. Until the twentieth century, most cocoa production continued to come from Central and South American countries. Since then, however, various African nations have become major cocoa producers. Even more recently, several Southeast Asian nations, Indonesia and Malaysia in particular, have become major producers, while Central and South American production has held steady or, in the case of Brazil, declined considerably. (See Fig. 16.3.)

World cocoa bean production in 2002–2003 reached an all time high of 3.1 million metric tons, up 8 percent from the previous year and almost double the production averaged throughout the 1970s. The leading cocoa-producing African nations—Ivory Coast, Ghana,

FIGURE 16.3

Leading Cocoa Producers, 2003

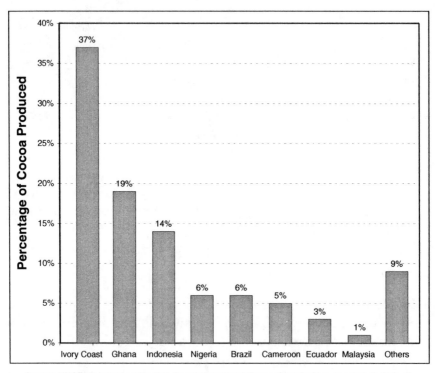

Source: UNCTAD, based on the data from International Cocoa Organization, quarterly bulletin of cocoa statistics.

Nigeria, and Cameroon—produced 2.1 million metric tons, about 67 percent of global cocoa output. The Ivory Coast alone accounted for 37 percent of this production. Africa represented 70 percent of world production in 2002–2003, Asia and Oceania produced 17 percent, while the Americas produced 13 percent.

It takes several years to produce cocoa because the cocoa tree does not produce enough beans to harvest until it is at least 5 years old. After that, the number of beans produced increases until the tree reaches its peak yield at 15 years of age. It will maintain that yield for another 15 years. A tree's production begins to decline after 40 or 50 years until the tree can no longer be used for commercial production.

Beans ripen from October through August, with two crops being harvested. The main crop runs from October through March and produces approximately 80 percent of the total global harvest. The mid-crop runs from May to August and produces the balance.

After the cocoa pods ripen, they are cut from the trees and opened. The beans are then removed, fermented, dried, packed into bags, and transported to a processing plant. In processing, beans are roasted, separated from the husks, and ground into a liquid known as chocolate liquor. As the liquor cools, it hardens into a cake. To produce cocoa, most of the fat or cocoa butter is removed from the liquor by hydraulic presses. In the manufacturing of chocolate, however, additional cocoa butter is mixed in with the cocoa.

World 2002–2003 cocoa consumption, as measured by global cocoa bean grindings, was estimated at 2,996 million metric tons. The four principal import markets—the United States, Germany, France, and the United Kingdom—account for 54 percent of overall demand. Russia, Japan, Brazil and Italy also import considerable amounts.

Virtually all the major bean producers export cocoa. Governments of the countries that produce the largest quantities of cocoa designate the amount of cocoa to be exported, and the marketing and sales policies of these nations differ considerably. In Ghana, Nigeria, and other West African countries, for instance, government marketing agencies purchase cocoa from farmers and then sell the exports to buyers at predetermined prices. Announcements of the size of the holdings by the marketing agencies, especially those by the Ghana Cocoa Marketing Board, are important indicators of the current crop size and available supplies for export. By contrast, Brazilian cocoa is sold through free markets, although the government may establish minimum selling prices and export quotas.

Cocoa bean stocks can be either visible or invisible. Visible stocks are held in public warehouses, and these supply figures are available to the public. A larger portion of cocoa bean stocks, however, is held in private warehouses. These privately held, invisible supplies can be very difficult to estimate.

TABLE 16.5

Major Cocoa Futures Contracts

Contract	Futures Exchange	Annual Volume in 2004
Cocoa futures	New York Board of Trade	2,389,050
No. 7 cocoa futures	Euronext LIFFE	2,643,199

Source: Data provided by Futures Industry Association, Inc.

Cocoa futures and options are traded on the New York Board of Trade. Cocoa futures and options also trade outside the United States at the Euronext LIFFE (London). (See Table 16.5.)

COFFEE

The Ethiopians were probably the first people to use coffee. Only later did its popularity spread from Ethiopia to various Arabian countries and into Europe. Nevertheless, by the seventeenth century, coffee was the main nonalcoholic drink of most of Europe and the Americas, as coffeehouses proliferated.

Because coffee production is concentrated in subtropical and tropical climates, while the major consumers tend to live in the United States and Europe, coffee is one of the most internationally traded of all commodities. Up until World War II, the United States and other Western countries met their growing taste for coffee with imports from South and Central America. Since then, several African and Southeast Asian countries have become major exporters as well.

In 2003–2004, these coffee-producing regions and others produced more than 100.7 million 60-kilogram bags worldwide, which was the lowest production year since 1996–1997. Brazil was by far the largest producer at 28.8 million bags, which was about 29 percent of world production. However, Brazil's production was significantly down from its peak year of 2002–2003, but it is expected to rebound in 2004–2005. Colombia, Indonesia,

Mexico, and India followed Brazil, producing about 11, 6, 5, and 4 percent of the world total, respectively. All are major coffee exporters. (See Fig. 16.4.)

There are two types of coffee: high-quality *arabica* and low-quality *robusta*. The high-quality group includes the mild coffees of Brazil, Colombia, and other South and Central American countries. The low-quality coffees are grown primarily in Africa and Southeast Asia.

Coffee trees, or bushes, begin to produce fruit about five years after planting. They thrive in subtropical climates at altitudes from 500 feet to more than 2,000 feet above sea level. Mature trees, 8 to 30 years old, produce about one pound of marketable coffee per year. Yield is affected adversely by frost,

FIGURE 16.4

Leading Coffee Producers, 2003

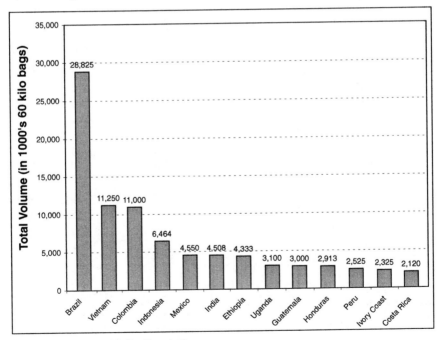

Source: International Coffee Organization.

high wind, drought, excessive rain, and various insects and diseases.

Coffee berries, each of which contains two coffee beans, are picked by hand at harvest and soaked in water. The beans are then removed from the pulp by friction and fermentation, dried and peeled, sized, and packed in 60-kilogram bags to protect the coffee from foreign odors and moisture. Coffee that is processed and ready for shipment and storage is known as *green coffee*. Green coffee can be stored for long periods of time with little change in quality. Later the coffee beans can be blended, roasted, and packaged for consumer sale.

The United States produces very little coffee, but consumes and imports more than any other country in the world. In 2003, U.S. coffee processors ground more than 19.3 million bags, raising green coffee roastings to a 30-year high. In 2003, the United States consumed nearly 17 percent of world green coffee production. Other major coffee-importing countries include Germany, Japan, France, Italy, Spain, the Netherlands, and the United Kingdom.

In the United States, coffee is consumed almost entirely as a beverage, though it is also used as a flavoring in food products. U.S. coffee is sold as beans or ground into a variety of processed

TABLE 16.6

Major Coffee Futures and Options Contracts

Contract	Futures Exchange	Annual Volume in 2004
Coffee "C" futures	New York Board of Trade	4,193,303
Coffee "C" options	New York Board of Trade	1,970,068
Arabica coffee futures	BM&F (Brazil)	620,997
Robusta coffee futures	Euronext LIFFE	3,054,386
Robusta coffee options	Euronext LIFFE	248,990
Robusta coffee futures	Tokyo Grain Exchange	427,466

Source: Data provided by Futures Industry Association, Inc.

forms, such as instant, decaffeinated, or freeze-dried. Coffee bean oil, extracted during processing, is used to manufacture soaps, paints, shoe polish, and medicine. Coffee is also used to produce a type of plastic called *cafelite.*

The International Coffee Organization (ICO), a voluntary alliance of coffee exporting and importing countries, sets export and import quotas in an effort to maintain market stability. The ICO evaluates current world supply and demand and determines production and marketing policies.

Coffee futures and options are traded at the New York Board of Trade. Outside the United States, various coffee futures and options contracts are traded at the BM&F (Brazil), Euronext LIFFE (London), and the Tokyo Grain Exchange. (See Table 16.6.)

FURTHER READING

Dean, William, *Terms of Trade: A Reference for the Forest Products Industry,* 2nd ed. New York: Random House, 1984.

Jacobson, Timothy Curtis, and George D. Smith, *Cotton's Renaissance: A Study in Market Innovation.* Cambridge, England: Cambridge University Press, 2001.

Savaiko, Bernard C., *Trading in Soft Commodity Futures.* New York: Wiley and Sons, 1986.

Sills, Erin, and Karen Lee Abt, *Forests in a Market Economy.* Boston: Kluwer Academic Publishers, 2003.

INFORMATION SOURCES

Cotton Incorporated	www.cottoninc.com
Florida Department of Citrus Economic and Market Research	www.floridajuice.com/ gr_market.php
International Cocoa Organization	www.icco.org

International Coffee Organization	www.ico.org
International Sugar Organization	www.sugarinfo.co.uk/iso
National Coffee Association of U.S.A., Inc.	www.ncausa.org
Ultimate Citrus Page	www.ultimatecitrus.com
U.S. Department of Agriculture (USDA)	www.usda.gov
U.S. Department of Commerce	www.doc.gov
USDA National Agricultural Statistics Service	www.usda.gov/nass
Western Wood Products Association	www.wwpa.org

CHAPTER 17

Energy Markets: Crude Oil, Gasoline, Heating Oil, Natural Gas, Electricity

Modern society depends, perhaps above all else, on energy—energy to light its way, heat its homes and factories, drive its various indispensable machines, and power its computers and electronic devices. The demand for energy in the United States alone is staggering—98.2 quadrillion Btus in 2003 for residential and commercial, industrial, and transportation use. U.S. demand is projected to rise to 111.8 quadrillion Btus by 2010. (See Fig. 17.1.) (One Btu, or British thermal unit, equals the amount of energy required to raise the temperature of one pound of water by one degree Fahrenheit. That energy equals 251.996 calories or 1054.8 joules. One quadrillion Btus thus equal 251,996,000,000,000,000 calories.)

This chapter covers some of the basic supply-and-demand factors that affect the price of crude oil, heating oil, gasoline, natural gas, and, more recently, electricity. (See Fig. 17.2.) To find out more about these energy sources, see suggestions for further reading at the end of the chapter.

FIGURE 17.1

U.S. Energy Consumption, Production, and Net Imports, 1949–2003

Overview, 1949-2003

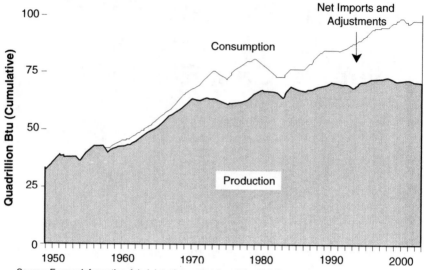

Source: Energy Information Administration, a division of the U.S. Department of Energy.

FIGURE 17.2

U.S. Energy Flow, 2004 (quadrillion Btu)

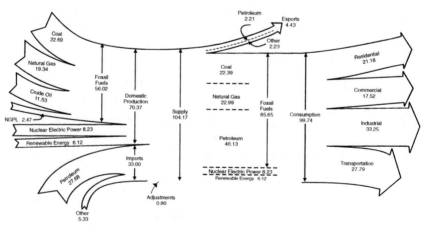

Note: NGPL represents natural gas plant liquids.

Source: Energy Information Administration, a division of the U.S. Department of Energy.

CRUDE OIL

Crude oil is petroleum (Latin for "rock oil") in its natural state. First used 5,000 years ago to coat the hulls of wooden ships and for religious and medical applications, petroleum did not find use as a source of light and heat until about 2,000 years ago. The first oil well dug deliberately to obtain crude oil, in Titusville, Pennsylvania, dates only from 1859. Yet in less than 140 years, crude oil exploration has spread around the world to the Middle East, North and South America, Europe, and Africa.

Since the 1970s, at least, crude oil has ranked among the most politically and economically critical raw materials in the world. That stems from the basic supply-and-demand situation that has emerged over the last several decades, as well as from the myriad products, many of them critically important, derived from so-called "black gold." Apart from the obvious fuels that are made from crude oil—among them gasoline, jet fuel, diesel oil, and heating oils—crude oil drives a large and varied petrochemical industry that produces a vast array of plastics, fertilizers, insecticides, waxes, adhesives, foods, cosmetics, pharmaceuticals, and textiles.

Oil Market's Structural Shift

A series of events beginning in the early 1970s brought about major changes in the structure of the energy markets. Prior to that time, a handful of major, multinational companies—most of them with global reach and a high degree of vertical integration—controlled both the major oil fields of the world and the production facilities. As a result, they could impose a "rack price" system on the rest of the marketplace. A rack price, at base, is a price by decree. Given their high degree of control over the industry, the major companies simply posted a price, and the rest of the marketplace had to accept it.

In the early 1970s, the price structure of crude oil changed dramatically, primarily because the ownership of oil production in the Middle East transferred from these operating companies to the governments of the oil-producing countries or their own national oil companies. With that transfer, the Organization of Petroleum Exporting Countries (OPEC) emerged as the major pricing power.

OPEC is a cartel of 11 oil-producing countries, including Algeria, Indonesia, Iran, Iraq, Kuwait, Libya, Nigeria, Qatar, Saudi Arabia, the United Arab Emirates, and Venezuela. Representatives of these nations meet periodically to discuss the worldwide economics of their industry and to establish policy for the group. The key evidence of that policy emerges in the form of production quotas for the member countries. The hope is that the discipline of group policy can hold prices at levels favorable to the economic needs of the members. Not surprisingly, any conference of the OPEC ministers attracts intense interest on the part of market analysts and oil product users throughout the world.

At the same time as this major shift of market power, OPEC, led by the world's largest oil producer, Saudi Arabia, had become the major oil supplier to the United States, Western Europe, and Japan. Because of increased oil demand, by the mid-1970s, OPEC was supplying two-thirds of the free world's oil and more than half of U.S. petroleum imports.

With OPEC's new authority came tremendous price increases and supply changes, which were influenced by political and economic events within the OPEC countries. Only after successive price hikes during the 1970s brought the average annual price of crude oil to a peak of $31.77 a barrel in 1981 did oil prices begin trending downward. In 1986, prices plummeted to $12.51 a barrel, driven by excess worldwide production, primarily by OPEC members seeking to regain lost market share.

After 1986, crude oil prices fluctuated. In 1990, the Iraqi invasion of Kuwait drove up the price of crude oil to $20.03 a barrel. Yet the ability of oil-producing nations to replace Iraqi and Kuwaiti oil, coupled with an economic recession that restrained petroleum demand, quickly pushed the price back down to $16.54 a barrel. Prices more or less remained in a $17 to $21 trading range until 1996, when low inventories, supportive weather conditions, and perceived political uncertainty pushed crude oil to a $27 a barrel post–Gulf War high. With the U.S. invasion of Iraq in 2003, crude oil prices again climbed, and reached all-time highs of more than $60 per barrel in 2005.

After such a long period under the rack price regime, the emergence of OPEC, attendant price shocks, and overall increasing price volatility seemed especially discomforting to the rest of the oil-consuming world. To help quiet that discomfort, a series of energy futures contracts began emerging during the late 1970s and early 1980s, beginning with the New York Mercantile Exchange's (NYMEX) heating oil, crude oil, and unleaded gasoline futures contracts. Natural gas, propane, and electricity contracts were later added to provide markets in other energy-related products. More recently, NYMEX introduced a long list of energy-futures-based contracts that can be used to create tailor-made swaps, calendar spreads, and delivery differentials for various combinations of natural gas, crude oil, petroleum, electricity, and coal market positions. Other major energy trading exchanges include the International Petroleum Exchange (IPE) in London, the Central Japan Commodity Exchange, and the Tokyo Commodity Exchange.

The emergence of the futures price discovery system in this marketplace, along with the political shifts of the era, focused market attention on supply-and-demand dynamics as never before and led to a major restructuring of the entire world marketplace for energy.

Typical Crude Oil Barrel Yield

The energy trade refers to petroleum products in terms of whether they come from the top, middle, or bottom of a barrel of crude oil. During refining, the lighter product at the top "boils off" at much lower temperatures than does the product at the middle and bottom of the barrel. For example, depending on the

grade of crude oil, gasoline "cracks out" at between 90 and 220
degrees Fahrenheit, while heating oil cracks out at between 450
and 650 degrees. Basically, going from the so-called light end of
the barrel to the heavy end, a 42-gallon barrel of crude oil produces yields in the ranges shown in Table 17.1 (omitting the gas
liquids like butane at the very top and the asphalt residue at the
bottom).

Crude oils, however, do vary. A barrel of Texas light sweet
crude oil produces relatively more on the light end and less on
the heavy end than does a barrel of Arabian heavy sour crude.
(*Sweet* and *sour* denote sulfur content, with sour crude oil having more sulfur than sweet.) Also, demand for higher-octane
unleaded gasoline has altered the demand pattern for crude oil,
as refiners must process more crude oil to produce a given
amount of that higher-octane gasoline than to produce an equal
amount of lower-octane leaded gasolines.

In addition, demand for products follows seasonal patterns.
Logically enough, heating oil is in greater demand in winter
than in summer, whereas demand for gasoline is higher in summer than in winter. Given typical barrel yields, seasonal factors
alone can shift the pattern of crude oil demand during the year.
Within the general pattern, a variety of weather and political
factors can motivate further shifts. A mild winter can drastically

TABLE 17.1

Range of Yields for Petroleum Products

Category (Common Products)	Percentage of Yield
Aromatics or gas liquids (butane)	—
Straight run gasoline	49–55
Naptha	3–6
Kerosene (jet fuel)	6
Medium distillates, or light gas oil (No. 2 heating oil, diesel fuel)	20–24
Heavy distillates, or heavy gas oil (residual or bunker fuel)	6–11
Residue (asphalt)	—

reduce heating oil demand. Economic crises can curtail travel and vacation plans. Increasing ecological sensitivity can alter consumers' fuel use, both in terms of driving patterns and in terms of household and industrial use.

Refiners can alter yields somewhat to adjust to those demand shifts, as the ranges in Table 17.1 suggest. Operators of newer refining technologies are better able to adjust than others, but the variation ranges are still relatively small.

Crude Oil Supply and Demand

World production of crude oil in 2003 averaged 67 million barrels a day, while demand ran close to 80 million barrels a day drawing on inventories as well as current production. (Barrels a day represents the maximum number of barrels of crude oil that can be processed during a 24-hour period. One barrel equals 42 U.S. gallons.) Looking at regional supply data shows OPEC's critical role in producing roughly 40 percent of the world's crude oil supply. (See Fig. 17.3.)

FIGURE   17.3

World Crude Oil Production, 1997–2003

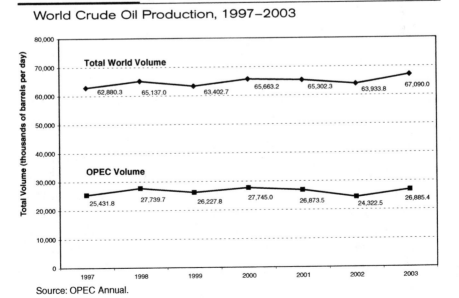

Source: OPEC Annual.

Whereas the world supply comes from relatively few locales, demand pulls that supply to every part of the world. In 2003, almost 25 percent of world oil production was used by the United States, which consumed roughly 20 million barrels per day, far more than any other nation. Yet the United States produced only about half that amount. As a result, imports play a large role in the U.S. energy picture. The United States has, however, reduced its dependence on OPEC by increasing its imports of oil from non-OPEC countries.

The world supply-and-demand situation can vary significantly from year to year and even from season to season. Ultimately, the price at any given moment depends on a complex interplay among supply-and-demand forces. For example, if demand is strong, stored supplies low, and prices relatively high, the OPEC nations will likely consider a production increase. The resultant increase in supply will lower prices, but such a move might also win increased market share for the OPEC nations and lead to a net gain from the suppliers' point of view.

Conversely, with prices at the low end of the range and a weaker supply-and-demand picture, the cartel will impose production limits to support prices. Historically, the cuts are more difficult to enforce than the boosts. Nevertheless, policy shifts along those lines remain an important part of the total market picture, and analysts, traders, and end users watch them carefully and issue detailed studies of developments and implications.

Because so many countries import so much of their crude oil supplies, transportation time and costs also play major roles in these markets. These factors have created interesting market share shifts among nations that produce crude oil.

For example, U.S. crude oil import shipments originating in South America take only 4 to 6 days to reach the U.S. Gulf Coast, as compared to 45 to 60 days for cargoes originating in the Middle East. The shorter transportation time affords refineries greater flexibility, comparable to "just in time" practices in other industries where suppliers set up operations closer to major customers. This change in purchasing practices is reflected in U.S.

crude oil import data. Market share gains by Venezuela, Mexico, Colombia, and Canada have come at the expense of Saudi Arabia and other more distant countries. (See Fig. 17.4.)

In January 1997, crude oil stocks briefly fell to levels not seen since the late 1970s, though they have risen since. Refiners appear to be increasingly comfortable with reduced supplies relative to the cost of holding more inventory. Furthermore, with the large incremental increases in global crude oil production originating in regions like the Americas, Africa, and the North Sea, the inventory situation is less risky, and thus more manageable than it would be without production from these regions. By using more oil from nearby sources, U.S. refiners can maintain lower inventories with a relatively lower level of risk because they can rely on shorter amounts of time to receive their orders.

Of course, energy market users watch the periodic reports issued by such organizations as the American Petroleum Insti-

FIGURE 17.4

U.S. Crude Oil Imports by Source, 1985–2003

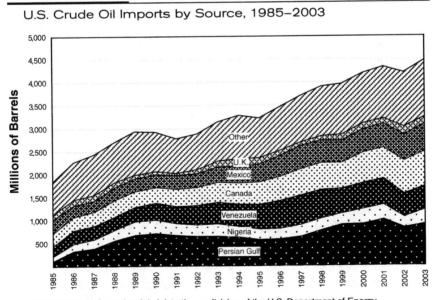

Source: Energy Information Administration, a division of the U.S. Department of Energy.

TABLE 17.2

Major Crude Oil Futures and Options Contracts

Contract	Futures Exchange	Annual Volume in 2004
Crude oil futures[1]	New York Mercantile Exchange	52,883,200
Crude oil options[1]	New York Mercantile Exchange	11,512,918
Crude oil one-month CSO (clarified slurry oil) options[1]	New York Mercantile Exchange	357,156
Brent crude oil futures[2]	International Petroleum Exchange	25,458,259
Crude oil futures[1]	Tokyo Commodity Exchange	2,284,572

[1]Data provided by Futures Industry Association, Inc.
[2]Data provided by CBOT.

tute, the International Energy Agency, and *Petroleum Intelligence Weekly* with great interest. All of those groups track supply, demand, inventories, refining activity, shipping fees, and other data of concern.

Crude oil futures and options trade at the New York Mercantile Exchange (NYMEX) and the International Petroleum Exchange (IPE) in London. Crude oil futures also trade at the Tokyo Commodity Exchange. (See Table 17.2.)

GASOLINE

Gasoline accounts for about half the yield of a barrel of crude oil. In the United States, individual consumers use about 75 percent of all gasoline produced, with peak demand during the summer travel season and lower demand during the winter months. Total U.S. motor gasoline consumption averaged 8.94 million barrels a day in 2003, up slightly from 2002. More than 90 percent of that total went for transportation. The remaining 10 percent went for construction and agricultural purposes.

Higher speed limits, sport utility vehicles, and a steady U.S. economy have all contributed to increasing consumption. Yet gasoline has changed significantly over the past decade. The production of unleaded gasoline, for instance, has increased as more and more cars using unleaded fuel were sold. In 1977, unleaded gasoline consumption was less than 30 percent of production. By 1990, unleaded gasoline had all but replaced leaded grades throughout the United States. (See Fig. 17.5 for an overview of gasoline prices.)

More recently, the U.S. Clean Air Act has mandated cleaner-burning reformulated gasoline, with about 10 percent oxygenate content, for heavily polluted areas. These oxygenates, typically MTBE (methyl tertiary-butyl ether) and ethanol, have become key parts of the overall gasoline pool. In 2004, California, New York, and Connecticut banned sale of MTBE gasoline because of its contamination of ground water supplies. State regulations on MTBE are expected to become widespread in the next decade. Gasoline producers have responded by substituting ethanol for MTBE in newer reformulations.

F I G U R E   17.5

Weekly U.S. Retail Gasoline Prices, Regular Grade
August 2003–February 2006

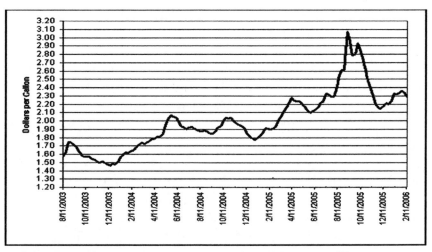

Source: Energy Information Administration, a division of the U.S. Department of Energy.

TABLE 17.3

Major Gasoline Futures and Options Contracts

Contract	Futures Exchange	Annual Volume in 2004
Unleaded regular gasoline futures	New York Mercantile Exchange	12,777,442
Unleaded regular gasoline options	New York Mercantile Exchange	904,466
Regular gasoline futures	Central Japan Commodity Exchange	15,869,951
Regular gasoline futures	Tokyo Commodity Exchange	23,648,587

Source: Data provided by Futures Industry Association, Inc.

Note that because gasoline and heating oil demands are inversely related—heating oil demand is greatest during the winter months, while gasoline demand peaks in the summer— refineries can alter their production to meet changes in demand. Gasoline is refined from lighter molecules of crude oil, while distillate fuels such as heating oil come from heavier molecules. The heavier molecules can, however, be transformed into lighter-end gasoline products by a catalytic cracking process. If gasoline demand—and price—increases, refiners can run the catalytic cracking at higher levels, thus increasing the production of lighter-end gasoline products.

Unleaded regular gasoline futures and options contracts trade on the New York Mercantile Exchange. Gasoline futures also trade on the Central Japan Commodity Exchange and the Tokyo Commodity Exchange. (See Table 17.3.)

HEATING OIL

Distillate fuels like heating oil, refined from the middle to the bottom of a barrel of crude oil, find use primarily as fuels for heating, diesel engines, railroads, and agricultural machinery. Heating oil, also known as No. 2 fuel oil, accounts for about 20 percent of total distillate fuel consumption and follows natural gas and electricity as an energy source of residential heating. In

2004, U.S. distillate fuel oil consumption averaged 4.2 million barrels a day, up slightly from 2003.

Generally speaking, the short-run demand for heating oil is relatively inelastic; that is, buyers' responsiveness to a change in price is relatively small. But given time, heating oil demand does respond to changes in crude oil prices. Individuals will alter their conservation habits, build more energy-efficient homes, and use more insulation to combat rising oil prices. During the 1980s, for example, consumers reduced their use of heating oil as a result of rising costs by switching to less expensive fuels.

While the short-run demand for heating oil is relatively inelastic, situations do occur in which heating oil prices will respond to short-term market conditions. For instance, a particularly harsh, cold winter can increase the demand for heating oil

TABLE 17.4

Winter Weather Scenarios: Warm (Mild), Normal (Base), and Cold (Severe) Cases
Illustrative Household Heating Demand and Costs

	Winter of 2002–2003	Winter of 2003–2004			% of Difference from Base	
		Mild	Normal	Severe	Mild	Severe
Natural Gas (Midwest)						
Consumption (mcf)	95.2	82.6	91.8	101.0	−10.0%	10.0%
Average price ($ per mcf)	8.39	8.77	9.17	9.67	−4.3%	5.5%
Expenditures ($)	799	724	841	977	−13.9%	16.1%
Heating Oil (Northeast)						
Consumption (gallons)	757	626	696	766	−10.0%	10.0%
Average price ($ per gallon)	1.33	1.25	1.33	1.42	−6.0%	6.3%
Expenditures ($)	1,010	785	927	1,084	−15.4%	16.9%
Propane (Midwest)						
Consumption (gallons)	941	816	907	998	−10.0%	10.0%
Average price ($ per gallon)	1.20	1.13	1.21	1.30	−6.6%	8.1%
Expenditures ($)	1,125	920	1,094	1,301	−15.9%	19.0%

Note: Scenarios involve assumptions of 10% greater and 10% lower heating degrees.
    mcf represents million cubic feet.
Source: Energy Information Administration.

TABLE 17.5

Major Heating Oil and Kerosene Futures and Options Contracts

Contract	Futures Exchange	Annual Volume in 2004
No. 2 heating oil futures[1]	New York Mercantile Exchange	12,884,511
No. 2 heating oil options[1]	New York Mercantile Exchange	800,277
Gas oil futures[2]	International Petroleum Exchange	9,355,767
Gas oil options[2]	International Petroleum Exchange	45,154
Gas oil futures[1]	Central Japan Commodity Exchange	1,056,257
Gas oil futures[1]	Tokyo Commodity Exchange	235,844
Kerosene futures[1]	Central Japan Commodity Exchange	15,454,906
Kerosene futures[1]	Tokyo Commodity Exchange	13,036,277

[1]Data provided by Futures Industry Association, Inc.
[2]Data provided by CBOT.

substantially, thus leading to large price increases. A particularly mild winter can result in lower demand and a price decline. (See Table 17.4.)

Heating oil contracts trade on the New York Mercantile Exchange, as well as on the International Petroleum Exchange, the Tokyo Commodity Exchange, and the Central Japan Commodity Exchange where it is called "gas oil." Kerosene (or jet fuel), another important and similar distillate from crude oil, is actively traded on the Central Japan Commodity Exchange and the Tokyo Commodity Exchange. (See Table 17.5.)

NATURAL GAS

Natural gas accounts for almost a quarter of all U.S. energy consumption, an amount that is likely to increase—both because of natural gas's competitive price relative to other fuels and because of tightening U.S. standards for fuel combustion, standards that natural gas (the cleanest burning of the fossil fuels) can best meet. In 2004, industrial, consumer, and residential users consumed 22.01 trillion cubic feet of natural gas, most of it produced domestically.

Natural gas is best known as fuel for cooking and heating in homes. Nevertheless, industrial demand accounts for the lion's share of use, about 38 percent of the market. Residential demand follows at 22 percent, with commercial, electric utility, and transportation demand at 14, 23, and 3 percent, respectively.

In contrast to the crude oil market, natural gas prices are influenced strictly by factors related to North America. Imports are relatively insignificant. Yet only since the Natural Gas Policy Act of 1978 has the natural gas industry gone from an almost totally regulated industry to one that primarily operates as a free market. Some federal and state rate structures remain, however, and several price categories exist. In addition, prices to consumers vary considerably by region because of such factors as transportation costs. (See Table 17.6.)

Most scientists believe that natural gas has been forming under the earth's surface for hundreds of millions of years and that the forces that created natural gas also created petroleum. Because of this, natural gas tends to be found with or near oil deposits. Note, however, that natural gas, a true gaseous form of matter, is very different from the gasoline that U.S. consumers typically refer to as "gas."

TABLE 17.6

U.S. Natural Gas Prices
(Dollars per thousand cubic feet, except where noted)

Sector	1999	2000	2001	2002	2003
Residential price	6.69	7.76	9.63	7.91	9.62
Commercial price	5.33	6.59	8.43	6.64	8.32
Industrial price	3.12	4.45	5.24	4.02	5.79
Electric power price (new definition)	2.62	4.38	4.61	3.68	5.55

Source: Energy Information Administration.

Because of the petroleum-natural gas relationship, though, some natural gas products can be derived directly from crude oil refining. The lightest hydrocarbon molecules in a barrel of crude oil (aromatics or gas liquids) are essentially a liquid form of natural gas. These natural gas liquids, or NGLs, as they are called, find widespread use as fuel and in the manufacturing of petrochemicals, including detergents, drugs, fertilizers, paints, plastics, synthetic rubber, acrylic, nylon, polyester, and other synthetic fibers.

Natural gas found apart from crude oil deposits can also yield NGLs. This is accomplished by pressurizing the gas into a liquid state. The liquid takes up much less space than the original gas and is easily transported in small pressurized containers. As the fuel is used, normal air pressure changes the liquid back to gas.

TABLE 17.7

Major Natural Gas Futures and Options Contracts

Contract	Futures Exchange	Annual Volume in 2004
Natural gas futures[1]	New York Mercantile Exchange	17,441,942
Natural gas options[1]	New York Mercantile Exchange	8,071,967
AECO-C/NIT basis swap futures[1] (Alberta basis swap)	New York Mercantile Exchange	488,699
Chicago basis swap futures[1]	New York Mercantile Exchange	174,498
Houston ship channel basis swap futures[1]	New York Mercantile Exchange	429,266
Henry Hub basis swap futures[1]	New York Mercantile Exchange	5,353,792
Northwest pipeline, Rockies basis swap futures[1]	New York Mercantile Exchange	652,511
SoCal basis swap futures[1]	New York Mercantile Exchange	569,540
Malin basis swap futures[1]	New York Mercantile Exchange	334,230
Natural gas monthly (NBP) futures[2]	International Petroleum Exchange	648,115

[1]Data provided by Futures Industry Association, Inc.
[2]Data provided by CBOT.

Two primary NGL compounds are propane and butane. Propane, butane, or a combination of the two—also known as liquefied petroleum gas (LPG), LP gas, or bottled gas—is used as a heating fuel in industry and homes. Those who live in mobile homes, farm areas, or other locations far from gas pipelines can purchase liquefied petroleum gas for cooking, heating, and other uses. Liquid petroleum gas represents approximately 4 percent of residential heating use, whereas nearly half of all homes use natural gas as a heating source.

Natural gas futures and options and propane futures trade on the New York Mercantile Exchange (NYMEX). Many of the most actively traded natural gas futures contracts are listed on the NYMEX ClearPort system, which allows market participants to directly negotiate their own prices based on different delivery points and dates. While prices are determined off-exchange, the trades are processed and cleared through the NYMEX clearinghouse in order to mitigate counterparty credit risk. Natural gas contracts are also listed on the International Petroleum Exchange in London. (See Table 17.7.)

ELECTRICITY

The newest energy market is the electricity market, created as a result of ongoing deregulation of electric utilities and nonutility power producers. Traditionally an industry of large, regulated utilities, with guaranteed pricing, the $200 billion electricity market has undergone and continues to undergo much of the deregulatory changes that the natural gas market underwent.

In the late 1970s, as a result of the Federal Public Utility Regulatory Policy Act, independent, nonutility power producers gained status as co-generators with the utilities, which were established as monopolies in the 1930s. Although the new nonutility generating companies remain small relative to the utility giants, their generating output doubled between 1988 and 1998. Some experts predict that they will account for half of all new generating capacity in the next decade.

With the Energy Policy Act of 1992, Congress opened the industry to wholesale sales, called "wholesale wheeling" in the industry, across the nation's transmission lines. Thus, competing suppliers—independent power producers, industrial co-generators, power marketers, even utilities selling outside their service territory—can sell wholesale electric power to various utilities and power providers throughout the United States. The next step, already being experimented with or phased in by some states, is "retail wheeling," where consumers can choose which power generator will supply their electricity. In 2003, 17 states had implemented restructuring to phase in retail wheeling. (See Fig. 17.6.)

Of course, free markets have something that regulated markets do not—namely, price risk. Already, state public service commissioners give more weight to market forces in setting rates. But an entirely deregulated electricity market, with wholesale and retail wheeling, will bring unprecedented price volatility and market risk to previously sheltered companies.

FIGURE 17.6

U.S. Electricity Flow, 2004 (quadrillion Btu)

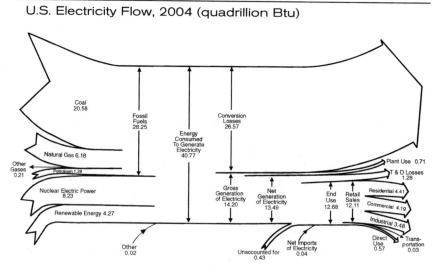

Source: Energy Information Administration, a division of the U.S. Department of Energy.

To help companies manage that risk, the New York Mercantile Exchange launched electricity futures and options in 1996. Currently, their PJM monthly electricity futures contract, which traded 234,207 contracts in 2004, is the most actively traded futures contract in electricity.

FURTHER READING

Brown, Stewart L., and Steven Errera, *Fundamentals of Trading Energy Futures and Options.* Tulsa, OK: PennWell Books, 2002.

Clubley, Sally, *Trading in Oil Futures and Options.* Cambridge, England: Woodhead Publishing, 1998.

Pilipovic, Dragana, *Energy Risk: Valuing and Managing Energy Derivatives.* New York: McGraw-Hill, 1997.

Wengler, John, *Managing Energy Risk: A Nontechnical Guide to Markets and Trading.* Tulsa, OK: PennWell Books, 2001.

INFORMATION SOURCES

American Petroleum Institute	www.api.org
Energy Information Administration	www.eia.doe.gov
International Energy Agency	www.iea.org
Energy Intelligence *(Petroleum Intelligence Weekly)*	www.piwpubs.com

Directory of Major
Futures Exchanges

TABLE A.1

U.S. Futures Exchanges

Exchange	2004 Annual Volume	2003 Annual Volume	Percentage of Change	Web Site
Chicago Mercantile Exchange	805,341,681	640,209,634	25.8%	www.cme.com
Chicago Board of Trade[1]	599,994,386	454,590,630	32.0%	www.cbot.com
New York Mercantile Exchange[2]	163,157,807	137,225,439	18.9%	www.nymex.com
New York Board of Trade	31,729,591	24,832,158	27.8%	www.nybot.com
EUREX US[3]	6,186,808	N/A	N/A	www.eurexus.com
Kansas City Board of Trade	3,089,103	3,099,805	–0.3%	www.kcbt.com
Minneapolis Grain Exchange	1,416,282	1,133,731	24.9%	www.mgex.com
CBOE Futures Exchange[4]	91,332	N/A	N/A	www.cboe.com/CFE

[1] CBOT market data 2003 and 2004 annual volume statistics.

[2] 2004 annual volume (NYMEX 134,023,050 + COMEX 29,134,757); 2003 annual volume (NYMEX 112,761,459 + COMEX 24,463,980).

[3] EUREX US launched February 2004.

[4] CBOE Futures Exchange launched March 2004.

Source: Futures Industry Association, Inc.

TABLE A.2

Futures Exchanges outside the United States

Exchange	2004 Annual Volume	2003 Annual Volume	Percentage of Change	Web Site
Korea Futures Exchange[1]	2,586,818,602	2,912,894,034	−11.2%	www.kofex.com
EUREX	1,065,639,010	1,014,932,312	5.0%	www.eurexchange.com
Euronext LIFFE, UK	386,959,234	335,825,947	15.2%	www.liffe.com
Euronext-Paris	318,512,628	277,881,912	14.6%	www.euronext.com
Mexican Derivatives Exchange	210,395,264	173,820,944	21.0%	www.mexder.com
BM&F, Brazil	183,427,938	120,785,602	51.9%	www.bmf.com.br
OMX Exchanges[2]	94,382,633	74,105,690	27.4%	www.omxgroup.com
Dalian Commodity Exchange	88,034,153	74,973,493	17.4%	www.dce.com.cn
Euronext-Amsterdam	83,267,638	79,444,756	4.8%	www.aex.nl
National Stock Exchange of India	75,093,629	43,081,968	74.3%	www.nse-india.com

[1]These contracts were transferred from the Korea Stock Exchange as of January 2, 2004, and are now traded on KFE.

[2]Effective July 2004 Helsinki and Stockholm Stock Exchanges are now reporting volume as OMX Exchanges. The 2003 and 2004 volumes have been adjusted to reflect this change.

Source: Futures Industry Association, Inc.

Specifications for Top-Traded Contracts

COMMODITY PRODUCTS

CBOT Corn Futures

Contract Size
5,000 bu

Deliverable Grades
No. 2 yellow at par, No. 1 yellow at 1½ cents per bushel over contract price, No. 3 yellow at 1½ cents per bushel under contract price

Tick Size
¼ cent per bushel ($12.50 per contract)

Price Quote
Cents per bushel

Contract Months
December, March, May, July, September

Last Trading Day
The business day prior to the 15th calendar day of the contract month

Last Delivery Day
Second business day following the last trading day of the delivery month

Ticker Symbols
Open auction: C
Electronic: ZC

Daily Price Limit
20 cents per bushel ($1,000 per contract) above or below the
previous day's settlement price; no limit in the spot month
(limits are lifted two business days before the spot month begins)

Trading Hours
Open auction: 9:30 a.m.–1:15 p.m. central time, Monday–Friday
Electronic: 6:30 p.m.–6:00 a.m. central time, Sunday–Friday
Trading in expiring contracts closes at noon on the last trading
day.

CBOT Soybean Futures

Contract Size
5,000 bushels

Deliverable Grades
No. 2 yellow at par, No. 1 yellow at 6 cents per bushel over
contract price, No. 3 yellow at 6 cents per bushel under contract
price

Tick Size
¼ cent per bushel ($12.50 per contract)

Price Quote
Cents per bushel

Contract Months
September, November, January, March, May, July, August

Last Trading Day
The business day prior to the 15th calendar day of the contract
month

Last Delivery Day
Second business day following the last trading day of the
delivery month

Ticker Symbols
Open auction: S
Electronic: ZS

Daily Price Limit
50 cents per bushel ($2,500 per contract) above or below the previous day's settlement price; no limit in the spot month (limits are lifted two business days before the spot month begins)

Trading Hours
Open auction: 9:30 a.m.–1:15 p.m. central time, Monday–Friday
Electronic: 6:31 p.m.–6:00 a.m. central time, Sunday–Friday
Trading in expiring contracts closes at noon on the last trading day.

CBOT Wheat Futures

Contract Size
5,000 bushels

Deliverable Grades
No. 1 and No. 2 Soft Red, No. 1 and No. 2 Hard Red Winter, No. 1 and No. 2 Dark Northern Spring, No. 1 Northern Spring at 3 cents per bushel premium and No. 2 Northern Spring at par; substitutions at differentials established by the exchange

Tick Size
¼ cent per bushel ($12.50 per contract)

Price Quote
Cents per bushel

Contract Months
July, September, December, March, May

Last Trading Day
The business day prior to the 15th calendar day of the contract month

Last Delivery Day
Seventh business day following the last trading day of the delivery month

Ticker Symbols
Open auction: W
Electronic: ZW

Daily Price Limit
30 cents per bushel ($1,500/contract) above or below the previous day's settlement price; no limit in the spot month (limits are lifted two business days before the spot month begins)

Trading Hours
Open auction: 9:30 a.m.–1:15 p.m. central time, Monday–Friday
Electronic: 6:32 p.m.–6:00 a.m. central time, Sunday–Friday
Trading in expiring contracts closes at noon on the last trading day.

CBOT Corn Futures Options

Contract Size
One CBOT corn futures contract

Strike Price Intervals
5 cents per bushel and 10 cents per bushel

Tick Size
⅛ cent per bushel ($6.25 per contract)

Exercise
Buyer may exercise the option on any business day. Option exercise results in an underlying futures position. In-the-money options on the last day of trading are automatically exercised.

Contract Months

December, March, May, July, September; a monthly option contract is also listed when the front month is not a standard option contract. The monthly option contract expires into the nearby futures contract.

Last Trading Day

For standard option contracts, the last Friday preceding the first notice day of the corresponding futures contract by at least two business days; for serial options, the last Friday preceding by at least two business days the last business day of the month preceding the option month

Ticker Symbols

Open auction: CY for calls; PY for puts
Electronic trading: OZC

Trading Hours

Open auction: 9:30 a.m.–1:15 p.m. central time, Monday–Friday
Electronic: 6:32 p.m.–6:00 a.m. central time, Sunday–Friday

CBOT Soybean Futures Options

Contract Size

One CBOT soybean futures contract

Strike Price Intervals

10 cents per bushel and 20 cents per bushel

Tick Size

⅛ cent per bushel ($6.25 per contract)

Exercise

Buyer may exercise the option on any business day. Option exercise results in an underlying futures position. In-the-money options on the last day of trading are automatically exercised.

Contract Months
September, November, January, March, May, July, August; a monthly option contract is also listed when the front month is not a standard option contract. The monthly option contract expires into the nearby futures contract.

Last Trading Day
For standard option contracts, the last Friday preceding the first notice day of the corresponding futures contract by at least two business days; for serial options, the last Friday preceding by at least two business days the last business day of the month preceding the option month.

Ticker Symbols
Open auction: CZ for calls; PZ for puts
Electronic: OZS

Trading Hours
Open auction: 9:30 a.m.–1:15 p.m. central time, Monday–Friday
Electronic: 6:33 p.m.–6:00 a.m. central time, Sunday–Friday

COMEX Gold Futures

Contract Size
100 troy ounces

Deliverable Grades
100 troy ounces of refined gold, assaying not less than 0.995 fineness

Tick Size
$0.10 (10 cents) per ounce ($10.00 per contract)

Price Quote
U.S. dollars and cents per troy ounce

Contract Months
Current calendar month; the next two months; any February, April, August, and October falling within a 23-month period; and any June and December falling within a 60-month period

Last Trading Day
The third to last business day of the delivery month

Last Delivery Day
Last business day of the delivery month

Ticker Symbols
GC

Daily Price Limit
$75.00 per ounce

Trading Hours
Open auction: 8:20 a.m.–1:30 p.m. eastern time, Monday–Friday
Electronic trading: 2:00 p.m.–8:00 a.m., Monday–Friday; session begins at 7:00 p.m. on Sundays

COMEX Silver Futures

Contract Size
5,000 troy ounces

Deliverable Grades
5,000 troy ounces of refined silver, assaying not less than 0.999 fineness

Tick Size
$0.005 (one-half cent) per ounce ($25.00 per contract)

Price Quote
U.S. dollars and half-cents per troy ounce

Contract Months
Current calendar month; the next two months; any March,
May, and September falling within a 23-month period; and any
July and December falling within a 60-month period

Last Trading Day
The third to last business day of the delivery month

Last Delivery Day
Last business day of the delivery month

Ticker Symbols
SI

Daily Price Limit
$1.50 per ounce

Trading Hours
Open auction: 8:25 a.m.–1:25 p.m. eastern time,
Monday–Friday
Electronic trading: 2:00 p.m.–8:00 a.m., Monday–Friday;
session begins at 7:00 p.m. on Sundays

NYMEX Light, Sweet Crude Oil Futures

Contract Size
1,000 U.S. barrels (42,000 gallons)

Deliverable Grades
Specific domestic and foreign crudes

Tick Size
$0.01 (1 cent) per barrel ($10.00 per contract)

Price Quote
U.S. dollars and cents per barrel

Contract Months
Thirty consecutive months based on a quarterly listing cycle

Last Trading Day
The third business day prior to the 25th calendar day of the contract month preceding the delivery month

Last Delivery Day
Last calendar day of the delivery month

Ticker Symbols
CL

Daily Price Limit
$10.00 per barrel

Trading Hours
Open auction: 10:00 a.m.–2:30 p.m. eastern time, Monday–Friday
Electronic trading: 3:30 p.m.–9:30 a.m., Monday–Thursday; session begins at 7:00 p.m. on Sundays

EQUITY INDEX PRODUCTS
CBOT Mini-Sized Dow Futures

Contract Size
Five ($5.00) times the Dow Jones Industrial Average (DJIA)
The DJIA is a price-weighted index of 30 of the largest, most liquid U.S. stocks.

Final Settlement Day
The third Friday of the contract month

Settlement
Cash settlement based on the final settlement day
The final settlement price is $5.00 times a special opening
quotation of the index.

Tick Size
Minimum price fluctuation is one point ($5.00 per contract)

Price Quote
One point equals $5.00 per contract

Contract Months
March, June, September, December cycle; four months listed at
all times

Last Trading Day
The business day preceding the final settlement day

Ticker Symbols
Electronic: YM

Daily Price Limit
Successive 10%, 20%, and 30% limits

Trading Hours
Electronic trading: 6:15 p.m.–4:00 p.m. central time,
Sunday–Friday

CME E-Mini S&P 500 Futures

Contract Size
Fifty ($50.00) times the Standard & Poor's 500 Stock Index

Final Settlement Day
The third Friday of the contract month

Settlement
Cash settlement based on the final settlement day
The final settlement price is $50.00 times a special opening
quotation of the index.

Tick Size
Minimum price fluctuation is 0.25 = $12.50 per contract

Price Quote
One point equals .01 index point = $0.50 per contract

Contract Months
March, June, September, December cycle; two months listed at
all times

Last Trading Day
The business day preceding the final settlement day

Ticker Symbols
Electronic: ES

Daily Price Limit
Price limit corresponding to a 5 percent increase or decrease of
the prior settlement price

Trading Hours
Electronic trading: 5:00 p.m.–3:15 p.m. and 3:30 p.m.–4:30 p.m.
central time, Monday–Thursday; 5:00 p.m.–3:15 p.m. central
time, Sundays and holidays

Eurex DJ EURO STOXX 50 Futures

Contract Size
EUR 10 times the Dow Jones EURO STOXX 50 Stock Index

Final Settlement Day
The third Friday of the contract month

Settlement
Cash settlement based on the final settlement day
The final settlement price is the average of the Dow Jones
EURO STOXX 50 Index values calculated between 11:50 a.m.
and 12 noon Central European Time (**CET**) on the last trading
day.

Tick Size
Minimum price fluctuation is 1 point = EUR 10 per contract

Price Quote
In points, with one decimal place

Contract Months
March, June, September, December cycle; three months listed
at all times

Last Trading Day
The final settlement day

Ticker Symbols
Electronic: ES

Trading Hours
Electronic trading: 8:50 a.m.–8:00 p.m. CET, Monday–Friday

INTEREST RATE AND CURRENCY PRODUCTS

CBOT 30-Year U.S. Treasury Bond Futures

Contract Size
One U.S. Treasury bond having a face value at maturity of $100,000 or a multiple thereof

Deliverable Grades
U.S. Treasury bonds that, if callable, are not callable for at least 15 years from the first day of the delivery month or, if not callable, have a maturity of at least 15 years from the first day of the delivery month

The invoice price equals the futures settlement price multiplied by a conversion factor plus accrued interest. The conversion factor is the price of the delivered bond ($1 par value) to yield 6 percent.

Tick Size
One thirty-second ($\frac{1}{32}$) point per 100 points ($31.25 per contract)

Price Quote
Points ($1,000) and $\frac{1}{32}$ of a point

Contract Months
March, June, September, December cycle

Last Trading Day
Seventh business day preceding the last business day of the delivery month

Last Delivery Day
Last business day of the delivery month

Delivery Method
Federal Reserve book-entry wire-transfer system

Ticker Symbols
Open auction: US
Electronic: ZB

Daily Price Limit
None

Trading Hours
Open auction: 7:20 a.m.–2:00 p.m. central time, Monday–Friday
Electronic: 6:00 p.m.–4:00 p.m. central time, Sunday–Friday
Trading in expiring contracts closes at noon on the last trading
day.

CBOT 10-Year U.S. Treasury Note Futures

Contract Size
One U.S. Treasury note having a face value at maturity of
$100,000 or a multiple thereof

Deliverable Grades
U.S. Treasury notes maturing at least 6½ years, but not more
than 10 years, from the first day of the delivery month

The invoice price equals the futures settlement price multiplied
by a conversion factor plus accrued interest. The conversion
factor is the price of the delivered bond ($1 par value) to yield
6 percent.

Tick Size
One-half of one thirty-second (½₃₂) point per 100 points ($15.625
per contract rounded up to the nearest cent per contract)

Price Quote
Points ($1,000) and one-half of ½₃₂ of a point

Contract Months
March, June, September, December cycle

Last Trading Day
Seventh business day preceding the last business day of the
delivery month

Last Delivery Day
Last business day of the delivery month

Delivery Method
Federal Reserve book-entry wire-transfer system

Ticker Symbols
Open auction: TY
Electronic: ZN

Daily Price Limit
None

Trading Hours
Open auction: 7:20 a.m.–2:00 p.m. central time, Monday–Friday
Electronic: 6:00 p.m.–4:00 p.m. central time, Sunday–Friday
Trading in expiring contracts closes at noon on the last trading
day.

CBOT 10-Year Treasury Note Futures Options

Contract Size
One CBOT 10-year Treasury note futures contract

Strike Price Intervals
One point

Tick Size
$\frac{1}{64}$ of a point ($15.625 per contract) rounded up to the nearest
cent per contract

Exercise

Buyer may exercise the option on any business day. Option exercise results in an underlying futures position. In-the-money options on the last day of trading are automatically exercised.

Contract Months

The first three consecutive months plus the next four months in the March quarterly cycle. There will always be seven months available for trading. The monthly option contract expires into the nearby futures contract.

Last Trading Day

For standard option contracts, the last Friday preceding the first notice day of the corresponding futures contract by at least two business days; for serial options, the last Friday preceding by at least two business days the last business day of the month preceding the option month

Ticker Symbols

Open auction: TC for calls; TP for puts
Electronic: OZNC for calls; OZNP for puts

Trading Hours

Open auction: 7:20 a.m.–2:00 p.m. central time, Monday–Friday
Electronic: 6:02 p.m.–6:00 a.m. central time, Sunday–Friday

CME Euro FX Futures

Contract Size

125,000 euro

Delivery

Physical delivery takes place on the third Wednesday of the contract month

Tick Size
Minimum price fluctuation is 0.005 = $12.50 per contract

Price Quote
Quoted in terms of the three-month Eurodollar index; 100 minus the yield on an annual basis for a 360-day year

Contract Months
March, June, September, December cycle; 40 months listed plus the four nearest serial months

Last Trading Day
The second London bank business day preceding the third Wednesday of the contract month

Ticker Symbols
Open auction: ECD
Electronic: GE

Daily Price Limit
No limits for open auction; 200 points for electronic

Trading Hours
Open auction: 7:20 a.m.–2:00 p.m. central time
Electronic trading: 5:00 p.m.–4:00 p.m. central time, Monday–Thursday; 5:00 p.m.–4:00 p.m. central time, Sundays and holidays

CME Eurodollar Futures Options

Contract Size
One CME Eurodollar futures contract

Strike Price Intervals
0.25 intervals

Tick Size
0.01 = $25.00 and 0.005 = $12.50

Exercise
Buyer may exercise the option on any business day. Option exercise results in an underlying futures position. In-the-money options on the last day of trading are automatically cash exercised.

Contract Months
March, June, September, December; eight months in the March quarterly cycle and two serial months not listed in the March cycle

Last Trading Day
Same as the underlying futures

Ticker Symbols
Open auction: CE for calls; PE for puts
Electronic: GE

Trading Hours
Open auction: 7:20 a.m.–2:00 p.m. central time
Electronic trading: 5:00 p.m.–4:00 p.m. central time,
Monday–Thursday; 5:00 p.m.–4:00 p.m. central time, Sundays and holidays

Eurex Euro-Bund Futures

Contract Size
One Euro-Bund having a face value at maturity of 100,000 euros or a multiple thereof

Deliverable Grades
Euro-Bunds maturing at least 8½ years, but not more than 10½ years

Tick Size
Minimum price change equals 0.01 percent (Eur 10)

Price Quote
In percent of the par value

Contract Months
March, June, September, December cycle; three months listed

Last Trading Day
Two exchange trading days preceding the delivery day of the delivery month

Delivery Day
The tenth calendar day of the delivery month; if this is not a trading day, the next following trading day

Ticker Symbols
Electronic: FGBL

Trading Hours
Electronic trading: 8:00 a.m.–7:00 p.m. CET, Monday–Friday

Euronext.liffe Three-Month (EURIBOR) Interest Rate Futures

Contract Size
1,000,000 EUR

Settlement
Cash settlement based on the European Bankers Federations' Euribor offered rate for three-month euro deposits at 11:00 Brussels time on the last trading day

Tick Size
Minimum price fluctuation is 0.005 = EUR 12.50 per contract

Price Quote
100.00 minus the rate of interest

Contract Months
March, June, September, December cycle plus 4 serial months
with 24 delivery months listed for trading

Last Trading Day
Two business days prior to the third Wednesday of the delivery
month

Trading Hours
Electronic trading: 7:00 a.m.–6:00 p.m. London time CET,
Monday–Friday

accrued interest—Interest earned between the most recent interest payment and the present date but which has not yet been paid to the lender.

actuals—An actual physical commodity someone is buying or selling, e.g., soybeans, corn, gold, silver, Treasury bonds, etc. Also referred to as *cash commodity*.

add-on method—A method of paying interest in which the interest is added onto the principal at maturity or on interest payment dates.

adjusted futures price—The cash-price equivalent reflected in the current futures price. The adjusted futures price is calculated by multiplying the futures price by the conversion factor for the particular financial instrument (e.g., bond or note) being delivered.

against actuals—A transaction generally used by two hedgers who want to exchange futures for cash positions. Also referred to as *versus cash*.

assign—To make an option seller perform his or her obligation to assume a short futures position (as a seller of a call option) or a long futures position (as a seller of a put option).

associated person (AP)—An individual who solicits orders, customers, or customer funds (or who supervises persons performing such duties) on behalf of a futures commission merchant, an introducing broker, a commodity trading advisor, or a commodity pool operator.

at-the-money option—An option with a strike price that is equal, or approximately equal, to the current market price of the underlying futures contract.

balance of payment—A summary of the international transactions of a country over a period of time, including commodity and service transactions, capital transactions, and gold movements.

bar chart—A chart that depicts the high, low, and settlement prices for a specific trading session over a given period of time.

basis—The difference between the current cash price and the futures price of the same commodity. Unless otherwise specified, the price of the nearby futures contract month is generally used to calculate the basis.

bear—Someone who thinks market prices will decline.

bear market—A period of declining market prices.

bear spread—In most commodities and financial instruments, this term refers to selling the nearby contract month and buying the deferred contract, to profit from a change in the price relationship.

bid—An expression indicating a desire to buy a commodity at a given price; opposite of offer.

book entry securities—Electronically recorded securities that include each creditor's name, address, Social Security or tax identification number, and dollar amount loaned (i.e., no certificates are issued to bond holders; instead the transfer agent electronically credits interest payments to each creditor's bank account on a designated date).

broker—A company or individual who executes futures and options orders on behalf of financial and commercial institutions and/or the general public.

brokerage fee—A fee charged by a broker for executing a transaction. Also referred to as *commission fee*.

brokerage house—An individual or organization that solicits or accepts orders to buy or sell futures contracts or options on futures and accepts money or other assets from customers to support such orders. Also referred to as *commission house* or *wire house*.

bull—Someone who thinks market prices will rise.

bull market—A period of rising market prices.

bull spread—In most commodities and financial instruments, the term refers to buying the nearby month and selling the deferred month, to profit from the change in the price relationship.

butterfly spread—The placing of two interdelivery spreads in opposite directions with the center delivery month common to both spreads.

buying hedge—Buying futures contracts to protect against a possible price increase of cash commodities that will be purchased in the future. At the time the cash commodities are bought, the open futures position is closed by selling an equal number and type of futures contracts of those that were initially purchased. Also referred to as *long hedge* or *purchasing hedge*.

calendar spread—(1) The purchase of one delivery month of a given futures contract and the simultaneous sale of another delivery month of the same commodity on the same exchange. (2) The purchase of either a call or put option and the simultaneous sale of the same type of option with typically the same strike price but with a different expiration month.

call option—An option that gives the buyer the right, but not the obligation, to purchase (go "long") the underlying futures contract at the strike price on or before the expiration date.

canceling order—An order that deletes a customer's previous order.

carrying charge—For physical commodities such as grains and metals, the cost of storage space, insurance, and finance charges incurred by holding a physical commodity. In interest rate futures markets, a carrying charge refers to the differential between the yield on a cash instrument and the cost of funds necessary to buy the instrument. Also referred to as *cost of carry* or *carry*.

carryover—Grain and oilseed commodities not consumed during the marketing year and remaining in storage at year's end. These stocks are "carried over" into the next marketing year and added to the stocks produced during that crop year.

cash commodity—An actual physical commodity someone is buying or selling, e.g., soybeans, corn, gold, silver, Treasury bonds, etc. Also referred to as *actuals*.

cash contract—A sales agreement for either immediate or future delivery of the actual product.

cash market—A place where people buy and sell the actual commodities, i.e., grain elevator, bank, etc. See also *spot* and *forward contract*.

certificate of deposit (CD)—A time deposit with a specific maturity evidenced by a certificate.

charting—(1) The use of charts to analyze market behavior and anticipate future price movements. Those who use charting as a trading method plot such factors as high, low, and settlement prices; average price movements; volume; and open interest. Two basic price charts are bar charts and point-and-figure charts. (2) Anticipating future price movement using historical prices, trading volume, open interest, and other trading data to study price patterns.

cheap—Colloquialism implying that a commodity is underpriced.

cheapest to deliver (CTD)—A method to determine which particular cash debt instrument is most profitable to deliver against a futures contract.

clear—The process by which a clearinghouse maintains records of all trades and settles margin flow on a daily marking-to-market basis for its clearing members.

clearing corporation—An independent corporation acting as a guarantor for all trades cleared by it, reconciles all clearing member firm accounts each day to ensure that all gains have been credited and all losses have been collected, and sets and adjusts clearing member firm margins for changing market conditions.

clearing margin—Financial safeguards to ensure that clearing members (usually companies or corporations) perform on their customers' open futures and options contracts. Clearing margins are distinct from customer margins that individual buyers and sellers of futures and options contracts are required to deposit with brokers. See also *customer margin.*

clearing member—A member of an exchange clearinghouse. Memberships in clearing organizations are usually held by companies. Clearing members are responsible for the financial commitments of customers that clear through their firm.

clearinghouse—An agency or separate corporation of a futures exchange that is responsible for settling trading accounts, clearing trades, collecting and maintaining margin monies, regulating delivery, and reporting trading data. Clearinghouses act as third parties to all futures and options contracts, acting as a buyer to every clearing member seller and a seller to every clearing member buyer.

closing price—The last price paid for a commodity on any trading day. The exchange clearinghouse determines a firm's net gains or losses, margin requirements, and the next day's price limits, based on each futures and options contract settlement price. If there is a closing range of prices, the settlement price is determined by averaging those prices. Also referred to as *settle price*.

closing range—A range of prices at which buy and sell transactions took place during the market close.

COM (Commodity Options Market) membership—A membership with Chicago Board of Trade that allows an individual to trade contracts listed in the commodity options market category.

commission fee—A fee charged by a broker for executing a transaction. Also referred to as *brokerage fee*.

commission house—An individual or organization that solicits or accepts orders to buy or sell futures contracts or options on futures and accepts money or other assets from customers to support such orders. Also referred to as *wire house*.

commodity—An article of commerce or a product that can be used for commerce. In a narrow sense, products traded on an authorized commodity exchange. Types of commodities include agricultural products, metals, petroleum, foreign currencies, and financial instruments, to name a few.

Commodity Credit Corp—A branch of the U.S. Department of Agriculture, established in 1933, that supervises the government's farm loan and subsidy programs.

Commodity Futures Trading Commission (CFTC)—A federal regulatory agency established under the Commodity Futures Trading Commission Act, as amended in 1974, that oversees futures trading in the United States. The commission is composed of five commissioners, one of whom is designated as chairperson. All members are appointed by the President subject to Senate confirmation, and the commission is independent of all cabinet departments.

commodity pool—An enterprise in which funds contributed by a number of persons are combined for the purpose of trading futures contracts or commodity options.

commodity pool operator (CPO)—An individual or organization that operates or solicits funds for a commodity pool.

commodity trading advisor (CTA)—A person who, for compensation or profit, directly or indirectly advises others concerning the value or the advisability of buying or selling futures contracts or commodity options. Advising indirectly includes exercising trading authority over a customer's account as well as providing recommendations through written publications or other media.

concurrent indicators—Market indicators showing the general direction of the economy and confirming or denying a trend implied by the leading indicators.

consumer price index (CPI)—A major inflation measure computed by the U.S. Department of Commerce. It measures the change in prices of a fixed market basket of some 385 goods and services in the previous month.

contract grades—The standard grades of commodities or instruments listed in the rules of the exchanges that must be met when delivering cash commodities against futures contracts. Grades are often accompanied by a schedule of discounts and premiums allowable for delivery of commodities of lesser or greater quality than the standard called for by the exchange.

contract month—A specific month in which delivery may take place under the terms of a futures contract.

controlled account—An arrangement by which the holder of an account gives written power of attorney to another person, often his or her broker, to make trading decisions. Also known as a *discretionary* or *managed account.*

convergence—A term used to refer to cash and futures prices that tend to come together (i.e., the basis approaches zero) as the futures contract nears expiration.

conversion factor—A factor used to equate the price of T-bond and T-note futures contracts with the various cash T-bonds and T-notes eligible for delivery. This factor is based on the relationship of the cash-instrument coupon to the required 6 percent deliverable grade of a futures contract as well as taking into account the cash instrument's maturity or call.

cost of carry (or carry)—For physical commodities such as grains and metals, the cost of storage space, insurance, and finance charges incurred by holding a physical commodity. In interest rate futures markets, cost of carry refers to the differential between the yield on a cash instrument and the cost of funds necessary to buy the instrument.

coupon—The interest rate on a debt instrument expressed in terms of a percent on an annualized basis that the issuer guarantees to pay the holder until maturity.

crop (marketing) year—The time span from harvest to harvest for agricultural commodities. The crop marketing year varies slightly with each agricultural commodity, but it tends to begin at harvest and end before the next year's harvest; e.g., the marketing year for soybeans begins September 1 and ends August 31. The futures contract month of November represents the first major new-crop marketing month, and the contract month of July represents the last major old-crop marketing month for soybeans.

crop reports—Reports compiled by the U.S. Department of Agriculture on various agricultural commodities that are released throughout the year. Information in the reports includes estimates on planted acreage, yield, and expected production, as well as comparison of production from previous years.

cross-hedging—Hedging a cash commodity using a different but related futures contract when there is no futures contract for the cash commodity being hedged and the cash and futures markets follow similar price trends (e.g., using soybean meal futures to hedge fish meal).

crush spread—The purchase of soybean futures and the simultaneous sale of soybean oil and soybean meal futures.

current yield—The ratio of the coupon to the current market price of a debt instrument.

customer margin—Within the futures industry, financial guarantees required of both buyers and sellers of futures contracts and sellers of options contracts to ensure fulfilling of contract obligations. Futures commission merchants are responsible for overseeing customer margin accounts. Margins are determined on the basis of market risk and contract value. Also referred to as *performance-bond margin.*

daily trading limit—The maximum price range set by the exchange each day for a contract.

day traders—Speculators who take positions in futures or options contracts and liquidate them prior to the close of the same trading day.

deferred (delivery) month—The more distant month(s) in which futures trading is taking place, as distinguished from the nearby (delivery) month.

deliverable grades—The standard grades of commodities or instruments listed in the rules of the exchanges that must be met when delivering cash commodities against futures contracts. Grades are often accompanied by a schedule of discounts and premiums allowable for delivery of commodities of lesser or greater quality than the standard called for by the exchange. Also referred to as *contract grades*.

delivery—The transfer of the cash commodity from the seller of a futures contract to the buyer of a futures contract. Each futures exchange has specific procedures for delivery of a cash commodity. Some futures contracts, such as stock index contracts, are settled in cash.

delivery day—The third day in the delivery process at the Chicago Board of Trade, when the buyer's clearing firm presents the delivery notice with a certified check for the amount due at the office of the seller's clearing firm.

delivery month—A specific month in which delivery may take place under the terms of a futures contract. Also referred to as *contract month*.

delivery points—The locations and facilities designated by a futures exchange where stocks of a commodity may be delivered in fulfillment of a futures contract, under procedures established by the exchange.

delta—A measure of how much an option premium changes, given a unit change in the underlying futures price. Delta often is interpreted as the probability that the option will be in-the-money by expiration.

demand, law of—See *law of demand*.

differentials—Price differences between classes, grades, and delivery locations of various stocks of the same commodity.

discount method—A method of paying interest by issuing a security at less than par and repaying par value at maturity. The difference between the higher par value and the lower purchase price is the interest.

discount rate—The interest rate charged on loans by the Federal Reserve Bank to a member bank.

discretionary account—An arrangement in which the holder of the account gives written power of attorney to another person, often his or her broker, to make trading decisions. Also known as a *controlled* or *managed account*.

econometrics—The application of statistical and mathematical methods in the field of economics to test and quantify economic theories and the solutions to economic problems.

electronic trading—The automation or enhancement of pit trading; such systems usually electronically match market bids and offers in accordance with open auction trading standards.

equilibrium price—The market price at which the quantity supplied of a commodity equals the quantity demanded.

Eurodollars—U.S. dollars on deposit with a bank outside the United States and, consequently, outside the jurisdiction of the United States. The bank could be either a foreign bank or a subsidiary of a U.S. bank.

European terms—A method of quoting exchange rates, which measures the amount of foreign currency needed to buy one U.S. dollar, i.e., foreign currency unit per dollar. Reciprocal of European terms is another method of quoting exchange rates, which measure the U.S.-dollar value of one foreign currency unit, i.e., U.S. dollars per foreign units.

exchange for physicals (EFP)—A transaction generally used by two hedgers who want to exchange futures for cash positions. Also referred to as *against actuals* or *versus cash*.

exercise—The action taken by the holder of a call option if he or she wishes to purchase the underlying futures contract or by the holder of a put option if he or she wishes to sell the underlying futures contract.

exercise price—The price at which the futures contract underlying a call or put option can be purchased (if a call) or sold (if a put). Also referred to as *strike price*.

expiration date—The date on which a futures contract expires. Options on futures generally expire on a specific date during the month preceding the futures contract delivery month. For example, an option on a March futures contract expires in February but is referred to as a March option because its exercise would result in a March futures contract position.

extrinsic value—The amount of money option buyers are willing to pay for an option in the anticipation that, over time, a change in the underlying futures price will cause the option to increase in value. In general, an option premium is the sum of time value and intrinsic value. Any amount by which an option premium exceeds the option's intrinsic value can be considered extrinsic value. Also referred to as *time value*.

face value—The amount of money printed on the face of the certificate of a security; the original dollar amount of indebtedness incurred.

federal funds—Member bank deposits at the Federal Reserve; these funds are loaned by member banks to other member banks. Also referred to as *fed funds*.

federal funds rate—The rate of interest charged for the use of federal funds.

Federal Housing Administration (FHA)—A division of the U.S. Department of Housing and Urban Development that insures residential mortgage loans and sets construction standards.

Federal Reserve system—The central banking system in the United States, created by the Federal Reserve Act in 1913, designed to assist the nation in attaining its economic and financial goals. The structure of the Federal Reserve system includes a board of governors, the federal open market committee, and 12 federal reserve banks.

feed ratio—A ratio used to express the relationship of feeding costs to the dollar value of livestock. See also *hog/corn ratio* and *steer/corn ratio.*

fill-or-kill—A customer order that is a price limit order that must be filled immediately or be canceled.

Financial Analysis Auditing Compliance Tracking System (FACTS)—The National Futures Association's computerized system of maintaining financial records of its member firms and monitoring their financial conditions.

financial instrument—The reference to transactions in the management of money and other assets. There are two basic types: (1) a debt instrument, which is a loan with an agreement to pay back funds with interest; (2) an equity security, which is a share of, or stock in, a company.

first notice day—According to Chicago Board of Trade rules, the first day on which a notice of intent to deliver a commodity in fulfillment of a given month's futures contract can be made by the clearinghouse to a buyer. The clearinghouse also informs the sellers who they have been matched up with.

floor broker (FB)—An individual who executes orders for the purchase or sale of any commodity futures or options contract on any contract market for any other person.

floor trader (FT)—An individual who executes trades for the purchase or sale of any commodity futures or options contract on any contract market for such individual's own account.

foreign exchange market—An over-the-counter market in which buyers and sellers conduct foreign exchange business by telephone and other means of communication. Also referred to as a *forex market.*

Tick Size
Minimum price fluctuation is 0.0001 = $12.50 per contract

Price Quote
One point equals 0.0001 per euro = $12.50 per contract

Contract Months
March, June, September, December cycle; six months listed at all times

Last Trading Day
The second business day preceding the third Wednesday of the contract month

Ticker Symbols
Open auction: EC
Electronic: 6E

Daily Price Limit
No limits

Trading Hours
Open auction and electronic trading: 5:00 p.m.–4:00 p.m. central time, Monday–Thursday; 5:00 p.m.–4:00 p.m. central time, Sundays and holidays

CME Eurodollar Futures

Contract Size
Eurodollar time deposit having a principal value of $1,000,000 with a three-month maturity

Delivery
Cash delivery on the last day of trading based on the British Banker's Association interest settlement rate

forward (cash) contract—A cash contract in which a seller agrees to deliver a specific cash commodity to a buyer sometime in the future. Forward contracts, in contrast to futures contracts, are privately negotiated and are not standardized.

full carrying charge market—A futures market in which the price difference between delivery months reflects the total costs of interest, insurance, and storage.

fundamental analysis—A method of anticipating future price movement using supply-and-demand information.

futures commission merchant (FCM)—An individual or organization that solicits or accepts orders to buy or sell futures contracts or options on futures and accepts money or other assets from customers to support such orders. Also referred to as *commission house* or *wire house.*

futures contract—A legally binding agreement, made on the trading floor of a futures exchange, to buy or sell a commodity or financial instrument sometime in the future. Futures contracts are standardized according to the quality, quantity, delivery time and location for each commodity. The only variable is price, which is discovered on an exchange trading floor.

futures exchange—A central marketplace with established rules and regulations where buyers and sellers meet to trade futures and options on futures contracts.

gamma—A measurement of how fast delta changes, given a unit change in the underlying futures price. See also *delta.*

give-up—A transaction in which one clearing firm places an order for execution on behalf of a different clearing firm which ultimately will carry the trade.

GLOBEX—A global after-hours electronic trading system.

grain terminal—Large grain elevator facility with the capacity to ship grain by rail and/or barge to domestic or foreign markets.

gross domestic product (GDP)—The value of all final goods and services produced by an economy over a particular time period, normally a year.

gross national product (GNP)—Gross domestic product plus the income accruing to domestic residents as a result of investments abroad minus income earned in domestic markets accruing to foreigners abroad.

gross processing margin (GPM)—The difference between the cost of soybeans and the combined sales income of the processed soybean oil and soybean meal.

hedger—An individual or company owning or planning to own a cash commodity, corn, soybeans, wheat, U.S. Treasury bonds, notes, bills, etc., and concerned that the cost of the commodity may change before the hedger buys or sells it in the cash market. A hedger achieves protection against changing cash prices by purchasing (or selling) futures contracts of the same or similar commodity and later offsetting that position by selling (or purchasing) futures contracts of the same quantity and type as the initial transaction.

hedging—The practice of offsetting the price risk inherent in any cash market position by taking an equal but opposite position in the futures market. Hedgers use the futures markets to protect their business from adverse price changes. See also *short hedge* and *long hedge*.

high—The highest price of the day for a particular futures contract.

hog/corn ratio—The relationship of feeding costs to the dollar value of hogs. It is measured by dividing the price of hogs ($/hundredweight) by the price of corn ($/bushel). When corn prices are high relative to pork prices, fewer units of corn are equal to the dollar value of 100 pounds of pork. Conversely, when corn prices are low in relation to pork prices, more units of corn are required to equal the value of 100 pounds of pork. See also *feed ratio.*

holder—The purchaser of either a call or put option. Option buyers receive the right, but not the obligation, to assume a futures position. Also referred to as the *option buyer.*

horizontal spread—The purchase of either a call or put option and the simultaneous sale of the same type of option, with typically the same strike price, but with a different expiration month. Also referred to as a *calendar spread.*

in-the-money option—An option having intrinsic value. A call option is in-the-money if its strike price is below the current price of the underlying futures contract. A put option is in-the-money if its strike price is above the current price of the underlying futures contract.

initial margin—The amount futures market participants must deposit into their margin accounts at the time they place an order to buy or sell a futures contracts. Also referred to as *original margin.*

intercommodity spread—The purchase of a given delivery month of one futures market and the simultaneous sale of the same delivery month of a different, but related, futures market.

interdelivery spread—The purchase of one delivery month of a given futures contract and simultaneous sale of another delivery month of the same commodity on the same exchange. Also referred to as an *intramarket* or *calendar spread.*

intermarket spread—The sale of a given delivery month of a futures contract on one exchange and the simultaneous purchase of the same delivery month and futures contract on another exchange.

intrinsic value—The amount by which an option is in-the-money. A call option is in-the-money if its strike price is below the current price of the underlying futures contract. A put option is in-the-money if its strike price is above the current price of the underlying futures contract.

introducing broker—A person or organization that solicits or accepts orders to buy or sell futures contracts or commodity options but does not accept money or other assets from customers to support such orders.

inverted market—A futures market in which the relationship between two delivery months of the same commodity is abnormal.

invisible supply—Uncounted stocks of a commodity in the hands of wholesalers, manufacturers, and producers that cannot be identified accurately; stocks outside commercial channels but theoretically available to the market.

lagging indicators—Market indicators showing the general direction of the economy and confirming or denying the trend implied by the leading indicators. Also referred to as *concurrent indicators*.

last trading day—According to the Chicago Board of Trade rules, the final day on which trading may occur in a given futures or option contract month. Futures contracts outstanding at the end of the last trading day must be settled by delivery of the underlying commodity or securities or by agreement for monetary settlement (in some cases by exchange for physicals, EFPs).

law of demand—The relationship between product demand and price.

law of supply—The relationship between product supply and its price.

leading indicators—Market indicators that signal the state of the economy for the coming months. Some of the leading indicators include: average manufacturing workweek, initial claims for unemployment insurance, orders for consumer goods and material, percentage of companies reporting slower deliveries, change in manufacturers' unfilled orders for durable goods, plant and equipment orders, new building permits, index of consumer expectations, change in material prices, prices of stocks, change in money supply.

leverage—The ability to control large dollar amounts of a commodity with a comparatively small amount of capital.

limit order—An order in which the customer sets a limit on the price and/or time of execution.

limits—(1) The maximum number of speculative futures contracts one can hold as determined by the Commodity Futures Trading Commission and/or the exchange upon which the contract is traded. Also referred to as *trading limit*. (2) The maximum advance or decline from the previous day's settlement permitted for a contract in one trading session by the rules of the exchange. According to the Chicago Board of Trade rules, an expanded allowable price range set during volatile markets.

linkage—The ability to buy (or sell) contracts on one exchange (such as the Chicago Mercantile Exchange) and later sell (or buy) those contracts on another exchange (such as the Singapore International Monetary Exchange).

liquid—A characteristic of a security or commodity market with enough units outstanding to allow large transactions without a substantial change in price. Institutional investors are inclined to seek out liquid investments so that their trading activity will not influence the market price.

liquidate—(1) To sell (or purchase) futures contracts of the same delivery month in which they were purchased (or sold) during an earlier transaction or to make (or take) delivery of the cash commodity represented by the futures contract. (2) To take a second futures or options position opposite the initial or opening position.

liquidity data bank—A computerized profile of CBOT market activity used by technical traders to analyze price trends and develop trading strategies. There is a specialized display of daily volume data and time distribution of prices for every commodity traded on the Chicago Board of Trade.

loan program—A federal program in which the government lends money at preannounced rates to farmers and allows them to use the crops they plant for the upcoming crop year as collateral. Default on these loans is the primary method by which the government acquires stock of agricultural commodities.

loan rate—The amount lent per unit of a commodity to farmers.

long—Referring to one who has bought futures contracts or owns a cash commodity.

long hedge—The purchase of futures contracts for the purpose of protecting against a possible price increase of cash commodities that will be purchased in the future. At the time the cash commodities are bought, the open futures position is closed by the sale of a number and type of futures contracts equal to those that were initially purchased. Also referred to as a *buying hedge*.

low—The lowest price of the day for a particular futures contract.

maintenance—A set minimum margin (per outstanding futures contract) that customers must maintain in their margin account.

managed account—Financial safeguard to ensure that clearing members (usually companies or corporations) perform on their customers' open futures and options contracts. Also known as a *controlled* or *discretionary account.*

managed futures—Represent an industry made up of professional money managers known as commodity trading advisors who manage client assets on a discretionary basis, using global futures markets as an investment medium.

margin—An amount of money deposited by both buyers and sellers of futures contracts to ensure performance of the terms of the contract. Margin in commodities is not a payment of equity or a down payment on the commodity itself but rather is a performance bond or security deposit.

margin call—A call from a clearinghouse to a clearing member, or from a brokerage firm to a customer, to bring margin deposits up to a required minimum level.

market order—An order to buy or sell a futures contract of a given delivery month to be filled at the best possible price and as quickly as possible.

Market Profile—A Chicago Board of Trade information service that helps technical traders analyze price trends. Market Profile consists of the time and sales ticker and the liquidity data bank.

market reporter—A person employed by an exchange and located in or near the trading pit. This person records prices as they occur during trading.

marking-to-market—Debiting or crediting on a daily basis a margin account based on the close of that day's trading session. Marking-to-market protects buyers and sellers from the possibility of contract default.

minimum price fluctuation—The smallest allowable increment of price movement for a contract.

money supply—The amount of money in the economy, consisting primarily of currency in circulation plus deposits in banks.

M-1 is the U.S. money supply consisting of currency held by the public, traveler's checks, checking account funds, NOW (Negotiable Order of Withdrawal) and super-NOW accounts, automatic transfer service accounts, and balances in credit unions. M-2 is the U.S. money supply consisting of M-1 plus savings and small time deposits (less than $100,000) at depository institutions, overnight repurchase agreements at commercial banks, and money market mutual fund accounts. M-3 is the U.S. money supply consisting of M-2 plus large time deposits ($100,000 or more) at depository institutions, repurchase agreements with maturities longer than one day at commercial banks, and institutional money market accounts.

moving-average chart—A statistical price analysis method of recognizing different price trends. A moving average is calculated by adding the prices for a predetermined number of days and then dividing by the number of days.

municipal bonds—Debt securities issued by state and local governments, and special districts and counties.

National Futures Association (NFA)—An industrywide, industry-supported, self-regulatory organization for futures and options markets. The primary responsibilities of the NFA are to enforce ethical standards and customer protection rites, screen futures professionals for membership, audit and monitor professionals for financial and general compliance rules, and provide for arbitration of futures-related disputes.

nearby (delivery) month—The futures contract month closest to expiration. Also referred to as *spot month.*

notice day—According to Chicago Board of Trade rules, the second day of the three-day delivery process when the clearing corporation matches the buyer with the oldest reported long position to the delivering seller and notifies both parties. See also *first notice day.*

offer—An expression indicating one's desire to sell a commodity at a given price; opposite of bid.

offset—To take a second futures or options position opposite to the initial or opening position. To sell (or purchase) futures contracts of the same delivery month purchased (or sold) during an earlier transaction or to make (or take) delivery of the cash commodity represented by the futures contract.

OPEC (Organization of Petroleum Exporting Countries)—OPEC emerged as the major petroleum pricing power in 1973 when the ownership of oil production in the Middle East transferred from the operating companies to the governments of the producing countries or to their national oil companies. Members are Algeria, Indonesia, Iran, Iraq, Kuwait, Libya, Nigeria, Qatar, Saudi Arabia, the United Arab Emirates, and Venezuela.

open interest—The total number of futures or options contracts of a given commodity that has not yet been offset by an opposite futures or option transaction or fulfilled by delivery of the commodity or option exercise. Each open transaction has a buyer and a seller, but for calculation of open interest, only one side of the contract is counted.

open market operation—The buying and selling of government securities, Treasury bills, notes, and bonds by the Federal Reserve.

open outcry—Method of public auction for making oral bids and offers in the trading pits or rings of futures exchanges.

opening range—A range of prices at which buy and sell transactions take place at the opening of the market.

option—A contract that conveys the right, but not the obligation, to buy or sell a particular item at a certain price for a limited time. Only the seller of the option is obligated to perform.

option buyer—The purchaser of either a call or put option. Option buyers receive the right, but not the obligation, to assume a futures position. Also referred to as a *holder.*

option premium—The price of an option—the sum of money that the option buyer pays and the option seller receives for the rights granted by the option.

option seller—The person who sells an option in return for a premium and who is obligated to perform when the holder exercises his or her right under the option contract. Also referred to as the *writer.*

option spread—The simultaneous purchase and sale of one or more options contracts, futures, and/or cash positions.

option writer—The person who sells an option in return for a premium and who is obligated to perform when the holder exercises his or her right under the option contract. Also referred to as the *option seller.*

original margin—The amount of money futures market participants must deposit into their margin account at the time they place an order to buy or sell a futures contract. Also referred to as *initial margin.*

out-of-the-money option—An option with no intrinsic value, i.e., a call whose strike price is above the current futures price or a put whose strike price is below the current futures price.

over-the-counter market—A market in which products such as stocks, foreign currencies, and other cash items are bought and sold by telephone and other means of communications.

par—The face value of a security. For example, a bond selling at par is worth the same dollar amount it was issued for or at which it will be redeemed at maturity.

payment-in-kind program—A government program in which farmers who comply with a voluntary acreage-control program and set aside an additional percentage of acreage specified by the government receive certificates that can be redeemed for government-owned stocks of grain.

performance bond margin—The amount of money deposited by both buyer and seller of a futures contract or an options seller to ensure performance of the term of the contract. Margin in commodities is not a payment of equity or down payment on the commodity itself, but rather it is a security deposit. See also *margin, clearing margin, customer margin.*

pit—The area on a trading floor where futures and options on futures contracts are bought and sold. Pits are usually raised octagonal platforms with steps descending on the inside that permit buyers and sellers of contracts to see one another.

point-and-figure charts—Charts that show price changes of a minimum amount regardless of the time period involved.

position—A market commitment. A buyer of a futures contract is said to have a long position and, conversely, a seller of futures contracts is said to have a short position.

position day—According to the Chicago Board of Trade rules, the first day in the process of making or taking delivery of the actual commodity on a futures contract. The clearing firm representing the seller notifies the Chicago Board of Trade clearing service provider that its short customers want to deliver on a futures contract.

position limit—The maximum number of speculative futures contracts one can hold as determined by the Commodity Futures Trading Commission and/or the exchange at which the contract is traded. Also referred to as *trading limit.*

position trader—A trader whose approach to trading is to either buy or sell contracts and hold them for an extended period of time.

premium—(1) The additional payment allowed by exchange regulation for delivery of higher-than-required standards or grades of a commodity against a futures contract. (2) In speaking of price relationships between different delivery months of a given commodity, one is said to be "trading at a premium" over another when one commodity's price is greater than that of the other. (3) In financial instruments, the dollar amount by which a security is traded above its principal value. See also *option premium*.

price discovery—The generation of information about "future" cash market prices through the futures markets.

price limit—The maximum advance or decline from the previous day's settlement permitted for a contract in one trading session by the rules of the exchange. According to the Chicago Board of Trade rules, an expanded allowable price range set during volatile markets.

price limit order—A customer order that specifies the price at which a trade can be executed.

primary dealer—A designation given by the Federal Reserve system to commercial banks or brokers/dealers who meet specific criteria. Among the criteria are capital requirements and meaningful participation in Treasury auctions.

primary market—Market of new issues of securities.

prime rate—Interest rate charged by major banks to their most creditworthy customers.

producer price index (PPI)—An index that shows the cost of resources that were needed to produce manufactured goods during the previous month.

pulpit—A raised structure adjacent to, or in the center of, the pit or ring at a futures exchange where market reporters, employed by the exchange, record price changes as they occur in the trading pit.

purchase and sell statement—A statement sent by a commission house to a customer when the customer's futures or options on futures position has changed. The statement shows the number of contracts bought or sold, the prices at which the contracts were bought or sold, the gross profit or loss, the commission charges, and the net profit or loss on the transaction.

purchasing hedge or long hedge—Futures contracts that are purchased to protect against a possible price increase of cash commodities that will be purchased in the future. At the time the cash commodities are bought, the open futures position is closed by the sale of a number and type of futures contracts equal to those that were initially purchased. Also referred to as a *buying hedge*.

put option—An option that gives the option buyer the right but not the obligation to sell (go "short" on) the underlying futures contract at the strike price on or before the expiration date.

range (price)—The price span during a given trading session; could be a week, month, year, etc.

reciprocal of European terms—One method of quoting exchange rates; it measures the U.S.-dollar value of one foreign currency unit, i.e., U.S. dollars per foreign currency units. See also *European terms*.

repurchase agreement (repo)—An agreement between a seller and a buyer, usually in U.S. government securities, in which the seller agrees to buy back the security at a later date.

reserve requirements—The minimum amount of cash and liquid assets as a percentage of demand deposits and time deposits that member banks of the Federal Reserve are required to maintain.

resistance—A level above which prices have had difficulty penetrating.

resumption—The reopening the following day of specific futures and options markets that also trade during the evening session at the Chicago Board of Trade.

reverse crush spread—The sale of soybean futures and the simultaneous purchase of soybean oil and soybean meal futures.

runners—Messengers who rush orders received by phone clerks to brokers for execution in the pit.

scalper—A trader who trades for small, short-term profits during the course of a trading session and rarely carries a position overnight.

secondary market—Market in which previously issued securities are bought and sold.

security—Common or preferred stock; a bond of a corporation, government, or quasi-government body.

selling hedge—The sale of futures contracts for the purpose of protecting against possible price decline of commodities that will be sold in the future. At the time the cash commodities are sold, the open futures position is closed by the purchase of a number and type of futures contracts equal to those that were initially sold. Also referred to as a *short hedge*.

short—(noun) Refers to one who has sold futures contracts or plans to purchase a cash commodity.

short—(verb) To sell futures contracts or initiate a cash forward contract sale without offsetting a particular market position.

short hedge—See *selling hedge.*

simulation analysis of financial exposure (SAFE)—A sophisticated computer risk-analysis program that monitors the risk of clearing members and large-volume traders at the Chicago Board of Trade. It calculates the risk of change in market prices or volatility to a firm carrying open positions.

speculator—A market participant who tries to profit from buying and selling futures and options contracts by anticipating future price movements. Speculators assume market price risk, and they add liquidity and capital to the futures markets.

spot—Usually refers to a cash market price for a physical commodity that is available for immediate delivery.

spot month—The futures contract month closest to expiration. Also referred to as *nearby* or *delivery month.*

spread—The price difference between two related markets or commodities.

spreading—The simultaneous buying and selling of two related markets in the expectation that a profit will be made when the position is offset. Examples include buying one futures contract and selling another futures contract of the same commodity but with a different delivery month; buying and selling the same delivery month of the same commodity on different futures exchanges; buying a given delivery month of one futures market and selling the same delivery month of a different, but related, futures market.

steer/corn ratio—The relationship of cattle prices to feeding costs. It is measured by dividing the price of cattle ($/hundredweight) by the price of corn ($/bushel). When corn prices are high relative to cattle prices, fewer units of corn equal the dollar value of 100 pounds of cattle. Conversely, when corn prices are low in relation to cattle prices, more units of corn are required to equal the value of 100 pounds of beef. See also *feed ratio*.

stock index—An indicator used to measure and report value changes in a selected group of stocks. How a particular stock index tracks in the market depends on its composition, the sampling of stocks, the weighing of individual stocks, and the method of averaging used to establish an index.

stock market—A market in which shares of stock are bought and sold.

stop-limit order—A variation of a stop order in which a trade must be executed at an exact price or better. If the order cannot be executed, it is held until the stated price or a better price is reached.

stop order—An order to buy or sell when the market reaches a specified point. A stop order to buy becomes a market order when the futures contract trades (or is bid) at or above the stop price. A stop order to sell becomes a market order when the futures contract trades (or is offered) at or below the stop price.

strike price—The price at which the futures contract underlying a call or put option can be purchased (if a call) or sold (if a put). Also referred to as *exercise price*.

supply, law of—See *law of supply*.

support—The place on a chart where the buying of futures contracts is sufficient to halt a price decline.

suspension—The end of the evening session for specific futures and options markets traded at the Chicago Board of Trade.

technical analysis—Anticipation of future price movement using historical prices, trading volume, open interest, and other trading data to study price patterns.

tick—The smallest allowable increment of price movement for a contract.

time and sales ticker—Part of the Chicago Board of Trade Market Profile system consisting of an online graphic service that transmits price and time information throughout the day.

time limit order—A customer order that designates the time during which it can be executed.

time-stamped—Part of the order-routing process in which the time of day is stamped on an order. An order is time-stamped when it is (1) received on the trading floor and (2) completed.

time value—The amount of money option buyers are willing to pay for an option in the anticipation that, over time, a change in the underlying futures price will cause the option to increase in value. In general, an option premium is the sum of time value and intrinsic value. Any amount by which an option premium exceeds the option's intrinsic value can be considered time value. Also referred to as *extrinsic value*.

trade balance—The difference between a nation's imports and exports of merchandise.

trading limit—The maximum number of speculative futures contracts one can hold as determined by the Commodity Futures Trading Commission and/or the exchange upon which the contract is traded. Also referred to as *position limit*.

Treasury bill—A Treasury bill is a short-term U.S. government obligation with an original maturity of one year or less. Unlike a bond or note, a bill does not pay a semiannual, fixed-rate coupon. A bill is typically issued at a price below its par value and is therefore a discounted instrument. The level of the discount depends on the level of prevailing interest rates. In general, the higher the short-term interest rates are, the greater the discount. The return to an investor in bills is simply the difference between the issue price and par value. Also referred to as *T-bill*.

Treasury bond—Government-debt security with a coupon and original maturity of more than 10 years. Interest is paid semi-annually. Also referred to as *T-bond*.

Treasury note—Government-debt security with a coupon and original maturity of 1 to 10 years. Also referred to as *T-note*.

U.S. Treasury bill—See *Treasury bill*.

U.S. Treasury bond—See *Treasury bond*.

U.S. Treasury note—See *Treasury note*.

underlying futures contract—The specific futures contract that is bought or sold by exercising an option.

variable limit—According to the Chicago Board of Trade rules, an expanded allowable price range set during volatile markets.

variation margin—During periods of great market volatility or in the case of high-risk accounts, additional margin deposited by a clearing member firm to an exchange.

versus cash—A transaction generally used by two hedgers who want to exchange futures for cash positions. Also referred to as *against actual* or *exchange for physicals*.

vertical spread—The purchase and sale of puts or calls of the same expiration month but with different strike prices.

volatility—A measurement of the change in price over a given period. It is often expressed as a percentage and computed as the annualized standard deviation of the percentage of change in daily price.

volume—The number of purchases or sales of a commodity futures contract made during a specific period of time, often the total transactions for one trading day.

warehouse receipt—Document guaranteeing the existence and availability of a given quantity and quality of a commodity in storage; commonly used as the instrument of transfer of ownership in both cash and futures transactions.

wire house—An individual or organization that solicits or accepts orders to buy or sell futures contracts or options on futures and accepts money or other assets from customers to support such orders. Also referred to as *commission house* or *futures commission merchant* (*FCM*).

writer—The person who sells an option in return for a premium and is obligated to perform when the holder exercises his or her right under the option contract. Also referred to as the *option seller.*

yield—A measure of the annual return on an investment.

yield curve—A chart in which the yield level is plotted on the vertical axis and the term to maturity of debt instruments of similar creditworthiness is plotted on the horizontal axis. The yield curve is positive when long-term rates are higher than short-term rates; however, the yield curve is negative, or inverted, when long-term rates are lower than short-term rates.

yield to maturity—The rate of return an investor receives if a fixed-income security is held to maturity.